D0906905

Quantitative Intelligence Analysis

SECURITY AND PROFESSIONAL INTELLIGENCE EDUCATION SERIES (SPIES)

Series Editor: Jan Goldman

In this post–September 11, 2001, era, there has been rapid growth in the number of professional intelligence training and educational programs across the United States and abroad. Colleges and universities, as well as high schools, are developing programs and courses in homeland security, intelligence analysis, and law enforcement, in support of national security.

The Security and Professional Intelligence Education Series (SPIES) was first designed for individuals studying for careers in intelligence and to help improve the skills of those already in the profession; however, it was also developed to educate the public in how intelligence work is conducted and should be conducted in this important and vital profession.

Books in the series include:

Communicating with Intelligence: Writing and Briefing in the Intelligence and National Security Communities, by James S. Major, 2008

A Spy's Résumé: Confessions of a Maverick Intelligence Professional and Misadventure Capitalist, by Marc Anthony Viola, 2008

An Introduction to Intelligence Research and Analysis, by Jerome Clauser, revised and edited by Jan Goldman, 2008

Writing Classified and Unclassified Papers for National Security, by James S. Major, 2009

Strategic Intelligence: A Handbook for Practitioners, Managers, and Users, revised edition by Don McDowell, 2009

Partly Cloudy: Ethics in War, Espionage, Covert Action, and Interrogation, by David L. Perry, 2009

Ethics of Spying: A Reader for the Intelligence Professional, edited by Jan Goldman, 2006

Ethics of Spying: A Reader for the Intelligence Professional, edited by Jan Goldman, 2006 (Volume #1) & 2010 (Volume #2)

Handbook of Warning Intelligence: Assessing the Threat to National Security, by Cynthia Grabo, 2010

Handbook of Scientific Methods of Inquiry for Intelligence Analysis, by Hank Prunckun, 2010

Keeping U.S. Intelligence Effective: The Need for a Revolution in Intelligence Affairs by William J. Lahneman, 2011

Counterintelligence Theory and Practice, by Hank Prunckun, 2012.

Words of Intelligence: An Intelligence Professional's Lexicon for Domestic and Foreign Threats, Second Edition, by Jan Goldman, 2011

Balancing Liberty and Security: An Ethical Study of U.S. Foreign Intelligence Surveillance, 2001-2009, by Michelle Louise Atkin, 2013

The Art of Intelligence: Simulations, Exercises, and Games, by William J. Lahneman & Ruben Arcos (eds), 2014

Quantitative Intelligence Analysis, by Ed Waltz, 2014.

Scientific Methods of Inquiry for Intelligence Analysis, Second Edition, by Hank Prunckun, 2014

Communicating with Intelligence: Writing and Briefing in National Security, Second Edition, by James S. Major, 2014

https://rowman.com/page/IJIE

Quantitative Intelligence Analysis

Applied Analytic Models, Simulations, and Games

Edward Waltz

ROWMAN & LITTLEFIELD
Lanham • Boulder • New York • London

This document has been approved by the DNI Prepublication Board
on 19 April 2013

The opinions expressed in this book are those of the author. They do not
represent the official position of the Office of the Director of National
Intelligence, the Department of Defense, or any other agency of the U.S.
Government.

Published by Rowman & Littlefield
A wholly owned subsidiary of The Rowman & Littlefield Publishing Group, Inc.
4501 Forbes Boulevard, Suite 200, Lanham, Maryland 20706
www.rowman.com

16 Carlisle Street, London W1D 3BT, United Kingdom

Copyright © 2014 by Rowman & Littlefield

All rights reserved. No part of this book may be reproduced in any form or by
any electronic or mechanical means, including information storage and retrieval
systems, without written permission from the publisher, except by a reviewer
who may quote passages in a review.

British Library Cataloguing in Publication Information Available

Library of Congress Cataloging-in-Publication Data
Waltz, Edward.
    Quantitative intelligence analysis : applied analytic models, simulations and
games / Edward Waltz.
        pages cm. — (Security and professional intelligence education series)
    Includes bibliographical references and index.
    ISBN 978-1-4422-3586-1 (cloth : alk. paper) — ISBN 978-1-4422-3587-8
(electronic)
    1. Intelligence service—Methodology.   2. Quantitative research.   I. Title.
    JF1525.I6W395 2014
    327.1201—dc23

                                                                    2014027175

∞ ™ The paper used in this publication meets the minimum requirements of
American National Standard for Information Sciences—Permanence of Paper for
Printed Library Materials, ANSI/NISO Z39.48-1992.

Printed in the United States of America

Dedication

Dedicated to the men and women of the U.S. Intelligence Community.
I am grateful to the Lord for the opportunity to share in their
challenges and learn from their courage, enthusiasm, and wisdom.

Table of Contents

List of Figures

List of Tables

Foreword

The U.S. Intelligence Community's (IC) use of analytic tools (e.g., modeling, simulation, and gaming) and structured analytic techniques (e.g., brainstorming, red teaming, competitive-hypotheses analysis, alternative scenarios/futures exercises) has evolved over seventy years from humble beginnings in the late 1940s to the verge of a golden age in the first decade of the twenty-first century.

In the early years of my career, most analysts held to the conviction that brainpower ultimately trumped evolving technologies and methodologies, and that the best check and balance to analytic mindset was more brainpower. This bias has gradually been swept away over the past quarter century, however, by the data-glutting revolution in information technology, by the brain-busting profusion of post–Cold War priority intelligence issues and new critical missions, by the maturation of analytic tradecraft with a firm emphasis on collaboration, by dramatic advances in neuroscience that clarify how the analyst's brain works, and by the veritable explosion in user-friendly software that models and enhances cognitive function rather than competes unfavorably with it. As Ed Waltz's in-depth research attests, analytic tools of synthesis and structured analytic techniques today, while still a work in progress, are core to IC workplace practices, training, and strategic planning.

The seeds for tools and techniques were planted early in the IC, though they were slow to take root. The legendary scholar and architect of the national intelligence estimates process, Sherman Kent, published the first edition of his seminal work, *Strategic Intelligence for American World Policy*, in 1949. Kent argued that intelligence analysis is a unique discipline requiring rigorous critical thinking and repeatable methodological approaches to deal with the often limited information and inherent uncertainty in a high-stakes business. Then as now, we could add that the protected intelligence environment is further hampered by adversaries who want to deceive us and by collectors, analysts, and customers who often bring their own strong biases to the game. For these reasons, there was never much debate about the need to question our analytic assumptions and to consider alternative outcomes, and this imperative was reflected in internal review processes, in systematic engagement with cleared outside experts, and in episodic red teaming and much less useful Team-A–Team-B exercises. In that early era, when man came up against models, I usually favored the expert analyst.

Computer programming and modeling made modest leaps forward beginning in the 1980s in parallel with developments in academia and think tanks. But IC models tended to be selective—with preference for econometric, military, technical, and long-term regional analysis—and were usually controlled by a few experts, generally outside the mainstream of production planning and analytic training. The average analyst was not enabled, and was not expected to be.

In my early years as an analyst and manager, there was often a wide gap between what we preached in the training classroom and what we practiced in the heat of the shop floor. Analysts on current, high-profile, regional accounts, where mindset-challenging "tools or techniques" would conceivably be most helpful, worked bulging inboxes under tight deadlines for managers and customers disinclined to make time for modeling, simulation, and gaming. Individual brainpower and expertise were the coin of the realm. Methodological approaches, by contrast, assumed time-consuming and credit-sharing collaboration, which was less valued, and were often seen to upset the established ops tempo of analytic production. Analysts under a heavy workload showed little appetite for new tools or methodologies, especially when they involved arcane software with onerous data-entry requirements for the analyst. To be accepted, the software had to be easy to feed, simple to use, and demonstrably effective in improving the analyst's performance—a simple formula that still holds true today. This undercurrent of resistance to tools and techniques, both from individual analysts and the bureaucracy itself, was endemic in the Community into the 1990s.

Attitudes and practices, however, have changed dramatically in recent years, along with the highly charged information environment in which analysts function. The IT-driven technology revolution transformed an information-scarce environment into an information-glut environment for intelligence analysts, making tools and techniques essential to the exploitation of increasing volumes of data. Put simply, with tools we swim, without them we sink in a vast and expanding ocean of data. Second, globalization and technical advances have enabled improved worldwide collection, including massive flows of valuable open-source information, on a wider range of traditional nation-state and transnational issues, as well as on newer policy priorities related to cyber and bioterrorist threats, humanitarian and refugee crises, natural disasters, competition for natural resources, international migration, international financial crises, human trafficking, infectious diseases, and environmental concerns including global warming. All this results in heightened expectations on stretched analysts, who are forced to recognize how tailored, user-friendly software and applications—which are now increasingly available and accessible to average analysts—can help them bring order and even innovation to the hyperactive information environment and chaotic world they face every day.

The range and depth of complex issues now covered by the IC, along with a trend toward integration of collection strategies, impels tool-enabled collaboration as never before. Most of these issues favor interactive analysis and cooperative solutions across the IC, the U.S. government, and the international community—a collaborative approach which is naturally advanced by modeling, simulation, and gaming. Most of these high-priority issues also call for long-term, strategic assessments for which advanced tools and techniques can be especially helpful in displaying and clarifying potential second- and third-level consequences. Software tools now empower analysts and their methodologist colleagues to access networked data and synthesize models in unprecedented ways. Intelligence customers today increasingly register their satisfaction with the wide variety of ways the IC has to represent and visualize analyzed data, including in daunting geospatial models, conceptual maps, temporal lines, and social networks.

Not surprisingly, the IC leadership today strongly advocates the use of high-value state-of-the-art tools and techniques to support its critical missions. In the wake of the 9/11 terrorist attacks, key recommendations of the 9/11 Commission and the WMD commission stressed the need for greater analytic rigor and called for increased focus on advanced tools and methodologies. The creation of the Office of the Director of National Intelligence and, to a lesser extent, the Department of Homeland Security established new focal points to drive improvement in analytic tradecraft across the IC and into the domestic intelligence arena. Finally, U.S. intelligence operations in Iraq and Afghanistan have achieved unmatched interagency collaboration and unparalleled fusion of intelligence disciplines (e.g., SIGINT, IMINT, MASINT, HUMINT, OSINT) in successful ISR (intelligence, surveillance, and reconnaissance) operations. We have new, battle-tested models for the integration of intelligence collection and analysis.

The future for tools and techniques has never been more exciting. These ISR successes "down range" have, in turn, spawned new critical, tool-dependent missions that must be sustained, including wide-area persistent surveillance, activity-based intelligence, GEOINT-focused human geography, precision analysis-supported targeting, and UAV-derived video exploitation. The demand for tools and techniques to enable rapid synthesis of "multi-INT" collection and analysis on these and other priority national-security issues will only grow in the years ahead.

Finally, I will return to the major breakthroughs in neuroscience over the past decade that have deepened our understanding of how the brain works and have resulted in the successful modeling of some brain functions. We also have learned, of course, that what we cannot yet model about the whole human brain is vast and humbling. Nonetheless, we have witnessed a major leap in sophisticated tool development that closely complements, rather than competes with, cognitive function; that is increasingly tailored precisely to the analyst's dynamic requirements; and that is both easy to use and to populate with relevant data. As a result, usage of tools is becoming more the norm and less the exception in the IC. Analytic gaming, once viewed by some of my smartest colleagues as distracting child's play, is now championed by leading analytic programs as both a key training tool and an effective instrument to challenge mindset in the workplace. Brainpower, once seen as the unchallenged coin of the realm, is now viewed as enhanced by the rigor of modeling, dynamic simulations, and interactive games that are the wave of the Intelligence Community's collaborative future.

It has been my privilege to work with Ed Waltz, a bold pioneer and a passionate innovator in the field of analytic tools, for most of the past decade. His technical mastery of the tools business, so evident in the text that follows, has been exceeded only by his tireless efforts to understand the pressure-cooker environment in which intelligence analysts toil every day. No one has worked harder, or with greater enthusiasm, to understand the practical and changing requirements of the working analyst in a fast-changing and dangerous world, or has been more productive in developing useful tools to address those requirements. As this book makes clear, Ed Waltz is a respected leader in a dynamic field to which he has made, and will continue to make, major contributions.

John Gannon
June 15, 2012

Dr. Gannon is a career intelligence officer who served in the most senior analytical positions at CIA and in the Intelligence Community: Deputy Director for Intelligence (DDI) at CIA, Chairman of the National

Intelligence Council, and Assistant Director of Central Intelligence for Analysis and Production. He headed the White House team in the Department of Homeland Security Transition Planning office standing up the Information Analysis and Infrastructure Protection Directorate, and was the staff director of the House of Representatives Select Committee on Homeland Security. President George W. Bush awarded him the National Security Medal, the nation's highest intelligence award. Following his thirty-year intelligence career in 2005, he joined BAE Systems and served in senior leadership positions as president of Intelligence & Security and vice president of Global Analysis.

Preface

My colleagues have often cautioned me not to mention in public the record I claim for the number of intelligence modeling and simulation tools I have developed for the U.S. Intelligence Community—that were never fully adopted. There are many other tool developers who may vie for my dubious record, because developing and transitioning useful analytic tools has proven a daunting challenge to many of us in the Community.

In 2005, the Intelligence Community sponsored a major analytic conference that featured technical papers on several dozen new analytic methods and tools. Judging the lack of attendance by operational analysts, a senior Defense Intelligence Agency (DIA) intelligence officer wryly told me that the event was like a power-tool convention with no carpenters present. Tool-developer enthusiasm for tools has always exceeded the interest of intelligence analysts, who have often viewed technology-based analytic support tools with healthy skepticism. Unwieldy technology, awkward graphical user interfaces, egregious manual data-entry demands, esoteric or hidden logic, and mysterious mathematics have put off many analysts who had real problems and even a willingness to try anything. But in the process of tool development, we have steadily learned from working with analysts at their desks, and computational modeling tools are increasingly being adopted in many analytic areas.

I have spent over a decade working with analysts on the most difficult problems in the Community, seeking to understand how they view their problems, how they think, organize their evidence, and conceive mental models that hypothesize the complex context and hidden subjects of their analysis. While gaining respect for their challenges and methods, I have worked with them to develop new methodologies and supporting tools (in that order of emphasis) that more explicitly represent their problems.

We have collaborated to capture their mental models and explore the relationships between real-world evidence and conceptual-world ideas and then evaluated those ideas against the evidence.

This book is my effort to provide a readable introduction to the use of modeling, analytic games, and simulation methods in intelligence analysis; it is also an encouragement to the analyst that mental models can be captured explicitly, manipulated dynamically, and shared to benefit collaborative analysis.

This is by no means a textbook on the technical methods of modeling and simulation; the focus here is on methodologies to apply modeling, analytic games, and simulation, not just the enabling technologies. I have cited excellent technical texts on operational analysis, modeling, and simulation throughout the book and encourage further study.

I am indebted to an excellent team of reviewers—a diverse team of experts in intelligence analysis and analytic methodology, operations research, mathematics, cognitive science, social science, and computational science. These experts have reviewed draft chapters and encouraged me throughout the development of this manuscript; each has been a part of my own education in this field. I am grateful to these colleagues, reviewers, and friends: Dr. Steven Bankes, Mike Bennett, Dr. Peter Brooks, Mark Gelston, Jon Goldstein, Dr. Doug Griffith, Professor Frank Hughes, Valdemar Johnson, Howard Kee, Dr. Craig Lawrence, Dr. Corey Lofdahl, John Paul Parker, Laura Smith, Tim Smith, Tim Waltz, and Jeffrey White. I want to thank Lt. Col. Kevin Frisbie (USAF Ret.) for the glossary he prepared for our analysts and planners; I adopted his excellent foundation and included many additional terms introduced in this volume.

My goal here is to encourage analysts to consider these methods and to show them how they can be applied by the use of case studies throughout. It is my hope that future generations of analysts, trained in quantitative methods and comfortable with synthetic worlds, will apply and extend these methods to enhance our nation's security in a complex world.[1]

Ed Waltz
Chantilly, Virginia

NOTE

1. For a view of the author's perspective of how intelligence analysts may apply modeling and simulation in 2025, see chapter 9, Synthetic Worlds in National Security Policymaking, in C. A. P. Smith, J. G. Morrison, and K. W. Kisiel (eds.), *Working Through Synthetic Worlds* (London: Ashgate, 2009).

1

✛

The Intelligence Analyst and Synthesis

Intelligence analysis is, at the core, a discipline about thinking. Like the disciplines of philosophy, theology, and mathematics, the product of the practitioner is the result of conceptual reasoning about observations in the real world, reasoning about the reasoning process itself (or metareasoning), and applying judgment to deal with the inherent uncertainties in the process. The intelligence analyst, unlike the philosopher, theologian, or mathematician, however, faces a particularly unique challenge: Often, the subject of inquiry (or the intelligence *target*) is actively evading discovery and understanding, employing means of denial to minimize observations and deception to introduce observation errors that distort the reasoning of the analyst. In these circumstances, the analyst seeks to provide a decision advantage to commanders, planners, and policy makers—the information and insight they need to make well-informed decisions.

This book is about a method of intelligence analysis that represents the analyst's understanding of observations and also represents the analyst's reasoning process explicitly—exposing *what the analyst believes* about the intelligence subject, and *how they arrived* at those beliefs and converged on analytic judgments. We focus on the specific methods of explicitly representing the objects of the analyst's mind—mental models—in terms of static models, dynamic simulations, and interactive analytic games.

We use the general term *model* to refer to detailed and often technical descriptions or representations of the analyst's thinking or the subjects of analysis. The models in the analyst's mind are *tacit*; the ones expressed by the analysts in words or graphics on paper or the computer monitor are *explicit*—represented tangibly, clearly, and precisely, readily

1

understandable by others. No presumptions are hidden, and nothing is implied. Explicit models are intended to be understandable explanations by the model creators—but explicit does not imply "correct." In fact, good explicit models reveal uncertainties, ambiguities, and other flaws of evidence, assumptions, or inference that can be hidden or easily ignored when they remain implicit.

Furthermore, models are the product of intelligence *synthesis*, the process of creative composition of a description of cause-to-effect. The intelligence analyst moves from observations and evidence to explanation. While *analysis* is a process of decomposition of a situation and evidence, *synthesis* is focused on composition of a hypothesis or explanation built on inference, context, and conjecture. The intelligence analyst cycles between the analysis of evidence and synthesis of propositions (expressed as hypothetical models) to explain situations and answer policy makers' needs for information.[1]

It is helpful here to distinguish three categories of models (table 1.1) distinguished by their intended use. *Prescriptive models* are used to represent how things should be; these models are used in engineering to define a system to be constructed, or in political science to describe how an organization or political system should function. *Descriptive models* are used by intelligence analysts to represent our understanding of a situation or

Table 1.1 Categories of Model Representations

Type	Prescriptive Model	Descriptive Model	Exploratory and Predictive Models
Definition	A model used to convey the required behavior or properties of a proposed system.	A model used to depict the structural properties of an existing system or type of system.	A model used to depict to some degree the behavior of an existing system or type of system.
Objective	Represent and specify the **characteristics** (requirements) for an item to be designed.	Represent the **structure** (elements and relationships) of the real world as observed.	Represent the **behavior** of the real world as observed, to some degree to enable exploratory and predictive analysis.
Examples	A scale model, written specification, computer aided design (CAD) model, a simulation of required behavior of a system.	Network model of a foreign government, a military or terrorist organization (actors and linkages).	Simulation of the behavior of a terrorist organization behavior under varying conditions to explore its behavior and identify vulnerabilities.

system and how it functions; we refer to these models in describing structure (elements and parts) and behavior. *Predictive or exploratory models* include those models that represent the dynamic behavior of a system, with sufficient accuracy for the intended purpose, to anticipate how it will behave under a given set of circumstances. These models are useful to national policy makers and operations planners who desire to explore the potential effects of their planned actions.[2]

Explicit models have long been used in intelligence; the mental models in the minds of analysts about distant targets are explicitly described in their narrative descriptions, annotated imagery, drawings, and the maps and tables of estimated orders of battle. Throughout the Cold War, mainframe computers were applied to process models and simulations of the Soviet military capabilities, crops, commodities, and economic production; these models were built by teams of programmers and the underlying models were accessible only to key analysts. Technology now allows individual analysts and analytic methodologists much greater access to the power of explicit, computational models.

MODELS IN INTELLIGENCE AND POLICY

The general distinctions between intelligence and policy (table 1.2) are well-known:

- *Intelligence* is tasked with understanding the state of the world in the presence of uncertainty, ambiguity, and determined efforts to deny or provide deceptive information. This process includes the collection and weighing of evidence to make inferential judgments about the current state of affairs. These inferences lead to hypotheses—explanations based on evidence that estimate the current state and forecast potential futures. National Intelligence Estimates, for example, are the formal expressions of U.S. intelligence about topics of paramount interest.
- *Policy* is tasked with understanding the implications of the current state of affairs—relative to U.S. values (or "interests"). A current or forecasted state may be threatening to the national interests, or may pose an opportunity to support those interests. The policy analyst must consider alternative policies (or courses of action) and project the consequences and risks to those actions before making a judgment that results in a policy decision. The U.S. National Security Strategy is the ultimate expression of security policy; it expresses not only the U.S. position, but also the means (plan, or chosen courses of action) to accomplish the ends of security.

Table 1.2 Distinctions between Intelligence and Policy

	Intelligence	Policy
Focus	What is, Now?	What could be in the future?
Role of Exploration Analysis and Synthesis	• Explore the evidence pool and context • Conjecture on the past and present • Create arguments, hypotheses, explanations, provide judgments • Support policy questions about potential futures, effects of causes	• Explore the explanations • Question explanations • Conjecture on feasible futures • Create and assess response options • Judge consequences
Role of Explicit Modeling Games and Simulation	• Describe situations and targets • Instantiate (populate) process models to explore and explain behaviors and effects • Simulate dynamic models of the past and future situations (including analysis of possible adversary courses of action)	• Review intelligence models and simulations to understand the details and dynamics of a situation • Model the properties of policies or courses of action (COAs) • Apply simulations or analytic games explore the envelope of potential effects of policies or COAs

Functions	Evidence, Context	Hypothesis (argument)	Explanation	Assessment	Projection	Response
Analytic Issues	*What do I know; and what do I assume? What is missing?*	*What are the hypotheses to explain the situation?*	*How do I judge between competing hypotheses?*	*What state are we in? Is it changing? What are the critical dimensions?*	*What are the effects and consequences? What are the future scenarios?*	*What are my options? By what factors do I weight the decision options?*

The modeling approaches described herein contribute to the kind of clarification, structuring, and understanding of planning and action that will support military planners and policy makers who deal with uncertainty.

The degree of interaction and influence between these elements of government has been widely discussed. Policy makers do not want biased analysis to influence their decision making; analysts do not want undue policy influence to pressure them to bias their assessments to conform to policy. Some have argued for a sharp distinction of roles to mitigate the potential for intelligence to improperly influence policy making by shaping the presentation of intelligence to the decision making.[3] Of course, the desire is for intelligence to remain objective and present "objective analyses" to policy makers, but intelligence must be aware of policy makers' interests and alternatives to provide relevant information. Respected CIA analyst Jack Davis summarized the role of intelligence analysis to contribute effectively to policy makers as follows:

Policymakers need support from intelligence to help deal with uncertainty. Thus, policy officials come to respect and rely on analysts and managers who appreciate this aspect of the decision process. Analysts and their analysis are deemed most useful when they:

- Clarify what is known by laying out the evidence and pointing to cause-and-effect patterns.
- Carefully structure assumptions and argumentation about what is unknown and unknowable.
- Bring expertise to bear for planning and action on important long-shot threats and opportunities.

By the same standard, the heavily engaged policymaker has little use for intelligence products that emphasize prediction over explanation and opinion over evidence. The policymaking process is particularly ill served by assessments that trivialize the challenge of uncertainty by burying honest debate in compromise language and by ignoring high-impact contingencies.[4]

THE TOOLS OF SYNTHESIS

As desktop computers have become available with access to networked data, software modeling tools enable individual analysts and their supporting methodologists to analyze data and synthesize models at high conceptual levels of abstraction without requiring a dedicated computer support team. Today, analysts can readily apply modeling tools for conceptual mapping of ideas (e.g., CMap™ concept mapper), analysis of quantitative data (e.g., Excel™ spreadsheets), description of geospatial data (e.g., Google Earth™ and ArcGis™ geospatial information systems), and representation of causal systems (e.g., iThink™ and VenSim™ system dynamics tools). These tools provide analysts and their methodologists with analytic power at their desktops. It is now feasible for individual analysts to more easily create, refine, maintain, and explain models of their thinking and their targets; these capabilities also enable them to maintain and compare multiple, rigorous hypotheses with the data they collect.

Consider, for example, just six common categories of models that are currently supporting collection planning, intelligence analysis, and operations planning across the Community.

- *Conceptual Descriptions* of a target system, its components, structure and process relationships between operations.
- *Geospatial Model* of locations, routes, boundaries (e.g., physical, human, social, cultural), and spatial features that characterize an area.

- *Temporal Timeline* representations of events, activities with duration, and dependencies describing threat activities.
- *Conceptual Map* of an analyst's thinking about the structural and behavioral elements of a target.
- *Nonphysical System Model* of intangible organizations, governments, populations, social groups and their causal relationships.
- *Social Networks* represent the variety of relationships (familial, organizational, attitude, transactions, etc.) between individuals in organizations, communities, societies, or online.

A recent report of the respected JASON (defense advisory group) committee emphasized the use of models that provide insight to their users and the importance of collaboration between these model users (e.g., intelligence analysts) and the model creators (e.g., intelligence methodologists):

> The main use of models in science is to develop intuition for hard problems. Models are used to illustrate, visualize, and analyze a problem, to help human experts see patterns in data, and to systematize an expert's thinking in a way that might reveal key gaps in knowledge about the problem. An insight model need not be complicated. A simple systematic cartoon on a napkin may suddenly reveal a missing facet of a problem. Other models may be complicated. A red-team exercise may reveal an unanticipated vulnerability; an agent-based simulation may help illustrate inefficiencies and bottlenecks in resource allocation; a social network analysis may help clearly visualize a pattern of connections between people in a large dataset.
>
> Experts develop their own ways of organizing and viewing their data as they think about a problem—such as drawing cartoons showing relationships, or developing a personal system of archiving and indexing data. Experts develop these models for themselves, and they learn from the experience of other experts in their field. Because experts spend most of their time doing their job rather than developing new tools, there is good reason to fund free-standing research and development projects into new (insight) models. From a programmatic standpoint of funding research, the main problem with standalone research projects that aim to create new (insight) models is that they separate the model's creator from the model's user community, so they tend to face an adoption barrier. Experts are rightly skeptical of new tools developed by non-experts, especially if a model appears complex, mathematical, and highly abstracted rather than hewing closely to real-world data analysis needs. Success of an insight tool should ultimately be judged by how many experts use it and find it indispensable in their work. "Useful to experts" necessarily includes many factors that become just as important as the scientific validity of the model—issues such as software quality and usability, in the case of computer models.[5]

Models can take on many forms, and computers have enabled a wide variety of means of representation and visualization of data and models for analysts—often the proliferation of these tools has been viewed with distain by analysts who are overworked and not enthusiastic about being a "data entry slave" to a tool. Indeed, the ratio of tools developed to tools used is high (as in any period of technology development), but the use of modeling tools is on the rise, and their added value is gaining appreciation by analysts.

The potential added value is not unique to the intelligence discipline. In the business world, analytic cultures built around quantitative models, predictive analysis and model-based optimization are found in finance, insurance, and retail sales where market data is readily available; in "Competing on Analytics," Thomas Davenport has enumerated the characteristics of a range of competitive businesses that that rely on modeling to gain strategic advantage.[6] The uses of these models in business include:

- *Explanation*: To frame the data (to view from various perspectives), evaluate, and then hypothesize about the underlying causes of observed data.
- *Hypothesis Testing*: To test hypotheses about data; to verify, falsify or refine those hypotheses (e.g., about buyers' behaviors).
- *Collaboration*: To share explanations of the business environment with others (e.g., stakeholders, customers, suppliers).
- *Prediction*: To forecast future possibilities, based on current beliefs in the current state, trends, and business processes.
- *Optimization*: To explore processes that will maximize an objective function (e.g., customer growth, revenue, profit).

These business applications have their direct parallels for analysts who seek to understand dynamic situations and targets (instead of markets), and for planners who want to project future threats (not sales) and assess the consequences of planned policies (not sales plans). At the core of all of these tools developed to compete on analytics are *models*—explicit, quantitative, and dynamic.

THE ORGANIZATION OF THIS BOOK

This text begins by introducing modeling definitions, the use of models in intelligence analysis and the challenges in their implementation. We then introduce the distinction between mental models, explicit conceptual models, and computational models—and their use to understand and explain the subjects of intelligence analysis (chapter 2). Next, we describe the structure of an analyst's mental models and the theoretical basis for capturing and representing the tacit knowledge of these models explicitly (chapter 3). The means to translate static conceptual models to computational representations are described, as well as the means by which these computational models (and simulation of their dynamics) enable collaborative, analytic reasoning, and learning (chapter 4). The use of these models in rigorous, structured analysis of difficult targets is described in chapter 5 with a practical illustration. Next, two kinds of models are distinguished: models that describe our analytic reasoning process (chapter 6) and models of the subjects of our analysis (chapter 7). Both of these chapters are supported by illustrations of models, and representative tools that may be used to implement them. Models and simulations play an important role in analytic games, and these applications are described in chapter 8. The role of models in support of collection and operations is introduced in chapter 9. The final chapter provides an approach to further implement the disciplines of modeling and simulation to the analytic community, with a recommended curriculum to teach the discipline.

NOTES

1. See Waltz, Ed., *Knowledge Management in the Intelligence Enterprise* (Boston: Artech, 2004). Chapter 5 explains the analysis-synthesis process based on its philosophical roots that distinguish between analytic or synthetic propositions, based on the direction in which they are developed. Propositions in which the predicate (conclusion) is contained within the subject are called "analytic" because the predicate can be derived directly by logical reasoning forward from the subject; the subject "contains" the solution. "Synthetic" propositions have predicates and subjects that are independent. The synthetic proposition affirms a connection between otherwise independent concepts. Challenging intelligence problems often require the synthetic proposition—represented by mental or explicit models—to support a judgment that explains how the evidence affirms a hypothesis or explanation.

2. We avoid the word *predictive* in this work where possible; it provokes unnecessary skepticism as it implies a precision that many models do not provide. Rather we will describe how the exploratory, anticipatory and analytic benefits of such models provide significant benefits and avoid the epistemological standards associated with the term "prediction."

3. Davis, Jack, "The Kent-Kendall Debate of 1949," *Studies in Intelligence* 35, no. 2 (Summer 1991) 37–50. Analysis that is more closely linked to policy has been called "opportunity analysis"—analysis focused on the identification of information to support policy initiatives—and some are concerned such analysis lacks necessary objectivity or limits the perspective of analysis and marginalizes the ability to "speak truth to power."

4. Davis, Jack, "The Challenge of Managing Uncertainty: Paul Wolfowitz on Intelligence-Policy Relations," *Studies in Intelligence* 35, no. 5 (1996) 35–42.

5. Office of Secretary of Defense, *Rare Events*, JASON Report JSR-09-108, (October 2009) 31–32.

6. Davenport, Thomas H. "Competing on Analytics," *Harvard Business Review,* (January 2006) 99–107. Also see Davenport, Thomas H., and Jeanne G. Harris, *Competing on Analytics: The New Science of Winning* (Cambridge, MA: Harvard Business Review Press, 2007).

2

✝

Modeling in Intelligence

An important objective of defense intelligence, expressed in the 2007–2012 DIA Strategic Plan, is the development and application of methods to support critical analytic thinking that is carefully structured and made explicit:

> Objective 3.3: DIA will develop expertise in the use of advanced analytic methods and techniques that build on past knowledge. This includes the integration of critical thinking models and diverse perspectives in the development of analytic output. The Agency will provide customers with analytic judgments that clearly identify opportunities, vulnerabilities, and uncertainties. DIA will . . . create an environment for analysts to use critical thinking and basic structured analysis techniques to mitigate bias, understand mindsets, and incorporate competing views to help guide the national dialogue regarding threats to the United States and its interests.[1]

The more recent 2012–2017 DIA Strategy explicitly defines *critical thinking* as the intellectual discipline of rigorously weighing evidence and assumptions, and assessing multiple hypotheses resulting in accurate, persuasive and policy-relevant conclusions. It also emphasizes the role of critical thinking in the mission of strategic warning:[2]

> Enhance the operational environment in which collectors and analysts use structured and unstructured data, and apply advanced analytic techniques to foster critical thinking and improve the quality of defense intelligence.

Perhaps the most rigorous of critical thinking and analytic structuring methods are those that demand explicit and complete representation of the analyst's conception of a complex situation; this requires representations with three characteristics:

1. Explicit—The representation is presented in a manner that reveals the context, available data, gaps in knowledge and assumptions in sufficient detail to explain the structure and behavior of the situation.
2. Coherent—The representation coheres to (is consistent with) all propositions that make up the hypothesis (e.g., the representations of a terrorist organization—financial, size, relationships, etc., are internally consistent).
3. Corresponding—The representation, in all of its aspects, corresponds to the available evidence and accounts for contradictory evidence.[3]

In this chapter, we emphasize that explicit representations, especially in the form of explicit conceptual models and computational models used in analytic games or simulations, support traditional narrative descriptions and provide a unique ability to achieve these properties. We distinguish the following terms, in the context of intelligence analysis:

- *Models* refers to cognitive, conceptual, mathematical, physical, or otherwise logical representations of systems, entities, phenomena or processes.

  o *Mental models* are cognitive structures of associated concepts held consciously or subconsciously, forming an analyst's perception of reality; they are not codified, they may be difficult to record and are often described as *tacit knowledge*.[4]
  o *Conceptual models* are an analyst's *explicit knowledge*, or codified and shareable representations of mental models that are used to describe, explain, and explore concepts. These models can be structured in narrative, logical, mathematical, graphical, numerical spreadsheet, or a variety of other codified forms illustrated later in this work.

- *Simulations* refers to those methods to implement models over time (i.e., a simulation is a model that changes over time, representing the dynamic behavior of a phenomena, process, or system).[5]
- *Computational models* refer to conceptual models and simulations implemented on computers that allow manipulation of the structure and dynamics to perform analysis, exploration, gaming, and

planning. (Note that static PowerPoint graphical models, while constructed on a computer, are *not* computational; spreadsheet models and simulations that allow manipulation of variables and computation of effects of manipulation are computational.)

- *Analytic games* refer to human-role competitive gaming methods that replicate a situation for intelligence collection managers and analysts to consider uncertainties, alternative explanations, internal processes, and outcomes of intelligence and policy activities. Unlike war games, conflict and opposing forces are not necessarily required—but the realities of obfuscation may be represented.

Note that we often use the generic term *model* throughout to broadly refer to static or time-dynamic models (simulations). A top-level taxonomy of modeling terms and an example will illustrate the use of these models in intelligence (figure 2.1). The figure illustrates the basic distinction between an analyst's perception of a situation in mental models, which are translated to explicit representations that can be further analyzed, shared, challenged, and refined.

We further distinguish the two major categories of explicit models: models that are applied to represent *our thinking* and models that represent *our subjects of analysis—situations, targets or target systems.* Those models of targets or situations may represent either physical systems (e.g., factory processes, weapon systems, drug production, etc.) or more intangible nonphysical systems (e.g., human organizations, economies, information environments, etc.)

The example (figure 2.1, bottom) illustrates the models used by an analyst to understand and explain a foreign terrorist organization's financing operations. The overall argument of how the evidence is used to infer the organizational operations is described by an inference diagram that links available evidence to the operations hypothesis. This model describes the analyst's *thinking*, by structuring the argument. The argument includes two components, one about how the finances are processed from donors and criminal activities, through laundering, to terrorist operators (A), and a second model about the structure of the human organization and the relationships between the actors involved (B). Notice that the financing-process model describes a largely *physical system* of movements of people, material, and financial transfers, while the organizational model represents the *non-physical* aspects of human relationships (power, trust, role, etc.). The models of the terrorist organization systems are linked to the model of the analyst's argument and form the basis for asserting that the analyst has developed an understanding of the target and its operations.

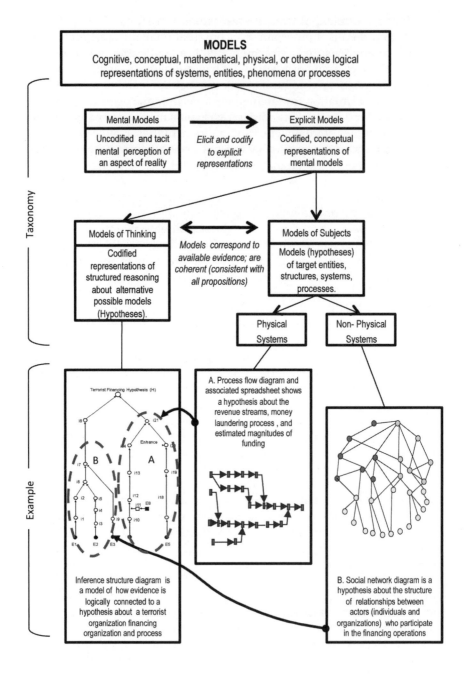

Figure 2.1 Basic taxonomy of the uses of models in intelligence

USING MODELS TO UNDERSTAND SYSTEMS

Models may represent *situations* (conditions and circumstances placed or situated within a context) by representing the contributing *systems* that create the situation. A typical intelligence problem can refer to understanding a foreign social movement and violent conflict with state governments; consider the situation-system distinctions:

- The *situation* is the political social and military conflict within the context of the country, its culture, economy, and political system.
- In this case, the relevant *systems* that give rise to the situation include diverse population groups, political organizations, the ministries of the state government, militaries, and paramilitary forces.

This systems-view of situations decomposes the situation into systems (those interrelated and interacting elements that behave as a distinguishable unit). And the models are abstractions of the real-world systems—designed to describe their real-world counterparts, their elements, structures, and behaviors.

We distinguish between *descriptive* models of these systems and *action* models (or simulations) that support two distinct categories of analysis (table 2.1). *Descriptive models* represent the targets of intelligence: entities, systems, and situations. When these models describe an entire situation, the models support *situation awareness* (SA), the perception of the elements in the environment within a volume of time and space, the comprehension of their meaning, and the projection of their status in the near future.[6] Endsley defines three levels of SA: Level 1 describes the perception of the elements in the current situation, Level 2 describes the current situation in context, explaining the meaning of the situation in an operationally relevant context. Such models are developed by intelligence analysts to describe to consumers a situation and the implications (e.g., the potential threat, vulnerabilities to attack, trends, and activities). Measures of the validity of the descriptive model must consider how accurately it represents the expert's mental model of the situation—and how accurately that mental model represents reality.

Action (or predictive) Models are implemented as computational simulations or analytic war games that are used to support plan or policy development. These models go beyond describing a situation; they represent the dynamic behavior of the systems that underlie the situation and enable the user to explore those behaviors to develop optional courses of action (COAs) to influence the situation. Of course, this requires a much higher degree of representation of the systems involved. Endsley refers to this level of understanding as Level 3 of situation awareness, while

Klein distinguishes this as *option awareness*, because the model is used to consider the space of options for action to influence the situation.[7]

Dynamic models used to evaluate options are considered "predictive" because they simulate the behavior of systems to forecast the transition of a situation from a current state to future states. But the use of the term "predictive" for these models has caused much consternation. Some models do provide accurate endstate "predictions" for a limited range of problems (e.g., physics-based fire control solutions), but most intelligence problems include social and technical components with sufficient uncertainty that a narrow range of future state or endstate predictions are not feasible. But the usefulness of these models to the analyst is not in their accuracy of prediction as much as in their insightful representations of the *dynamics* of a situation and the *potential* endstates or effects. This is particularly true in models that include human behavior and social interactions among humans.[8]

Measuring the validity of such models should be based on their contribution to the stated purpose for the model—or usefulness (this is generally to understand the dynamic factors of a situation, the interaction between elements, the dynamic stability, and the range of effects of

Table 2.1 Characteristics of Descriptive and Action Models

Characteristics	Model (Descriptive Model)	Simulation (Action Model)
Operational Use: *Addresses question:*	To understand *What is . . .*	To plan and decide policy *What if . . . What might be . . .*
Analytic Use of models	To explain structure, properties, makeup, and purpose (intent)	To explore behavior; To predict effects and outcomes
Function	Describe the elements, structure, capabilities, and operation of a system	Describe the behavior of a system, its outputs (independent variables) and response to conditions and inputs (dependent variables)
Abstract spaces considered in analysis	Situation Space—the space of possible operating states of the system	Option Space—the space of options available to a decision maker to affect the system
The measure of model validity	The effectiveness of describing an expert's mental model. The accuracy of representing reality: the situation structure, interrelationship between elements, and their properties	Statistical accuracy of behavior to known past behaviors ("degree of fit"); completeness of behavior to represent a theory ("coverage of representation")

alternative actions). The validity of the model is therefore not measured only by accuracy compared to the real world but by the degree to which it supports a clearly defined analytic purpose.[9] In fact, models that do not meet a high standard of accuracy or realism can provide a mechanism for computational experiments to understand the effects of uncertainty in the model.[10] *Exploratory modeling* is the process of building models to conduct computational experiments on uncertain models to reveal how a situation would behave under varying assumptions and hypotheses. The very process of experimenting with an imperfect model and comparing to reality may lead to insights that will refine the model—and the understanding of the target or situation.[11]

The benefits of simulating dynamic situations have been researched by cognitive psychologist Dietrich Dörner; focusing on human cognitive shortcomings that lead to serious planning errors (figure 2.2).

Organizing for Complex Action

Dietrich Dörner's research has shown that a common set of errors occurs in analysis and planning processes in complex situations, where there are many interdependent actors (or elements) and interactions, and the situation lacks transparency into the structure of underlying systems that are highly dynamic and not well-represented beyond general mental models or rules-of-thumb. Decision errors result from: 1. cognitive processes that simplify and economize our mental model of the situation, 2. emotive processes that bias us to maintain our sense of competency about the situation, 3. our limitations of memory, and 4. our failure to focus on the most critical aspects of a problem. These errors can be mitigated using a process that emphasizes explicit modeling to represent the structure and dynamics of the system – and simulation to immerse the analyst and planner in the behavior of the system. Dörner teaches that these errors can be mitigated with a proper understanding of the situation and rigorous planning to develop courses of action. The rigorous process includes five basic steps to organize for complex action. The process flow allows for feedback from any step to prior steps and reiteration as the planner learns:

1. **Formulate Goals** – Define what you are trying to ultimately achieve, explicitly, specifically, and distinguish the relationship between goals and subgoals.
2. **Formulate models of the System and gather information** – Describe the system you are trying to control, collect what information is necessary to understand its behavior.
3. **Predict and extrapolate**- Using the system model, explore the modeled *behavior* – compare this behavior to empirical data and expert knowledge, and refine as appropriate until the model provides the best understanding of the target system. Assess the effects of actions, and identify critical conditions that influence outcome.
4. **Plan actions** – Prepare a draft plan and try it on the model or simulation; iterate and refine the plan. Decide on best course of action, recognize the risks and uncertainties and THEN ACT.
5. **Watch results and review the effects of your action** and compare to goals and expectations; this results in learning and revision of the models and strategy. The planner must be prepared to revise goals and plans as the system is better understood.

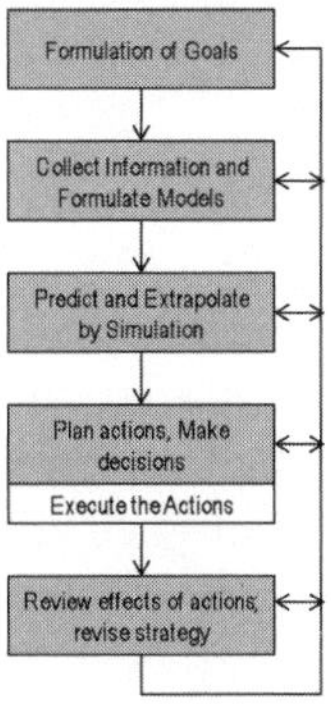

SOURCE: Dörner, Dietrich, *The Logic of Failure: Recognizing and Avoiding Errors in Complex Situations* (NY: Basic Books, 1997).

Figure 2.2 Organizing for complex action

Dörner conducted experiments to measure the improvement in planning and controlling complex situations attributable to the use of simulations to immerse analysts and planners in the dynamics of complex systems.[12] His research identified fundamental cognitive properties that limit our ability to fully understand complex system behaviors, yet give us overconfidence in our ability to control them (see figure 2.2). Simulations are a core of Dörner's explicit and rigorous process to help planners organize to develop a course of action for complex situations.

An overview of a representative model-based approach to intelligence analysis, then, includes the traditional analytic decomposition of evidence and synthesis of hypotheses backed by explicit models of the target situation. The stages in a notional process include the following (figure 2.3, paragraph numbers correspond to functions in the figure):

1. *Define Intelligence Problem*—The intelligence issue and need must be explicitly defined, providing the context, the level of knowledge required by the consumer for decision or action, the time sensitivity (long-term, *ad hoc* short-term, or time sensitive), and the planned use of the intelligence (e.g., policy guidance, cueing, surveillance, targeting, etc.).[13]

2. *Identify Information and Knowledge Needs*—Based on the problem and conceptual hypotheses about the situation, the analyst must derive the specific knowledge required to satisfy the need, identify current information available and gaps. In addition the analyst must identify uncertain factors or key variables that are judged to be critical, and the sensitivities of outcomes to be examined. This derivation will establish the boundaries (context) for any models of the situation, the initial range of alternatives that may be considered, and the analytic purpose for any supporting modeling; the purpose may be, for example: to provide a description of the structure of a situation, to provide an explanation of target behavior, to identify target locations and operations, to forecast likely trajectories of a situation, etc.[14]

3. *Collection*—Information needs are translated to a collection plan defining requirements across sources, tasking to specific sources, and then collection. Quantitative data are processed and modeled (e.g., regression modeling to determine statistical dependencies between variables to infer causality), producing data models (Step 3a). Qualitative data are analyzed to extract information and produce structural models (e.g., social networks extracted from text and digital

sources) (Step 3b). Data and these models are correlated, linked, and combined to provide information to support the next stage.

4. *Synthesis*—Appropriate methods of structuring the information for analysis are selected to organize the information, distinguish relevant information (evidence), organize the analysis process, and synthesize hypothetical alternative explanations. These preliminary hypotheses: 1) determine the needs for situation-target modeling and 2) may reveal information gaps not previously apparent and may result in additional tasking requests.

5. *Target Modeling*—For identified supporting models of the target or situation, the analyst decomposes the situation into abstracted components (elements, systems), and justifies the appropriate theories of causality (process theory) and assumptions to be adopted for dynamic models. The analyst and supporting analytic methodologist (modeler) selects and specifies the appropriate model representation, granularity, parameters, and method of validating the model for the analytic purpose defined earlier in step 2.

6. *Inferential and Exploratory Analysis*—The process of assembling evidence by inference to hypotheses (evidence marshalling) proceeds to consider the support for alternative hypotheses. This data-driven *inferential analysis* process carefully develops the inferences that proceed from evidence to hypothesis conclusions. The complementary model-driven *exploratory analysis* process performs exploratory experiments on models that represent the hypotheses—comparing the structure and expected behavior produced by the models to the evidence. These analytic methods are mutually supportive; the data-driven analysis explores what conceptual hypotheses can be supported by the evidence; the model-driven approach explores the concepts and describes what the evidence should look like if the hypothesis were true.

7. *Judgment and Reporting*—The analyst must apply analytic judgment to provide an assessment that responds to the stated need, and assigns a level of confidence in the assessment. The analyst must also describe the evidence used and the analytic method that proceeded from evidence to judgment. In reporting model-based analysis, it is critical that the analyst understand the audience perspective of modeling—and report the use of models in exploration and support to inferences in terms that the audience appreciates. For example, the use of a graph may not be appropriate for a non-technical audience, but the graph translated into a narrative explanation followed by a clear argument is more appropriate.

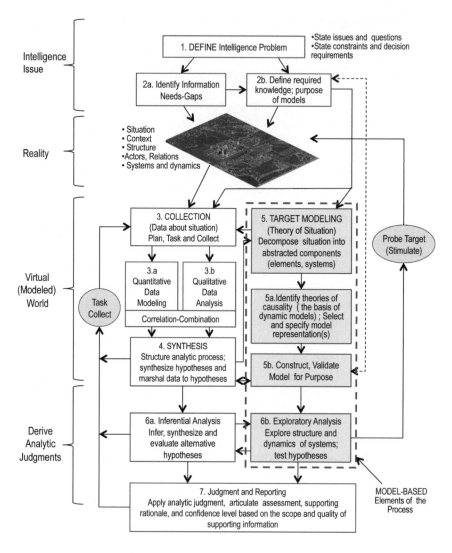

Figure 2.3 Model-based analysis within the analytic process

Notice that two top-level feedback loops are included. First, the synthesis and analysis activities often clarify the information requirements, discovering new information requirements that will produce additional collection tasking to resolve uncertainties. Second, the exploratory analysis process may reveal selected stimuli that might be used to design "probes" that will test target hypotheses, and provide the information to confirm or disconfirm a hypothesis about the target.

The description above has been deliberately abstract to cover a wide range of intelligence problems; to provide a more concrete illustration of this process implemented in a specific problem, a use case is provided at the conclusion of this chapter. Before the use case, we introduce the contribution of model-based methods to performing this analytic process in a collaborative manner and to the explanation of intelligence judgments.

USING MODELS TO ENABLE ANALYTIC COLLABORATION

A core element of the Office of Director of National Intelligence (ODNI) strategic plan is to create a culture of collaboration and provide all analysts with a common collaborative analytic environment.[15] The DNI Directorate for Analysis envisions this environment providing the ability for analysts to conduct "thinking in public," which will result in the "emergence of emphasis" in their analysis.[16] The concept of "thinking in public" succinctly describes the deepest level of analytic collaboration achievable; the work environment will allow collaborators to "see analytic thinking as it evolves." While analytic collaboration has been a long-stated goal of the Community; it is critical to distinguish three levels of analytic collaboration, in order of increasing depth (table 2.2); public, or *shared thinking*, is the deepest level. Operation at this level requires sustained leadership to incentivize collaboration to overcome competitive attitudes that oppose sharing. Indeed, competition, not collaboration, is often the natural state of equilibrium in some organizations due to the very structure that places organizational units in competition for resources and attention.

Table 2.2 Three Levels of Analytic Collaboration

Level of Collaboration	Description	Requirement
1. Shared Products	Analysts share judgments in the finished products of analysis.	Sharing policies; shared repositories for explicit data; search, association, and retrieval tools
2. Shared Data	Analysts share the raw data across sources that are the basis for analysis and their assessment of that data.	
3. Shared Thinking	Analysts share and collaboratively create explicit models of their perceptions of reality. The models represent alternate hypotheses, based on the data available and conjecture; uncertainties and the basis for meaning are shared.	Intellectual trust; means to explicitly represent and share mental models; means to collectively manipulate shared models

Activities to develop Community-wide enterprise architectures deal with the first two levels, providing shared repositories for the exchange of data and products, with appropriate metadata and tools for retrieval and automated association of related information. But the third level of collaboration, shared thinking in public workspaces, requires additional capabilities beyond the enterprise architecture:

- *Explicit representations of mental models*—Analysts must have the means to explicitly translate their tacit mental models to explicit representations in a wide variety of forms (narratives, conceptual maps, alternative competing hypothesis matrices, social structures, process simulations, etc.) that can be exposed and understood by others, especially those with different perspectives, contexts, and mental modeling modes. These models represent sharable explicit hypotheses, conjectures that expose 1) the selection of relevant data as evidence, and reject others; 2) uncertainty in, and the absence of evidence; and 3) assumptions and contextual perspective.
- *Collaborative model building*—Beyond sharing these models with others, analytic collaborations must have the means to jointly create models that represent the alternative hypotheses of teams. Just as a word processor document can be shared, and alternate versions edited and modified for review, teams must be able to create, copy-paste and modify alternative models.
- *Culture of analytic trust*—In her classic knowledge-management text *Wellsprings of Knowledge*, Dorothy Leonard-Barton distinguishes the "small *V*" intellectual performance virtues (agility, innovation, discipline in reasoning and judgment, etc.) from the "big *V*" virtues of personal integrity (consistency, honesty, and reliability), truthfulness, and trustworthiness that are required for the deepest levels of collaboration.[17] Beyond information sharing and new analytic methodologies, an environment of public thinking and shared creation of knowledge will require the highest level of these virtues among collaborators, and this requires sustained, effective leadership.

The result of public thinking is the "emergence of new areas of emphasis" as well as the emergence of analytic lines not apparent in closed, private thinking.[18] Indeed, the process of public thinking described above will enable analysis that is exploratory—a reasoning process of searching alternatives for the purpose of discovery of explanations not immediately apparent. This discovery process is emergent—revealing analytic lines of reasoning not apparent to individuals but revealed in the process of shared exploration. The process integrates two elements:

1. A *structured argumentation process* that first identifies relevant data (evidence) within the contexts defined by hypotheses, and then decomposes the evidence by inference to refute or support those hypotheses (modeling the analyst's thinking), and
2. A *hypothesis exploration process* to explicitly represent hypotheses (as arguments, or models) to allow exploration of both their structure and dynamics by simulation, and the anticipation of expected behaviors and observable evidence (modeling the analyst's target or situation). This imaginative process also sets new contexts by which the argumentation process can determine relevance of raw data.

As we described earlier, the first element is *analytic*, or top-down, decomposing raw data to fundamental facts, each with associated credibility that can be later assembled into hypotheses. The second element is *synthetic* or bottom-up creation of models (or, imagining) of the envelope of possible explanations that encompass, and even exceed, possible explanations from the currently available facts.

This process immerses the analyst not only in the interaction within a complex target situation and possible behaviors, but also in the exploration of excursions and alternative situations that present new contexts for filtering data. The process of analytic inference is complemented by a process of synthetic imagination; the first process applies *models of our thinking*, while the second applies *models of the subject or situation*.

USING MODELS TO EXPLAIN ANALYTIC JUDGMENT

Clear, yet comprehensive, explanations are demanded by intelligence consumers; veteran analyst Jack Davis has succinctly noted that analysts must make sure that arguments are made transparent and sound, supporting evidence is authentic and ample, and plausible alternative outcomes are given their due.[19]

Intelligence briefings that employ explicit static models and dynamic simulations to answer on-the-spot questions address five key categories of questions that consumers want to know (table 2.3). In each category, the model allows the briefer to focus on a specific aspect of understanding the situation; using a model, the briefer may illustrate causality ("show me"), demonstrate outcomes of a particular set of circumstances ("what if"), explain why a situation is most sensitive to particular factors ("how much"), or show the structural or dynamic differences between alternative hypotheses (models) of a particular situation, and the differences in potential courses of action.

The Joint Requirements Oversight Council (JROC), acknowledging the benefits of modeling to support model-based approaches to planning, has defined the application of modeling and simulation to planning as, "the ability to use live, virtual, and constructive simulations to identify and assess the success or failure of potential courses of actions, before, during, and after the planning process."[20] Interactive briefings using the simulations are particularly well suited to presenting the effects of alternative courses of action (diplomatic, information, military, economic, etc.) and allow the briefer to immediately illustrate the effects of audience queries about potential actions. Such simulations are currently used to illustrate the benefits of alternative collection strategies, visualizing complex collection geometries to immerse the audience in the issues of the brief. The ability to answer a decision maker's *specific questions* within the brief also provides a means to build confidence in the method of analysis and the model on which the analysis is based.

Table 2.3 Using Models to Answer Decision Makers' Questions

Decision Maker Questions	Use of the Model or Simulation in Real-time Interaction during the Brief
"What is"	• Describe the structure, properties and interrelationships of the elements of a target, target system, or situation.
"Show me"	• Illustrate the dynamics of a situation; illustrate one trajectory or a range of scenarios.
"What if?"	• Demonstrate how a particular trajectory unfolds, under conditions defined by the decision maker; explain the consequences or effects.
"How much?"	• Explain the sensitivity of outcomes to key factors. • Explain the marginal utility of gain attributable to key factors.
"Which one?"	• Show alternative views of a situation (alternative hypotheses) to compare and contrast the dynamics, sensitivities, and effects to alternative course of action.
"How confident are you? How do I know the results are valid?"	• Explain the basis for model components, the sources of information used, the theories of structure and causality applied, and assumptions behind the results (internal validity); cite evidence of comparisons of the model to real-world behaviors (external validity).

CHALLENGES TO THE USE OF MODELS

While the use of models and simulations for analytic collaboration and within analytic reports, assessments, and briefings provides significant benefits, these benefits are not gained easily or without cost. Unlike assessments based on the estimates of subject matter experts, who are challenged about their tacit experience, the briefer who uses a simulation will be (and should be) challenged about the validity of the data and abstractions applied in the explicit model.

Skeptics of model-based analysis abound, perhaps rightly so. The explicit representation of uncertain things and the hidden elements and math behind many models have deterred the adoption of modeling and simulation methods for decades in many fields. The best antidote for responding to skeptics is a clear and sound explanation of the methodology, supported by data and comparison of model results to reality. John Sterman, a pioneer in the modeling field developed a checklist for model consumers in his "Skeptics Guide to Computer Models" that has prepared modelers to help skeptics overcome their disbelief (figure 2.4).

Checklist for the Model Consumer

Computational modeling pioneer John Sterman's classic "Skeptics Guide to Computer Models" has withstood the test of time as the introduction for skeptical users of computational models. Sterman offers the following checklist for model consumers to consider when applying models to analytic problems. The same questions should be asked of subject matter experts when evaluating mental models of experience.

- What is the problem at hand? What is the problem addressed by the model?
- What is the boundary of the model? What factors are endogenous? Exogenous? Excluded? Are soft variables included? Are feedback effects properly taken into account? Does the model capture possible side effects, both harmful and beneficial?
- What is the time horizon relevant to the problem? Does the model include as endogenous components those factors that may change significantly over the time horizon?
- Are people assumed to act rationally and to optimize their performance? Does the model take non-economic behavior (organizational realities, non-economic, motives, political factors, cognitive limitations) into account?
- Does the model assume people have perfect information about the future and about the way the system works, or does it take into account the limitations, delays, and errors in acquiring information that plague decision makers in the real world?
- Are appropriate time delays, constraints, and possible bottlenecks taken into account?
- Is the model robust in the face of extreme variations in input assumptions?
- Are the policy recommendations derived from the model sensitive to plausible variations in its assumptions?
- Are the results of the model reproducible? Or are they adjusted (add factored) by the model builder? Is the model currently operated by the team that built it? How long does it take for the model team to evaluate a new situation, modify the model, and incorporate new data?
- Is the model documented? Is the documentation publicly available? Can third parties use the model and run their own analyses with it?

SOURCE: Sterman, J. D. "A Skeptic's Guide to Computer Models" in Barney, G. O. et.al. (eds.), *Managing a Nation: The Microcomputer Software Catalog* (Boulder, CO: Westview Press, 1991) 209-229. Accessed Online at web.mit.edu/jsterman/www/Skeptic's_Guide.html on 07 February 2012.

Figure 2.4 Checklist for the model consumer

Confidence in an expert's estimates are based on trust in experience, depth of knowledge, and prior track record of estimates, but the confidence in abstract models is based on their sources of data, the depth of their representation, the pedigree of theories of behavior used, and their track record in representing reality. The value of the interactive brief hinges on the credibility of the model used; if the decision maker does not have confidence in the model, the results are suspect and the briefer will spend precious time defending the model, rather than explaining results.

The briefer must recognize that audiences of the interactive brief have varying levels of personal confidence in the value of models (table 2.4); it is the briefer's responsibility to explain the appropriate use of a model or simulation for a given problem and not exceed the audience's belief in the model used. Indeed, an essential role of the briefer is to establish a level of confidence in the model and its appropriate application for the subject under analysis.

Consider our earlier example of an analyst briefing the J2 on estimated flows of funds to a terrorist organization, using a complex spreadsheet model that distinguishes sources and channels of funding as well as consumption rates of terrorist cells. If the J2 values the explanatory benefits of the model, but is skeptical about the accuracy of the source data (Level

Table 2.4 Levels of Confidence in the Value of Computational Models

Level of Capability Provided by Models	Confidence or Belief in the Value and Contribution of Models
1. Description	Allows an expert to explicitly represent, construct, refine, and describe to others the particular details (e.g. entities, complex relationships, and dynamics) of a situation or system.
2. Collaboration	In addition to being descriptive, the models enable analysts to share their concepts: analytic teams are able to express, exchange, challenge, and jointly modify and develop particular details (e.g. entities, complex relationships, and dynamics) of a situation.
3. Explanation	Beyond collaboration, the models enable individual experts and teams to explain complex situations to audiences; both the structure and the dynamics can be explained in depth, with drill down to details.
4. Exploration and Anticipation	Models enable individual experts and teams to conduct exploratory analyses of situations, evaluating changes in the structure and dynamics and the effects of a range of conditions. Provides deep understanding of situation behaviors; allows analysts to anticipate potential futures they might not envision otherwise.
5. Prediction	Once appropriately validated for a specified use, models can predict, within limits, future outcomes; the model may also be used to optimize outcomes of actions.

3), it may be unwise for the analyst to brief the use of the model to explore the dynamic effects of targeting different channels to anticipate effects (Level 4) (see table 2.4). Until the J2 gains confidence in the accuracy of the magnitude of funding and flows in the model, the model may be a source of distraction rather that an aid to understanding.

The author has taught a modeler's catechism in modeling and simulation workshops (See figure 2.5) to enumerate the key challenges that face those who seek to represent reality in abstract, computational models.[21] The list is organized in terms of the seven fundamental questions that are posed to the modeler who is asserting that quantitative models provide insight into the real-world that they purport to represent.[22] The questions are serious, sobering and worth review by the modeler before beginning to model, throughout the modeling and analysis process, and especially, before presenting the results in the interactive briefing.

Waltz's Modeler's Catechism

QUESTION: What are the questions an analyst and modeler must always be prepared to answer when reporting the results of a model-based analysis:

ANSWER: You must be prepared to answer seven categories of questions:

1. Abstraction – *How did you abstract the concrete real-world into abstract model components and their relationships? How do you know the model is complete, sufficient and at appropriate level of fidelity and causal granularity to represent the effects of reality that you desire?*

2. Justification (of data and model instantiation) – *How do you justify and where did you obtain the data set to model conditions and processes? How much confidence do we have in these parameters? How do you keep them up-to-date?*

3. Validation – *How can you validate that the model corresponds to real world structure and dynamic behavior? Is it repeatable? (*Validation is the process of determining the degree to which a model or simulation is an *accurate representation* of the real world from the perspective of the intended uses of the model or simulation.)

4. Realization – *How do you deal with complexity arising from human free will in decision-making, and the high order of interactions between humans and their systems? Do you allow for non-linearity, self-organization and the emergence of surprising behavior?*

5. Experimentation-Setting – *How do you select the range of conditions over which you assess behaviors? What is your methodology to choose critical parameters of variation, and the excursions which you will consider?*

6. Sensemaking – *How do you derive meaning from the large envelope of possible predictions of outcomes? How do you distinguish outcomes of consequence – and the critical behavioral dynamics of the complex adaptive systems?*

7. Instantiation – *How will you track and update the model with near real time changes in the fluid environment? Can you automatically populate or instantiate the models with intelligence feeds? How will you translate intelligence data into model abstraction? How much effort is required to keep the model up to date? (This question is often posed by skeptics as, "Who will feed this beast?")*

Figure 2.5 Waltz's Modeler's Catechism

DETERMINISM, CAUSALITY, AND PREDICTION

Before we proceed, it is important to identify the fundamental presumptions about our knowledge of the world and the limits of our thinking and modeling of the real world. Philosophers, scientists, and mathematicians have long sought to describe and represent things in the world, their relationships, and behaviors. They have produced a rich and deep literature that deals with the ontological and epistemological aspects of three related concepts that we introduce here: Determinism, Causality, and Prediction.

Determinism—A fundamental consideration in philosophy is the question "Are all effects (everything that happens) the direct result of causes such that nothing else could happen?" If so, even in a limited subset of the world, this philosophy results in a deterministic world in which all events or effects are the result of prior causes. On a small scale, we consider some manmade processes as *deterministic* (when they are operating properly); in fact, analysts count on vehicles, aircraft, weapons, and other targets of intelligence to be deterministic to a degree. But many manmade and natural systems are indeterminate; uncertainties in the structure of systems, the interaction between many agents, and the free will of those agents render them *non-deterministic*. In these cases, the effects of a set of causes may only be statistically determined. Economists, social scientists, and pharmaceutical researchers routinely apply statistical methods in efforts to learn if specified treatments or interventions (causes) can achieve a desired effect on a population or system. While we may apply deterministic models to aid our understanding, we carefully recognize the limitations of applying such models in an indeterminate world. More often, we apply statistical models that provide us with insight into the limits of our ability to understand the precise behavior of a system.[23]

Causality—The concept of determinism is inherently related the concept of causality; that which can be determined requires knowledge of two kinds of events: a cause and the effect it determines. A cause is generally defined as an event that:[24]

- is present before, or at least at the same time, as its effect;
- is associated with its effect;
- acts on its effect;
- can be necessary—that is, without it the effect will not occur;
- can also be sufficient—that is, with it the effect will result, regardless of the presence or absence of any other factors.

We commonly speak of a *causal chain* (or *pathway*), which simply specifies the structure of the causes that produce an effect. In the simple chain

X → Y → Z, Z is determined (caused) by Y *only*, and Y is determined by X *only*. Mathematicians represent more complex causal structures in structural equation models (SEM) that represent causal structures in directed acyclic graphs (a network of causal relations among variables that represent cause-effect events or factors) and an associated system of nonlinear equations that describe the variances and covariances among variables. Researchers focus on a causal variable of interest, Z, and seek to specify every causal factor that is correlated with Z in alternative SEM models (alternative causal hypotheses). The model guides trials and the collection of data for hypothesis testing to compare how well the covariance matrix is fit by alternative models.[25]

But confirming causal relations in intelligence problems poses serious challenges for analysts. Consider the types of practical causal thinking that analysts must address when observing a signature (S) in a foreign country and trying to determine if it can provide absolute assurance that it is evidence that the country is conducting a certain activity (A). The analyst must consider (at least) five possible causal structures that produce S (figure 2.6 illustrates basic causal structure diagrams). The first possibility (Case 1) is that the activity directly causes the signature. In physical processes, it is often the case that an activity will produce such a unique and discriminating signature (acoustic, spectral, etc.). But the signature may be the result of an intermediate event (Case 2) and the signature is not directly caused by the activity. In this case, the signature may be of a phenomenon that is removed from the actual activity itself (e.g., a waste product, a byproduct, a required supporting activity, etc.), but its causal relationship can be established by the causal chain.

There may also be a more complex situation (Case 3) in which an intermediate process (M) *mediates* between A and S. In this case, the signature is an effect of A and M, combined. Furthermore, the analyst must consider (Case 4) that S is, in fact, not at all caused by A, but is observed to be correlated with A because *both* are caused by an unobserved government policy. For example, the signature of deception operations may be highly correlated with activity A, but it is caused by a coordinated government policy of deception, not a direct effect of the activity itself. Finally, (Case 6) the signature may be determined by both the policy and the intermediate activity that the policy also determines.

Pearl has pioneered formal methodologies for representing causal theories in directed acyclic graphs, a supporting causal calculus, and SEM methods for inferring causal chains from observed data.[26] These methods provide more precise representation and analysis of causal statements and have enabled the proper use of Bayesian inference to model causal structures.

Case	Causal Structure Diagram
1. **Direct Causation**: the activity (A) is the direct cause of an observed signature (S)	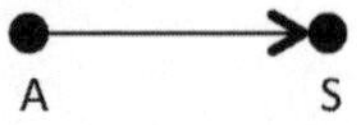 A ●———➤● S
2. **Causal Chain**: the activity (A) causes an intermediate event (I) that is the cause of observed signature (S)	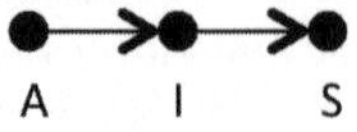 A ●➤● I ➤● S
3. **Mediated Cause**: there exists an intermediate process (M); the signature (S) is a result of the combined cause of Activity (A) and the intermediate process (M)	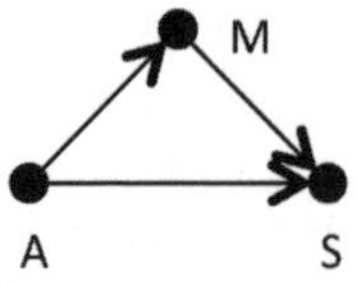 M; A and S diagram
4. **Correlated Cause**: A and S are not causally related, but are correlated because government policy (P) causes the activity (A) AND causes the signature (S).	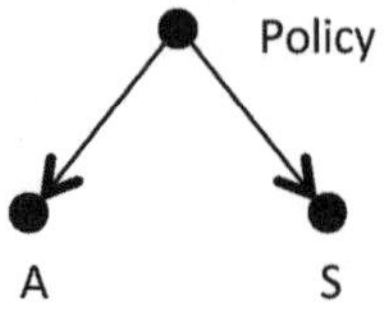 Policy; A and S diagram
5. **Combined Cause**: the signature (S) is caused by the combined effect of government policy (P) and the intermediate activity (A)	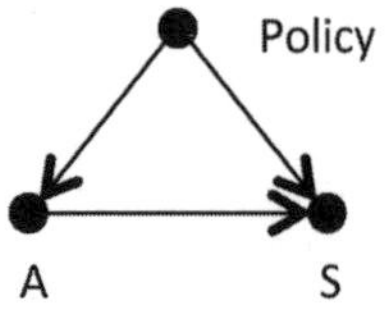 Policy; A and S diagram

Figure 2.6 Typical causal structures that consider causal relationships between an activity and a signature

Prediction—The ability to predict proceeds from causal knowledge. Accurate prediction includes the aspects of predictive precision (that the effects can be specified) and predictive certainty (that effects will always happen under the prescribed conditions). Of course, if things in the world are *to a degree* determinate and causal connections can be learned *to a degree* between events, then expected events (effects) can be predicted *to a degree* based on known conditions (causes). To the intelligence analyst, this means, for example, if a foreign weapon program is *to a degree* determinate, and causal connections can be learned between the program's activities and signatures that are causally effects of the program activities, then a model of the weapon program can predict *to a degree* the effects of sanctions against the program.

The modeling practices in this book take a commonsense approach to these three fundamental concepts, accepting that some intelligence subjects are deterministic *to a degree*, and that some causal models can be inferred from data and others developed theoretically *to the benefit of analytic thinking*. Furthermore, these models can be used to produce predictive data that will also be to the benefit *of analytic thinking*. Throughout, we avoid making claims of model-based prediction in the sense of predictive precision (and predictive certainty). The discussions about these concepts are carefully placed as topics are introduced throughout the book. In chapters 3 and 4, commonsense causal thinking in mental models is described, including mental simulations that estimate effects based on causal concepts. Structuring and representing arguments about causal thinking and the role of counterfactual thinking about alternative causes are discussed in chapter 6. In chapter 7, the challenges of causal inference from empirical data are described and the practical role of prediction by empirical and theoretical models in intelligence is introduced. The role of causal understanding and prediction in probing target systems and testing hypotheses for model-based fusion is explained in chapter 9.

CASE STUDY: UNDERSTANDING TERRORIST ORGANIZATION

To illustrate the model-based analytic process introduced earlier in figure 2.3 we consider how an analytic team might approach a specific problem in understanding the behavior of a hypothetical terrorist organization's financing operations to understand the effects of various policies (or courses of security-military actions) to attack their financial resources.

SITUATION: In the past 9 months, the rapidly emerging terrorist organization FPBZ (Frango Politic bena Zannati) has emerged as a potent threat around a foreign city in the country of Frango, threatening U.S. citizens and businesses there, and even the stability of the friendly host government. The ruthless violence, number of operations conducted, and rapid growth in recruitment and operations has surprised the host government and has overwhelmed its security.

The following paragraphs follow the numbered steps in figure 2.2 and described earlier in this chapter.

1. *Define Intelligence Problem*—U.S. policy makers have specified the intelligence issue elements as:

   - *Core issue* is the threat posed by the little-known FPBZ and the implications for U.S. relations with a weakening Frango.

- *Policy makers' need* is intelligence on FPBZ, specifically: 1) the structure and composition of the organization, 2) the financing and recruitment systems, and 3) the vulnerabilities of the organization.
- *Use of intelligence* will be to develop near-term (1–4 months) courses of action to severely disrupt the organization's operations and support the Frango government; the level of detail is to support operational (not targeting) actions.

2. *Identify Information and Knowledge Needs* — The analytic team that receives the analysis tasking surveys the immediately available information on the Frango situation (context) and FPBZ activities (target). The team identifies critical gaps in collection and knowledge about FPBZ and lists the key factors that must be learned: 1) FPBZ intentions (ideological or financial) and leadership core, 2) FPBZ financial and membership strength, 3) resource streams (domestic and foreign), and 4) relationships to foreign entities. The team defines the analytic purpose for supporting analytic games or models: 1) to describe the FPBZ structure and resources that are sustaining operations, and 2) finance, recruitment, and operations dynamics to evaluate the relative effects of courses of action to attack the leadership, the funding sources, or the recruitment process.

3. *Collection and Processing* — The collection plan includes the following:

   - Organize existing holdings on the FPBZ; task HUMINT (human intelligence) and SIGINT (signals intelligence) collectors to focus on FBPZ targets; organize all open-source media reporting for the past nine months in holdings on FPBZ activities and incidents, then set open-source filters to capture future collections; task GEOINT (geospatial intelligence) sources to update the Frango foundation data in FPBX operating areas and overlay all incident and intercept data. Request, via U.S. embassy, access to captured FPBZ actors to interrogate on recruitment and finance subjects.
   - Quantitative data — analyze FPBZ activity and incident statistics over the past year to develop trends in type of attacks; if possible overlay on geospatial map layer to locate hot spots and characterize those spots. (Step 3a).
   - Qualitative data — organize, enumerate, and develop a network structure of known and suspected FPBZ actors, by geographic locations (Step 3b).

4. *Synthesis* — Review the existing data sets and bring in counterterrorism and regional subject matter experts for a workshop to de-

velop conceptual models of FPBZ and the socio-cultural context in which rapid recruitment is occurring. This event produces several theories of how FPBZ operates, deriving alternative hypotheses for organization operation. Key questions are: 1) Is the group internally funded by known extortions and criminal activities, or it is externally funded by supporting terrorist groups? 2) Is the recruitment process driven by ideological appeal or economic incentives? 3) Is the objective of the group to gain territory and political power or to sustain an emerging and lucrative narcotics cartel in an adjacent country? Based on these considerations, the analytic team chooses three structuring methods:

- Decomposition—Apply methods of explicit target modeling in three areas; develop: 1) an explicit social net models of FPBZ, 2) a geospatial model of activity locations and properties, and 3) a computational model of the funding-recruitment process to understand the dynamics that have led to unusually rapid growth—and to explore how alternative courses of action can degrade the organization.[27]
- Hypothesis Testing—Apply the method of Analysis of Competing Hypotheses (ACH) to compare evidence to hypotheses and explicitly describe the analytic rationale for each hypothesis.
- Challenge Analysis—conduct monthly red team analysis workshops to evaluate current judgments.

5. *Target Modeling*—An analytic methodologist collaborates with the analyst to develop a dynamic model of the funding-recruitment process that considers: 1) inflow of resources by extortion and donations, domestic and possibly foreign, 2) operations, 3) recruitment and membership, 4) state security impact on recruitment and operations. The methodologist selects a general terrorism model from the model library (that represents a widely supported theory of terror organization operations) and tailors it to the Frango-FPBZ situation, based on data being collected. The chosen model is a system dynamics model that best represents the finance-recruitment–operations behaviors at the appropriate granularity to meet the purposes stated earlier; the model dynamics are externally validated to a degree by simulating the prior year's situations and comparing the model to actual FPBZ incident-generating, recruitment, and operational capabilities observed in empirical data.

6. *Inferential and Exploratory Analysis*—The team marshals the accumulating evidence derived from collection against each of two emerging hypotheses:

- Terror Hypothesis—FPBZ is an ideologically driven organization seeking to prove itself to become syndicated by a major terrorist group in the region and has secured only initial external funding for the current burst of activities.
- Narco Hypothesis—FPBZ is a financially driven organization that presents an ideological front to recruit economically frustrated young men; its real intentions are to open an export path through Frango for a neighboring narcotics cartel. FPBZ has penetrated the Frango Ministry of Interior and Security; its rapid growth in operations has occurred with the support of security forces.

The analytic methodologist adapts two versions of the dynamic models (one per hypothesis) to compare empirical data against each. The methodologist also conducts exploratory simulations to develop *probes* that could test each hypothesis—operational actions that could confirm, falsify, or refine either hypothesis. The analytic team reviews the growing body of evidence to compare evidence to the hypotheses and the behavioral dynamics of the competing simulations. At this time, the simulations are also used to identify the sensitivities of the organizational strength and stability to conceptual courses of action.

7. *Judgment and Reporting*—The analytic team prepares periodic reports to national policy makers, providing assessments of FPBZ capabilities and operations—and projected capabilities. When appropriate, the assessments include the relative effect of COAs based on simulated attacks on leadership, funding sources, or the recruitment process. As evidence accumulates to confirm the Terror Hypothesis, the analytic team provides briefings that include simulation clips of the effects of leadership and external financial attacks on the organization—allowing decision makers to understand the dynamics of the organization and the sensitivity of its weak leadership to financial support.

SUMMARY

We have introduced the value of implementing explicit models to support difficult intelligence problems and the ways that models, analytic games, and simulations contribute to reasoning, collaboration, and presentation. Subsequent chapters develop the details of this methodology and the development and applications of these capabilities as tools. In the next chapters, we pause to discuss the critical role of the models that all analysts use—the mental models of their experience, exposure to intelligence data, and even models of their own thinking. In a real sense, the explicit models that we describe throughout this work are simply extensions of the analyst's mental models—explicit, dynamic, and shareable with others.

NOTES

1. Strategic Plan 2007–2012: Leading the Defense Intelligence Enterprise, Defense Intelligence Agency, PCN 2822 (2008) 13, 14.
2. 2012–2017 Defense Intelligence Strategy, Defense Intelligence Agency, PCN 23800 (June 2011) 3, 6.
3. These characteristics are based on the need for a representation that is available for peer review (explicit) and satisfy the fundamental bases for evaluating belief. The coherence and correspondence theories of truth in epistemology are complementary approaches to objective truth; both hold valuable insights into basic principles for evaluating intelligence hypotheses and explicit models that represent them.
4. The term "tacit knowledge" follows philosopher Michael Polanyi's process of *tacit knowing* (developing the personal knowledge of experience, inexplicable intuition, etc.) and refers to knowledge that may be difficult to explain or is entirely inexplicable. We do not imply that all tacit knowledge is translatable to explicit knowledge in models, but we emphasize the value and process of translating such knowledge as is possible to explainable and shareable models.
5. Definitions of models and simulations are adapted from the Defense Modeling and Simulation Office (DMSO) Modeling & Simulation Glossary, which is now maintained by the Modeling and Simulation Coordination Office (M&SCO).
6. Endsley, Mica R. "Theoretical Underpinnings of Situation Awareness: A Critical Review," in M. R. Endsley and D. J. Garland (eds.), *Situation Awareness Analysis and Measurement* (Mahwah, NJ: Lawrence Erlbaum, 2000) 3–32.
7. Klein, Gary L., Jill L. Drury, Mark Pfaff, and Loretta More, "COAction: Enabling Collaborative Option Awareness," *Proc. of 15th International Command and Control Research and Technology Symposium*, Santa Monica, CA, June 22–24, 2010.
8. Robert Axelrod, recognized pioneer in computational social modeling, has wisely noted "A moral of the story is that models that aim to explore fundamental [social] processes should be judged by their fruitfulness, not by their accuracy. For this purpose, realistic representation of many details is unnecessary and even counterproductive. . . . The intention is to explore fundamental social processes." Axelrod, Robert, *The Complexity of Cooperation* (Princeton: Princeton University Press, 1997) 6.
9. See the discussion of validation of action models in chapter 8 of National Research Council, *Behavioral Modeling and Simulation: From Individuals to Societies*. Committee on Organizational Modeling from Individuals to Societies, Greg L. Zacharias. Jean MacMillan and Susan Van Hemel, eds. Board on Behavioral, Cognitive, and Sensory Sciences. Division of Behavioral and Social Sciences and Education (Washington, DC: The National Academies Press, 2008). This book

develops the approaches to "validation for use" and distinguishes the validation criteria for understanding an exploration purpose, and for action (planning).

10. For a classic article on the beneficial analytic uses of imperfect models, see Hodges, James S., *Six (or So) Things You Can Do with a Bad Model*, RAND Note N-3381-RC (Santa Monica, CA: RAND, 1991).

11. See the original articulation of this method in Bankes, S., "Exploratory Modeling for Policy Analysis," *Operations Research*, Vol. 41. No. 3 (May–June 1993) 435–49. See also an application to planning in Davis, Paul K., Steven C. Bankes and Michael Egner, "Enhancing Strategic Planning with Massive Scenario Generation: Theory and Experiments" (Santa Monica, CA: RAND, 2007).

12. Dörner, Dietrich, *The Logic of Failure: Recognizing and Avoiding Errors in Complex Situations* (New York: Basic Books, 1997). Dörner is a professor at the University of Bamberg, Germany, and a winner of the Gottfried Wilhelm Leibniz Prize, the most respected German research prize for extraordinary scientific performance.

13. For a general introduction to steps 1–3, see Krizan, Lisa, *Intelligence Essentials for Everyone*, Occasional Paper Number 6 (Washington, DC: Joint Military Intelligence College, June 1999) 7–20.

14. It is critical in this stage that requirements be broad, rather than focused on supporting favored hypotheses. Commenting on collection requirements prior to concluding that Iraq had an active WMD program in 2002, senior intelligence officers have noted, "Collection was not focused or conceptually driven to answer questions about the validity of the premise that the WMD programs were continuing apace. This problem is well illustrated by a comprehensive collection support brief describing intelligence needs . . . [it] describes in great detail the information required to support analysis of Iraq's weapons programs. The intent of the brief was to expose gaps in knowledge about what was believed to be aggressive, ongoing Iraqi weapons programs. The revealed gaps in knowledge were not, however, raised as requirements to address what was not known nor did such gaps raise doubts about prevailing intelligence judgments." Kerr, Richard, Thomas Wolfe, Rebecca Donegan, and Aris Pappas, "Issues for the US Intelligence Community: Collection and Analysis on Iraq," *Studies in Intelligence*, Vol. 49, No. 3, 47–54.

15. Director of National Intelligence, *United States Intelligence Community 500-Day Plan*, October 10, 2007.

16. Office of the Director of National Intelligence, Deputy Directorate for Analysis, Technology Office, "Building an Integrated Intelligence Service," Draft (March 17, 2006) 4.

17. Leonard-Barton, Dorothy, *Wellsprings of Knowledge* (Boston: Harvard Business School Press 1995) 24–26; 51–53.

18. Office of the Director of National Intelligence, Deputy Directorate for Analysis, Technology Office, "Building an Integrated Intelligence Service," 4.

19. Davis, Jack, "Improving CIA Analytic Performance: Analysts and the Policymaking Process," *Occasional Papers*: Vol. 1, No. 2, (Washington, DC: Sherman Kent Center for Intelligence Analysis, 2002).

20. Definition from Joint Capability Areas Tier 1 & Tier 2 Lexicon, Joint Requirements Oversight Council (Pentagon: Washington, DC, August 24, 2006). Modified from JP 1-02 & JP 2-01; JCA CRC March 2006.

21. Waltz, Ed, "Modeling Complex Systems," Unpublished DARPA Report for Dr. John Allen (September 2004).

22. Catechism—From the Greek *katecheo*, meaning "to sound aloud"—a succinct summary of teachings on key aspects of computational modeling that a student should recite, remember, and apply.

23. For a deeper philosophical treatment of determinism and causality, the reader is referred to Bunge, Martin, *Causality and Modern Science*, Third Revised Edition, (New York: Dover, 1991). Of particular relevance to the intelligence problems described in this book, see chapters 11 and 12 (respectively); "Causality and Scientific Explanation" and "Causality and Scientific Prediction." For a readable theological perspective on cause and chance, see Sproul, R. C. *Not a Chance: The Myth of Chance in Modern Science and Cosmology* (Grand Rapids, MI: Baker Books, 1994).

24. These properties extend beyond the basic properties defined by Scottish philosopher David Hume (1711–1776). His definition included three properties: If E is said to be the effect of C, then: 1) by *Association*, C and E must have temporal and spatial contiguity; 2) by *Direction*, C must precede E temporally, and 3) there must be *Constant Conjunction* such that If C, then E for all situations.

25. Spirtes, P., C. Glymour, and R. Scheines, *Causation, Prediction, and Search.* 2nd ed. (Cambridge, MA: MIT Press, 2000); McClendon, McKee J., *Multiple Regression and Causal Analysis* (Utasca, IL: Peacock Publishers, 1994).

26. Pearl, J. *Causality: Models, Reasoning, and Inference*, 2nd ed. (New York: Cambridge University Press, 2009); also see Pearl, J. "The Foundations of Causal Inference" *Sociological Methodology*, 40, (2010) 75–149.

27. For a detailed example of the implementation of a modeling approach similar to this example, see Grynkewich, Alex and Chris Reifel (USAF), "Modeling Jihad: A System Dynamics Model of the Salafist Group for Preaching and Combat Financial Subsystem," *Strategic Insights*, Naval Postgraduate School, Vol. V, No. 8. (November 2006).

3

Mental Models in Intelligence Analysis

Before we discuss the methods of *explicit representation* by modeling and simulation, it is prudent to make four fundamental assertions about the role of modeling in the analysis and presentation of intelligence:

- The use of explicit models can be an aid to thinking (providing structure and dynamics to the representation of reality, supporting the disciplines of rigor of analysis and explanation).
- Explicit models are shareable artifacts of thinking, objects of information that relate raw data and our thinking about the data.
- Explicit models, therefore, can be an aid to shared thinking by teams of analysts or by the intelligence briefer and the audience at the time of the briefing.
- But explicit models *are never a replacement for thinking itself*; they are but powerful aids and artifacts to discipline and empower the critical thinker.

In this chapter, we introduce the object of our thinking—often described as mental models, mindsets, conceptions, cognitive representations, frames, analytic lines, images, or just ideas—and we describe their critical role in intelligence analysis.

MODELS OF THINKING

The essence of analysis is thinking; this and the following chapter explain how explicit external models of our internal *mental models* can enhance the process, both as an aid to thinking as well as a shareable artifact of the process—enabling collaborative thinking. The intelligence analyst is required to acquire information about a situation, develop a representation of that situation, and present it to policy makers, often with the implications of alternative policies that can influence the situation.[1] The process proceeds from:

- the external reality (e.g., the foreign target), to
- an internal small-scale representation (the analyst's mental model), to
- an explicit external representation (presented in the intelligence report).

While we often think of models as representations of objects (e.g., a mental model of a toy dog), a more general functional definition, provided by Rouse and Morris, is focused on representing real-world objects as systems (e.g., a mental model of a real dog, its physical structure, its behavior, and its processes of eating, drinking, barking, playing, etc.):

> *Mental models* are the mechanisms whereby humans are able to generate descriptions of system purpose and form, explanations of system functioning and observed system states, and predictions of future system states.[2]

A more specific definition focuses on our mental models of real-world systems that focus on their structure and dynamic behavior:

> *A mental model* of a dynamic system is a relatively enduring and accessible but limited internal, conceptual, representation of an external system whose structure maintains the perceived structure of that system.[3]

The intelligence analyst applies a variety of mental mechanisms (cognition) to move from collected information and prior knowledge to understanding. *Perception* is the process that provides self-awareness and understanding about the environment, resulting in the formation of abstract concepts, expressed as mental models, about the environment. *Intuition*, sometimes called "immediate cognition" is the process of knowing or recognizing without the use of rational processes; it is a recognition process that compares the perceived cue to stored patterns of experience and recognizes those that match. *Reasoning* is the use of the logical, rational, and analytical faculty of the mind to form conclusions, inferences, or judgments by analyzing evidence and arguments. *Inference* is the reasoning process that specifically manages (creates, modifies, and maintains) beliefs in the process of learning and problem solving.

Figure 3.1 compares three views of human cognition: Aristotle (384–322 BC), American pragmatist philosopher William James (1842–1910), and the current view adopted by researchers such as Daniel Khaneman and Amos Tversky.[4] Aristotle considered these mechanisms of cognition, distinguishing between physical objects of the world and the abstract ideas that the mind creates once the senses perceive the object.[5] He recognized that the mind creates abstractions, or symbols to represent the world as we perceive it, explaining three processes of the intellect that proceed from sensation to knowledge:

- *Apprehension* is the process by which the mind perceives and understands a sensed physical object or situation and creates a mental abstraction.
- *Predication* is the process of making declarations or propositions about the object or situation—characterizing the object and its behavior.
- *Reasoning* is the process, then, of applying logical principles to the propositions to create new conclusions, or syllogisms, using the methods of deduction and induction.

In James' view, the mind's predispositions and preconceptions form mental abstractions that are then related to other abstractions in the process of thought to establish beliefs; reflection on these beliefs influences our predispositions and preconceptions and the way we apprehend further sensed information.

The view introduced by Stanovich and West is the current two-process theory of cognition that distinguishes the two distinct cognitive capabilities (intuition and reasoning), or systems of cognition.[6]

System 1, called *intuition*, or intuitive thought, is the largely unconscious operation in the analyst's mind that recognizes a pattern of previous experiences. It is involuntary and provides responses and impressions to things we see, read, hear, and smell; it gives us the immediate "sense" of a situation. For example, an image analyst may see a new overhead image of a military facility and immediately have the "impression" that an activity is about to begin, before a thorough analysis of the image—system 1 has matched this image (showing placement of vehicles, activity at buildings, and traffic flows) to associate the pattern of behavior on the base to one similar to that, just prior to a major exercise. A foreign-area analyst receives a report that a foreign government is about to take a specific action, but the analyst "knows" that they will not make that decision because it does not match any pattern of previous behavior for

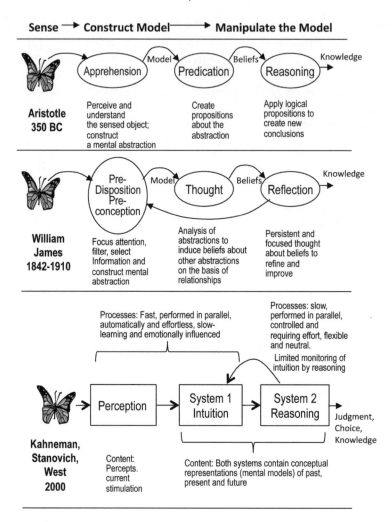

Figure 3.1 Three basic concepts of human thought[7]

that risk-averse government body, which has been deeply studied by the analyst.[8] This mental operation is immediate, unconscious, and triggered by perception and draws on knowledge (mental models or patterns) that the analyst may not be able to easily articulate. The more an intelligence analyst is exposed to a subject, the more the system learns associations between ideas (mental models) and the features of these models and distinguishes the nuances between them. As the student can complete the phrase "cats and ____" without effort, the experienced Pol-mil analyst can recognize and complete the pattern of diverse activities for a political shakeup without effort. System 1 recognition is immediate.

System 2 is called *reasoning* or deliberate thought—the basis for what we consider deep or critical thinking in intelligence analysis. Analysts are familiar with the mostly conscious activities that marshal the resources of system 2: for example, search for information on a subject, create feasible hypotheses to explain what we know, organize and structure evidence against hypotheses, enumerate all known influences on a situation, examine the potential effects or consequences of an operational action, study and develop a model of how finances flow from A to B, or evaluate the comparative risks of actions X, Y, or Z. The best practices we develop to conduct these activities (analytic tradecraft, checklists, procedures, structured analytic methods, quantitative models and simulations, and analytic games) are all methods to guide the focus of our attention to system 2 mental activities. In contrast with system 1, these activities are intentional, purposeful, conscious, and require mental effort. Any student being introduced to linear algebra or T. S. Eliot's *The Wasteland* is familiar with the difficult mental "effort" of system 2 focus. In fact, the mental work we call *study* requires system 2 to focus attention, the attention of system 1 to step through the patterns of a subject (e.g., the patterns of knowledge in a textbook) as system 2 creates mental models of explicit knowledge that can be retrieved to later answer questions and solve problems using that knowledge.

The characteristics of these systems identified by psychologists and the roles of mental models in each are distinguished in table 3.1.

Kahneman and Tversky pioneered the recent study of human cognitive performance and the roles of each system. In particular, they theorized about how humans make judgments and choices and the limitation of the mental mechanisms used. They defined the *availability heuristic* as a mental strategy (or system 1 shortcut that bypasses more rigorous analytic reasoning) to aid in predictive judgments, such as judgments about the likelihood of certain future or counterfactual events. People tend to bias the likelihood of the occurrence by the "availability" of similar circumstances and past instances (or cases) that come to mind. The more easily a person can recall similar cases, the higher a person will estimate the likelihood of the event.[9]

One important form of the availability heuristic is the *simulation heuristic* by which we run "mental simulations" to construct scenarios to reason about hypothetical situations: to predict future situations, or address "What if" questions about counterfactual situations.[10] This mechanism is used when making judgments about situations where a person has no prior experience to draw on and so a cause-and-effect simulation is constructed to assess the situation. The ease with which a person can

Table 3.1 Comparison of System 1 and 2 Processes and Roles of Mental Models

System 1 Intuition	System 2 Reasoning
Attributes of Intuitive Thought: • **Automatic effortless** operation; the analyst is not consciously aware of the operation. • **Fast and immediate** in response to perception, something "comes to mind" and leaves an "impression." • **Applies tacit knowledge** that can often not be explained. • **Applies associative memory** to relate perceived cues to tacit knowledge from previous experiences and make matches. • **Focused on present time** perceptions as they occur. • **Operation not controlled** by the analyst, but responsive to perceived stimulus.	**Attributes of Deliberate Thought:** • **Deliberate effort** of the analyst to consciously focus the attention of a mental operation on a subject. • **Slow and purposeful** action of the analyst to focus and rationally "make sense" of information. • **Constructs explicit representations** of knowledge that can be articulated. • **Applies rational, logical constructs** to analyze information and synthesize explicit models of internal knowledge. • **Considers causality over time** in the past, present and into the future. • **Operation that is controlled** by the analyst and able to be modified and structured.
Role of Mental Models: • **Compares models** (complex patterns) based on prior experience to recognize current perception. • **Adds models** of sensed perception as experience grows; models are tagged with associated emotions or attitudes (e.g., fire-danger; ice cream-tasty). Triggered emotions can *initiate* or *inhibit* reasoning.	**Role of Mental Models:** • **Constructs and manipulates models** as an artifact of thinking about a subject. • **Runs mental models** over time as simulations to reason about hypothetical situations.

build such hypothetical causal simulations influences the likelihood with which the person estimates the likelihood of the event. Kahneman and Tversky showed how these heuristics lead to incorrect decisions and judgments; of course the most obvious is that likelihood estimates are based on the ability of a person to recall from memory (availability of similar cases) or to easily simulate an event (availability of a simulation). We tend to overestimate scenarios where dramatic changes take place and then underestimate the likelihood of a scenario where smaller changes that contribute to the outcome take place.

Of course, system 1 and 2 work together; system 1 is sensory-perception driven, passing impressions to system 2, while system 2 is more concept driven, focusing the attention of system 1 on subjects to be observed and understood. System 2 examines the impressions of system 1 and may establish them as beliefs, then build even larger (and stronger) models of belief by associating many impressions. (Later in this chapter we will introduce the term *mindset* to describe these models.) System 2 provides oversight of the cognitive process and should check the first impressions provided by system 1—but it is a "lazy controller," in Kahneman's terms, and often lets system 1 errors of judgment pass without appropriate vetting, even when a simple check can reveal the error. (This is why external cognitive devices, such as the simple checklist, can discipline system 2 to systematically review our analysis and find the assumptions or errors of intuitive judgment.)

Researcher Gary Klein's studies of decision makers have provided practical explanations of how the two systems often work together and the role of static mental models and dynamic mental simulations. Klein's "recognition primed decision making" (RPD) process posits that humans follow a naturalistic process for many categories of decisions—a process that engages both systems 1 and 2 quickly, enabling the comparison of alternative options. System 1 recognitions cue or "prime," a process that engages deliberate system 2 considerations. The process is a blend of the two systems, used by experts who are under time pressure and must make decisions with serious consequences; the experts must rely on their prior experience (mental models of a range of situations) to associate similar situations (or interpolate between them) and then choose a feasible course of action.

The RPD process can be summarized as follows:[11]

- Experience over time builds a subject-matter expert's mental models of situations in a domain of expertise (e.g., an intelligence analyst's repeated observations of the different behaviors or activities of a foreign military site over time). The mental model includes patterns of behavior and cues or attributes that uniquely distinguish them.
- When confronted with a particular situation (e.g., a sudden flurry of activity at the site), the analyst is cued to compare the current situation with the patterns built by experience and chooses the closest pattern matches as candidate explanations.
- The match activates action scripts that project out over time mental simulations of the implications or effects of this current situation, using the previously experienced patterns (e.g., prior rapid activations, emergencies, or training exercises at the military site). These mental simulations help the analyst address the key questions that must be answered: What will happen over the next twenty-four hours? What level of deployment can be achieved? What happens if we respond with a particular course of action? The analyst may mentally run many simulation trajectories, experimenting and exploring a range of possible consequences of the current situation.[12]

Mental simulation extends static mental models by using methods of story building (narrative descriptions of event sequences, complete with alternative branches and resulting sequels within a given context), analogical reasoning (comparing the situation to an analogous situation in the same domain), or metaphorical reasoning (comparing the situation to a different domain, to extend beyond previously experienced patterns).[13]

MENTAL MODELS AS ARTIFACTS OF THINKING

Scottish psychologist Kenneth Craik (1914–1945) postulated that the constructed mental symbols that Aristotle described were "small-scale models" that described: 1) the mind's perception of the external reality, 2) a hypothesis about reality, or 3) a purely imagined reality (e.g., a fantasy, a novel, a future vision to be fulfilled). Craig further described how the mind must be able to manipulate these mental models to understand and evaluate different versions of reality and even simulate the effects of actions on these models (e.g., mental simulations—the theater of the mind). These cognitive functions of model construction, manipulation, and simulation allow the mind to describe, explain and attempt to predict, and imagine even counterfactual situations.[14] Our internal models encompass a wide range, from simple patterns or signatures (e.g., names, colors, smells, textures) to complex counterfactual or fantasy simulations of hoped-for (or dreaded) events (figure 3.2).

More recent research by cognitive scientists has focused on the structures of these mental abstractions, or structures of belief, to understand how the mind organizes information into models. The research has focused on how the mind creates models at different levels of abstraction and how the mind structures and manipulates different kinds of information (e.g., linguistic models, imagery or pictorial models, causal models, logical models). An additional area of cognitive research also seeks to explain how models deal with uncertainty and how the mind reasons about uncertain models and uncertain evidence.[15]

Philosopher Michael Polanyi (1891–1976) identified the property of these mental models as *tacit knowledge*, arguing that the (system 1) "tacit way of knowing" is internal and personal, and that our models are framed by our own unique experience, and individual context. Therefore, the process of explicitly articulating our mental models can be limited by our ability to express things framed by our unconscious experience. Asserting that *"we can know more than we can tell,"* Polanyi believed tacit knowing was a precursor to discovery and preceded the logical form of reasoning. As in Aristotle's apprehension, or William James's preconception, tacit knowing is the formative stage of the mind's modeling.

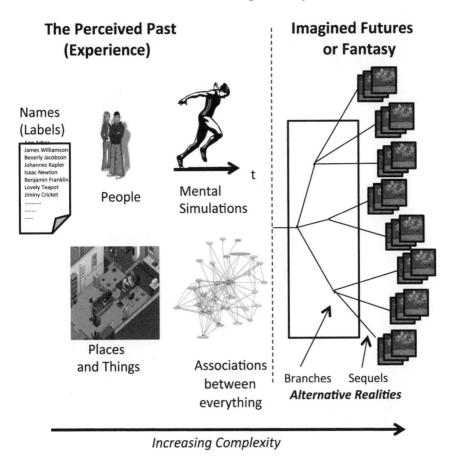

The Perceived Past (Experience)

Imagined Futures or Fantasy

Names (Labels)

James Williamson
Beverly Jacobson
Johannes Kepler
Isaac Newton
Benjamin Franklin
Lovely Teapot
Jiminy Cricket

People

Mental Simulations

t

Places and Things

Associations between everything

Branches   Sequels
Alternative Realities

Increasing Complexity

Figure 3.2 The wide range of complexity of mental models

Polanyi illustrated the difficulties, by using the example of the victim of a robbery who has a clear mental model of the thief but is not an artist. A police artist is required to elicit and capture the mental image of the face of the thief, although the victim is unable to explicitly represent the model.[16] Polanyi's work has been widely adopted by the knowledge-management community to distinguish between internal tacit knowledge used by system 1 and the explicit knowledge that system 2 operations express explicitly to be captured and codified and then shared with others.

While mental models provide us with an impressive power to choose and make judgments, they are not infallible; in fact, they are limited. Consider one cognitive scientist's warning about his observations of these models:[17]

1. Mental models are incomplete.
2. People's abilities to "run" their models are severely limited [i.e., mental simulations].
3. Mental models are unstable: People forget the details of the system they are using, especially when those details (or the whole system) have not been used for a period.
4. Mental models do not have firm boundaries; similar devices and operations get confused with one another.
5. Mental models are "unscientific": People maintain "superstitious" behavior patterns even when they know they are unneeded because cost little in physical effort and save mental effort.
6. Mental models are parsimonious: Often people do extra physical operations rather than the mental planning that would allow them to avoid those actions; they are willing to trade-off extra physical action for reduced physical complexity.

The combined effect of incomplete mental models, system 1 recognition errors (biases or illusions) and system 2 laziness, brings risk to intelligence analysis. Richards Heuer's now classic text, *The Psychology of Intelligence Analysis*, introduces the cognitive shortfalls that bias an intelligence analyst's judgment and presents a remedy in the method of Alternative Competing Hypotheses (ACH) that explicitly structures and models the relationship between evidence and hypotheses, disciplining the analyst to critically consider alternatives.[18] Heuer explicitly addresses the role of mental models in analysis, noting:[19]

> People [intelligence analysts] construct their own version of "reality" on the basis of information provided by the senses, but this sensory input is mediated by complex mental processes that determine which information is attended to, how it is organized, and the meaning attributed to it. What people perceive, how readily they perceive it, and how they process this information after receiving it are all strongly influenced by past experience, education, cultural values, role requirements, and organizational norms, as well as by the specifics of the information received. This process may be visualized as perceiving the world through a lens or screen that channels and focuses and thereby may distort the images that are seen. To achieve the clearest possible image . . . analysts need more than information. . . . They also need to understand the lenses through which this information passes. These lenses are known by many terms—mental models, mind-sets, biases, or analytic assumptions.

Heuer's work focused the attention of the Intelligence Community on the role of mental shortcuts and limitations of mental models in analysis. In this book we emphasize the benefits of using explicit models to provide discipline and rigor to overcome the limitations of mental models alone (figure 3.3).

Using Models and Simulations to Discipline our Cognitive Systems

My early days of analysis in the 1980's were devoted to simulating then-future US and Soviet air combat engagements where the US would confront a numerically superior Soviet air attack. My research was focused on the effects of alternative sensor suites and data fusion systems to gain a long-range identification long beyond visual range, and therefore a first-to-shoot advantage. Developing the computer simulations required detailed modeling of the signatures of a wide range of phenomena of fighter aircraft (e.g. radar cross sections infrared, signals, flight behavior, and others) and the on-board sensors that would detect them; the months spent developing each aircraft model, the sensor model, and the correlation, fusion and identification algorithms forced our team to painstakingly understand the implication of each signature on identification, and the joint contribution of signatures. For some of these combinations, the effect was obvious, for others that were dependent on sensor-target geometry, flight dynamics, range and environmental conditions - the effect was not at all obvious. Simulations allowed us to set a range of stressful conditions to find the mix of sensors and combat geometries that provided the greatest advantage. Integrating basic criteria-to-shoot decision making models and missile flyout simulations, we could compute the aggregate P_k (kill probabilities) and exchange rates for a range of scenarios. Analysis of Variance (ANOVA) procedures were applied over a large number of simulations and conditions to determine the statistical significance of our results.

As our team began running simulations of various encounter geometries, sensor mixes, and the effects of weather and the electromagnetic combat environment, I realized that the model began producing results that were not intuitive to my excited Air Force sponsor, but were not surprising to me. After all, I had spent months understanding the unique signatures of each Mikoyan and Sukhoi fighter. I had established the geometries of combat encounters, and had learned the conditions when the combination of sensors could combine to produce spectacular results, and when there was no joint contribution at all.

I realized that the model building process had been my teacher – disciplining me to address each detail, cross-checking each combination of sensor signatures, and conducting hand check tests to verify the proper operation of the fusion algorithms, and the validity of their results. My system 2 could not be lazy, or the simulation would show my sloppiness. The model-building and simulation results taught my system 1 process many mental models of air combat encounters and results, making me a good judge of when improved identification could have an impact on air combat outcomes.

See papers by Ed Waltz in the *Proceedings of the Combat Identification Systems Conference*, October 1984 and *Proceedings of the 54th Military Operations Research Symposium*, June 1986.

Figure 3.3 Using models and simulations to discipline our cognitive systems

INTELLIGENCE ANALYSTS AND THEIR MENTAL MODELS

Consider three examples to illustrate how intelligence analysts develop and manipulate mental models and simulations:

- A MASINT (measurement and signature intelligence) analyst who uses unattended ground sensors to monitor road traffic develops a daily activity model of traffic patterns around the clock, inferring a model of causality by correlating traffic levels to events (e.g., military movements at night when there is low civilian traffic). The analyst may also run mental visual simulations of what the traffic patterns "look like" on the roadmaps of the area.

- A GEOINT analyst responsible for monitoring a foreign facility reviews periodic images of the site to track construction, level of traffic, and other characteristics to understand the facility's purpose, capability, and activity. Over time, the analyst may build several static mental models: a "mind's eye" visual model of the buildings, roads, parking lots, and walkways; a timeline of the progressive construction activities, a basic model of the organization structure, based on number and types of buildings (R&D, machining, production), and a financial model of the cost to operate the facility (facility capitalization, labor, materials flow). The analysts may also mentally visualize a simulation of what the daily activity inside the buildings at the facility looks like and how a major event might unfold at the site, the flow of vehicles and the routes they would take.

- An all-source analyst monitoring a foreign government institution develops models of "how they work" in the form of relationship structures among major actors in the institution, a narrative story of the process and rules by which they operate, and the logic of their culturally based decision-making calculus. In this case, the analyst mentally simulates the process of decision making across the organization, considering the time for meetings and debates, phone conversations, and the arrival at political consensus on policy.

While the mental models provide these analysts a framework for conceptualizing their intelligence subjects, analysts must always be aware that the models may be in error in numerous ways, and the model must always be subject to critique, refinement, and revision. The analyst's job is to test and evaluate these models, exposing them to scrutiny by others, and subject to refinement or revision as new information is obtained.

In a classic *Studies in Intelligence* article entitled "Combating Mind-Set," analyst Jack Davis described mental models using the term *mindset* to refer to "the distillation of the intelligence analyst's cumulative factual and conceptual knowledge into a framework for making estimative judgments on a complex subject."[20] Davis described how mindset includes a commitment to a reference viewpoint on a subject and how creating this reference is a vital and indispensable element of human reasoning in intelligence analysis. But he also warned analysts to be ever aware that mindset introduces a bias against contradictory evidence—or competing mindsets. The power of a mental model also brings this *confirmation bias* vulnerability—the analyst's predisposition toward evidence that will fill in model gaps and reinforce the mental model, rather than treating contradictory evidence with equal importance (e.g., evidence that does not fit the model, or worse yet, suggests another more difficult model not yet conceived).

Davis suggested two strategies to combat the vulnerabilities of our models—mindset and confirmation bias:

- *Mindset Enhancement*—acknowledging the limitations of the human mind (and the mental models they create) in three important areas: volume of stored information that can be recalled, number of variables that can be coherently managed together, and the ability to simulate the dynamics of the models and the effects or consequences. Here, Davis endorsed the need for "simple tools and procedures" to aid the analyst.
- *Mindset Insurance*—acknowledge where high uncertainty exists, and provide decision makers with "values other than, or in addition to single outcome predictions."

The explicit modeling and simulation approaches recommended in subsequent chapters address each of Davis's remedies for the vulnerabilities of a rigid mindset: the use of explicit models to represent, expose, and extend mental models and the use of explicit simulations to provide briefings that explain the behaviors of a situation and range of effects, rather than a single outcome.

NOTES

1. By *policy*, we refer to a wide range of actions that include diplomatic, information, military, economic, financial, intelligence, legal, and other courses of action.

2. Rouse, W. B. and N. M. Morris, "On Looking into the Black Box: Prospects and Limits in the Search for Mental Models" *Psychological Bulletin* 100(3), (1986) 349–63; definition is on page 351.

3. For a thorough review of the variety of definitions of mental models in the cognitive science literature, see: Doyles, James K. and David N. Ford, "Mental Models Concepts for System Dynamics Research" *System Dynamics Review* Vol. 14, No. 1, (Spring 1998): 3–29; the definition quoted is on p. 17ff.

4. Kahneman, Daniel, "A Perspective on Judgment and Choice", *American Psychologist*, Vol. 58, No. 9, (Sept. 2003) 697–720.

5. Aristotle expressed this in his *Metaphysics*, written in 350 BC.

6. Stanovich, K. E. and R. West, "Individual Differences in Reasoning: Implications for the Rationality Debate?" in Gillovich, Thomas, D. Griffin and D. Kahneman (eds.) *Heuristics and Biases: The Psychology of Intuitive Judgment*, (New York:

Cambridge University Press, 2002) 421–40. For a review of the range of dual-process theories of cognition for dual processing reported within the literature in cognitive and social psychology, see Evans, Jonathan St. B. T., "Dual-Processing Accounts of Reasoning, Judgment, and Social Cognition," *Annual Review of Psychology*, 59 (2008) 255-78.

7. Figure adapted from Waltz, Ed "The Fundamentals of Reasoning, Detection and Multisensing", chapter 2 in Hyder, Waltz and Shahbazian (eds), *Multisensor Data Fusion*, (Kluwer Academic Publishers, Netherlands, 2002), 38.

8. The operation of this system was popularized in Malcom Gladwell's book, *Blink: The Power of Thinking Without Thinking* (New York: Little, Brown and Company, 2005), although the word "intuition" never appears in the book because journalist Gladwell prefers the term "rapid cognition." The book extolled the virtues of intuition to such a point that it could appear to be the most reliable form of thinking; the book placed little emphasis on the conditions under which system 1 is reliable and *when it is not*. A more recent, balanced, and technical treatment of both systems is provided by psychologist Daniel Kahneman himself in *Thinking Fast and Slow* (New York:Farrar, Straus and Giroux, 2011). Kahneman readily acknowledges system 1 is "the hero of the book" for its impressive automatic capability but also describes the power of blended system 1 and 2 thinking, in which intuition and reasoning complement each other.

9. Kahneman, Daniel, Paul Slovic, and Amos Tversky, *Judgment under Uncertainty: Heuristics and Biases* (New York: Cambridge University Press, 1982). The earlier work of these researchers in the 1970s formed the foundation for their pioneering studies in cognition. See Tversky, A. and D. Kahneman, "Judgment under Uncertainty: Heuristics and Biases," *Science* 185, (1974) 1124–31. Kahneman won the Nobel Prize in Economics (2002) for describing the irrational judgments that people make, by conducting basic experiments that demonstrate cognitive processes, shortcuts, and categories of errors of judgment.

10. Kahneman, Daniel and Amos Tversky, "The Simulation Heuristic," in Kahneman, Daniel, Paul Slovic, and Amos Tversky, *Judgment under Uncertainty: Heuristics and Biases*, (Cambridge: Cambridge University Press, 1982) 201–9.

11. *Naturalistic decision making* refers to the descriptions of how experienced people actually make decisions in operational settings (often under time pressure) where information is ambiguous, conditions are changing over time, and plausibility of achieving goals is also changing; this is in contrast with analytic decision making that refers to a range of structured, logical methods that are available to decision makers.

12. Klein, G. A., and B. W. Crandall, "The Role of Mental Simulation in Naturalistic Decision Making," in Flach, J., P. Hancock, J. Caird, and K. Vicente (eds.), *Local Applications of the Ecological Approach to Human-Machine Systems*, (Hillsdale, NJ: Lawrence Erlbaum Associates, 1995).

13. Klein, Gary, *The Power of Intuition: How to Use Your Gut Feelings to Make Better Decisions at Work* (NewYork: Doubleday, 2004); see also Klein, Gary A., Judith Orasanu, and Roberta Calderwood, (eds.), *Decision Making in Action*, (Norwood, NJ: Ablex, 1993).

14. Craik, K., *The Nature of Explanation* (Cambridge: Cambridge University Press, 1943).

15. For an introduction to this research, see Johnson-Laird, P. *Mental Models: Towards a Cognitive Science of Language, Inference and Consciousness* (Cambridge, MA: Harvard University Press 1983).

16. Polanyi, Michael, *The Tacit Dimension*, (Garden City, NY: Doubleday, 1966).

17. Norman, Donald A. "Some Observations on Mental Models" in Gentner, Dedre, and Albert Stevens, *Mental Models*, (Mahwah, NJ: Lawrence Erlbaum Associates Cognitive Science Series, 1983) 8. This text focused on the early efforts of artificial-intelligence researchers to explicitly capture and computationally represent mental models of systems that people commonly use.

18. Richards J. Heuer, Jr., *Psychology of Intelligence Analysis* (Washington, DC: Center for the Study of Intelligence, 1999).

19. Ibid., 13.

20. Davis, Jack, "Combatting Mind-Set," *Studies in Intelligence*, Vol. 36, No. 5, (Washington, DC: Center for the Study of Intelligence 1992) 33–38.

4

Translating Mental Models to Explicit Sharable Models

Just how do analysts translate their mental models to explicit ones? And how do they expose the tacit knowledge of their accumulated experience so it can be captured, codified, and shared with others? The translation process must map mental abstractions to a tangible representation on a chalkboard, on paper, or in a computer tool; the process moves from internal to external, from an informal mental conception to a more formal conceptual form.

As in other disciplines of the arts and sciences, intelligence analysts depict their mental models of reality in a variety of common forms:

- *Forms of Discourse*—the most common form uses the power of the written word to describe the analyst's model; the *narrative* text generally relates a *story* (including a set of actors, their relationships, and a sequence of events from a particular point of view), an *argument* (a reasoning process that supports a conclusion), or a *description* (an enumeration of the attributes that define and characterize a subject). The intelligence report is often an *exposition*, providing the basis for an intelligence estimate or judgment.
- *Graphical Forms*—A wide variety of forms of graphical visualization are available to describe physical structure, human relationships, temporal sequences, causality, output behavior, spatial locations, etc. The most common ones used in intelligence reporting include annotated maps, organization charts, materiel flow diagrams, network diagrams, tabular spreadsheets, and quantitative charts—bar graphs, pie charts, and statistical charts of probability distributions.[1]

- *Mathematical Forms*—quantitative models are expressed in mathematical relationships, ranging from enumerations (e.g., rank ordering of relative power of political leaders, estimates of the sizes of terrorist groups), to mathematical functions (e.g., an equation describing the relationship between poppy crop acreage, poppy yield, and opium production).

It should be noted that analysts often have preferences for the forms they use to represent concepts based on their personal style, formal training, experience, and the culture of their organization. Sherman Kent once noted that the ranks of analysts are made up of "poets and mathematicians."[2] Graduates of the liberal arts (humanities, natural sciences, and social sciences) are trained in the clarity of prose and tend to prefer the narrative forms, while those trained in the physical sciences and engineering prefer the graphical and mathematical forms. These are but expressions of the major approaches to solving problems in each domain (the use of language, the use of mathematics).

It was George Berkeley (a CIA "mathematician") who later wrote in *Studies in Intelligence* urging the development of a board to govern definitions:

> If a nuclear physicist were to write that "A few whatchamacallits created a new thingamajig when they bounced off a slew of whoosies," we might suggest that his terminology needed honing. Yet day in and day out we let reporters of political events (me included) get away with talking about "democracy," "nationalism," "insurgency," "dictatorship," "totalitarianism," "the right," "the left," "the slightly left of center," "probability," "possibility," and many other concepts that lack any universally accepted definitions. Why? My guess is that it's because the poets don't care—they like to keep words nice and loose—and the mathematicians haven't united to do something about it.[3]

For *appropriate problems*, this text describes how to translate mental models and "nice and loose" narratives to conceptual models that are tighter (more precise) and useful to clarify situations, understand uncertainties, and provide more insight into what can be done to improve their intelligence value.

FRAMING AND REPRESENTING AN INTELLIGENCE PROBLEM

The analyst's mental models form a "frame" or structure to describe a situation, subject, or event. *Framing* a problem is the process of conceiving or structuring an idea or concept (mental model). It includes the elements of forming boundaries, identifying constituent elements, creating a structure or relationships between elements, and imagining a subject as a system (figure 4.1). U.S. Army doctrine teaches planners to explicitly frame their problem (situation) as the initial step of any planning process to develop a comprehensive understanding of the situation:

> *Problem framing* establishes an initial hypothesis about the character of the friendly, adversarial, and wider environmental factors that define the situation. Problem framing also explores cultural narratives, institutional histories, propensities, and strategic trends in order to postulate a general structure of the factors and their relationships . . . the initial framing of the problem establishes only a starting hypothesis and a baseline for learning about the problem as the force operates. It sets the parameters for reframing—readjusting the commander's appreciation of the problem—as the commander's understanding expands and the situation changes over time.[4]

Problem Framing in the Sciences

Problem framing concepts are applied across the sciences, distinguishing the importance of structuring a problem, explicitly acknowledging the boundaries and perspective of the problem, and the influence of the frame on solutions. Frames control the context within which we evaluate data for its relevance as evidence.

Philosophy of Science – Historian Arthur Koestler described the discovery processes of science in terms of the ability to view information from different frames of reference; Koestler illustrated the rapid "aha!" of scientific discovery as the ability to see the data in a new frame that explains the data and their relationships.[i]

Organization Science –Management researcher Karl Weick has studied the means that organization employ to place information in context and create understanding - the process that Weick called *sensemaking*. He defined perspective as a generalized interpretive orientation (or frame) - the minimal sensible structure that people use to filter, focus attention, and adapt to data. [ii]

Mathematics – The Dempster-Shafer theory of evidence provides a mathematical means of quantifying and assembling evidence to derive probabilistic measures of belief in individual elements of evidence and in propositions (arguments) assembled from a mass of evidence. [iii] The theory defines a *frame of discernment* as the set of all possible situations that delimits a set of possible states of the world, exactly one of which is assumed to be true at any one time. The frame of discernment is the set of feasible perspectives from which to assemble evidence into propositions to be evaluated. The theory is structured as follows:

1. The analyst defines the Frame of Discernment - the mutually exclusive set of alternative explanations (S) of the set of items of evidence (e)
2. The Belief (S) summarizes all reasons to believe (S) and is represented by a basic probability, or mass m (S) that is derived as a sum of all supporting evidence
3. The Plausibility of (S) = 1 – Bel (S') or, 1 minus all contradictory evidence is computed
4. The Degree of Support for a proposition (S) is then expressed on an interval ($0 \leq$ Belief $\leq$ Plausibility ≤ 1)

---

[i] Koestler, Arthur, *The Act of Discovery* (NY: Macmillan, 1964).

[ii] Weick, Karl, *Sensemaking in Organizations*, (Thousand Oaks, CA: Sage, 1995).

[iii] Shafer, Glenn, *Mathematical Theory of Evidence*, (Princeton Univ. Press, 1976).

Figure 4.1 Problem framing in the sciences

Framing and reframing is the iterative process of learning—moving from initial hypotheses to refined versions that represent changes in the scope of the situation of interest, changes in information about the situation, and changes in confidence in understanding (degree of belief) over time. The framing process uses various mental-model structures to represent the situation, called *schemas*—the mentally constructed structures that represent aspects of the world.[5]

To the cognitive scientist and psychologist, a schema describes the kind of mental model used by a person to understand something in the real world and the way they may then explicitly represent their mental model by narrative description, by drawing, or even by a mathematical representation. To the computer scientist, a schema may refer to the kind of structural or quantitative representation used to describe something in the real world, as perceived in the analyst's mind.[6]

The most common forms of discourse (schemas) are used throughout intelligence reporting, for example:

- Description—The basic form to depict or explain a subject; the form may include a variety of devices, for example:

    o List—An enumeration (e.g., the organization has conducted operations A, B, C, and D.)
    o Sequence—Description of sequential action (e.g., they conducted surveillance using method A and then B, before probing security features and finally issuing attack type J.)
    o Simile—A figure of speech that explicitly compares two different things (e.g., political party A in Polistan is diffusing power like political party B in Lanmandia diffused power after World War II.)
    o Tabular—Organization of nonquantitative information in tabular form to present structure and relationship.

- Narrative—A description of an incident or event, a series of events, or a situation to place them in a logical or temporal order. The presentation is in the form of a story with relevant context to provide a coherent explanation.
- Exposition—A form that includes descriptive information and an explanation of the subject, a hypothesis, or an analytic judgment based on the descriptive information.
- Argument—a coherent series of statements leading from a premise to a conclusion (e.g., the logical syllogism form *modes ponens*—All A are B; X is A, therefore X is B).

More complex topics require greater sophistication in representation, and numerous *computational schemas* have been developed to provide structure to represent (and aid in construction of) our mental models:

- Spreadsheet—Arrangement of quantitative data in a mathematical matrix (or array) of rows and columns containing mathematical relationships between entries (e.g., spreadsheet of estimated narcotics production and distribution volumes for major drug cartels).
- Complex data—Relational database schemas; extensible markup language, etc., representations.
- Relational—Graph theoretic schemas that represent entities as points (or vertices) and relationships between entities as links (or edges); these schemas allow graph-to-graph matching, network attribute computation, and other operations.
- Timeline—Sequence schemas that label chronologies of events along a linear timeline and can compute temporal relationships between events and make inferences about sequential behavior.
- Formal Argument—Directed graph representation of the inference linkages that proceed from evidence to propositions
- Mathematical—Equation relating dependent to independent variables.
- System—Diagrams relating system inputs, the interconnection of internal processes, and outputs; the diagrams may be instantiated with quantitative attributes to translate the graphic form to a computable simulation (e.g., Bayes networks, systems dynamics models)

These and other common schemas used in intelligence analysis are summarized in table 4.1. Selecting a schema to organize evidence or to represent a mental model is the first step in developing an explicit representation.

To illustrate how these forms can provide different perspectives of a situation, consider the descriptive text of a foreign threat organization and four graphical and quantitative forms (that supplement the description with details) (figure 4.2).

In this case, the graphical and quantitative schemas supplement the discourse:[7]

- Relational Model—social network schema provides the relationships between primary actors in the KPM organization; this model may be used to compute social network metrics that characterize the connection properties of individuals and the entire network.
- Causal Model—causal loop schema shows the major relationships between interdependent organizations and systems; where these relationships (flows) and process magnitudes (stocks) can be quantified, a dynamic model of the process can be developed to explore dynamics, stability, and the effects of interventions.

Table 4.1 Representative Categories of Explicit Models

Form	Schema	Description (Intelligence Applications)
Prose (Discourse)	Narrative (Story)	Description that places a situation in a logical or temporal order with context (historical or forensic analysis; background to intelligence estimate)
	Description	Depict or explain a subject (order of battle; target summary; event or forensic analysis)
	Exposition	Descriptive information with explanation of a subject, hypothesis, or an analytic judgment (intelligence estimate)
	Logical Argument	Coherent series of statements leading from a premise to a conclusion (used to explain intelligence judgments)
Graphical	Map; Geospatial Overlay	Placement of entities, boundaries, physical features, routes, or events in geospatial context (geospatial analyses, e.g., thematic maps, hotspot analyses, area limitation analysis)
	Concept Map	Diagram showing the relationships among concepts
	Gantt Chart	Time-based plot of activity and events (forensic analysis of situation; generic temporal model of a threat or target activity)
	Causal Loop Diagram	System diagram of interrelationships between subsystem elements—expressed as feed forward and feedback paths of cause and effect (model of military system to assess operation targeting vulnerabilities)
	Social (Relational) Network	Network diagram of entities and relationships (organization relationships—roles, relations, transactions, etc.)
	Data Flow Chart	Diagram of flow of information, decisions, actions, and activities of an organization or system (target system data flow analysis)
	State Diagram	Diagram of system states and transitions between states (e.g., operational process states of a military system)
Mathematical (Quantitative)	Spreadsheet	Arrangement of quantitative data in a mathematical matrix or array (e.g., intelligence estimate of narcotics source, production, and transit parameters)
	Bar, Pie, Radar Diagram	Comparison plots of multiple variables, where spatial dimensions are proportional to the values that they represent (used to represent comparative data in intelligence estimates)
	Heatmap	Spatial plot of gradients of intensity (e.g., geospatial plot of distribution activities or incidents)
	Probability Distribution	Statistical chart of the probability of a random variable taking certain values (e.g., estimated distribution of the frequencies at which a target signal will occur)
	Scatter Plot; Cluster Diagram	Display of values for multiple variables for a set of data to reveal correlation (e.g., plot to locate clusters of threat behaviors in multidimensional data)

Discourse Schema

K2 (KMP- Kuanikka) Cartel

The K2 cartel was formed in 1997 in response to the rise in power of the PLJ Party and loss of access for illicit shipment in northern port cities. Cartel leader Mulitic Kartika conducted a ruthless campaign to establish operational cells in the north by 2002 before moving southward. By 2007 the cartel network had access to northern ports and the western frontier. [Narrative]

The KMP party is influenced by K2 cartel and the major drug traffickers (Paulo Carchini, L.M Fereiko) and at least 3 wealthy families (A, B, C) connected to legitimate import-export trade. A,B, and C are believed to involved in human trafficking. Immar Kuanikka, Minister of the Interior, has financial ties with family B, and is known to have a close relationship with Paulo Carchini. The Ministry of Interior is a corrupt organization that maintains judicial influence and controls the leadership of the Sorgenna Jiapo Hirata (SJH) or national police. The largest groups of cells are located in the Southern province, Port city of Hisu and located along the Western Frontier. Estimated annual revenues of the cartel exceed 100M USD, with the largest number of contributing cells along in the North and port cities. [Descriptive]

We assess that the cartel is vulnerable to leadership disruption because:
•Rising tensions between northern shippers and western frontier producers in competition for share of profits
•Recent counternarcotics operations have severely restricted cartel income.
•Violent clashes have already been reported between at least 6 cells across the cartel. [Argument]

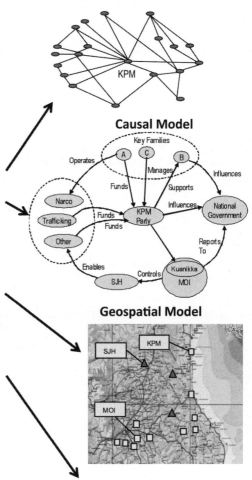

Relational Model

Causal Model

Geospatial Model

Quantitative Model

	Estimated	Estimated Annual Revenue (USD millions		
Provincial Zone	Cells	Drug Trade	Human Trafficking	Other Illicit
North and Port	90	50	10	5
East Boundary	25	10	5	unknown
Western Frontier	75	10	5	5
South	25	5	0	unknown
Totals	215	75	20	10

Figure 4.2 Five common forms used to translate and capture mental models

- Geospatial Model—An overlay of locations of organizations, events, and routes provides spatial context.
- Quantitative Model—The intelligence estimate of process values (stocks, rates, etc.) for different elements of the organization provide a comparison of relative contributions of each.

TACIT-EXPLICIT CAPTURE AND INTERACTION

The very process of capturing a mental model explicitly requires a creative interaction between the internal (mental) and the external representation. This process of *externalizing* that which is tacit and internal is found in the creative phase of writing, invention, scientific discovery, artistic expression, and for the intelligence analyst—the synthesis process of hypothesis creation from available evidence.

The experienced novelist, for example, translates the kernel of a story-line in his mind to a polished fiction, replete with vivid details, imagery, and action; the process requires development by interaction between the concept (mental model) and the external and detailed manuscript that cannot be fully carried in the mind—between the creative process of writing, and the critical process of review and rewriting. The novelist reviews supporting materials for background and to support creative elaboration of the story. The novel emerges from an iterative internal-external and creative-critical process to become an explicit representation that exceeds the original kernel of the mental model in scope, scale, and detail. Even as the novelist interacts with his manuscript, the analyst interacts with the emerging explicit representation of her internal model by writing, graphing, or quantifying to express a hypothesis (figure 4.3).

Research in the cognitive processes involved in research, writing, and revising is relevant to intelligence analysis (research) and synthesis (mental modeling, diagnosing the model, detecting errors like inconsistencies, and revising). Cognitive strategies for good writing fluency focus on the iterative revision process as an author interacts with the manuscript to revise and refine. Research shows that expert authors have an advantage of long-term memory of the topic, and have developed strategies to:[8]

- Learn by experience when to totally ignore a problem, defer a problem to later, immediately research and develop corrections or refinements for critical problems, or initiate a total revision.

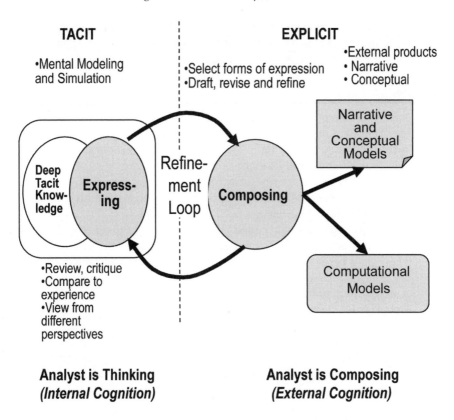

Figure 4.3 Tacit-Explicit externalization

- Distinguish between "detect/rewrite" (simplest solution to problematic text, but can also overload working memory if the writing task is complex) or "diagnose/revise" (more complex approach requires considerations of many options, and many changes throughout a manuscript).
- Invoke prior experiences to categorize problems in the text, and select previously applied approaches to solve the issue.

These principles apply to expert intelligence analysts who refine their mental models by explicitly representing them (in narrative or other explicit model forms) and revising them—detecting problems, diagnosing issues, and invoking prior experience to refine the model to an accurate representation of the evidence (correspondence) and one that is internally consistent (coherence).

This process for an individual can be viewed as an interaction between the internal memory of the writer or analyst and the *external* memory of the developing manuscript. When we consider group activities, cognitive psychologists distinguish three categories of memory involved in this process:[9]

- *Individual memory*—the ability of an individual to encode, store, and recall information (perceptions, conceptions, experiences). Individual memory retains tacit knowledge and the integrated memory objects we call mental models.
- *External memory*—the use of external symbols and mechanisms (e.g., written text, sketches, computer-based visualizations, etc.) to augment individual memory.
- *Transactive memory*—also called "group mind," is the set of individual memories, operating in combination with the communication that takes place between individuals. It is this collective and shared memory that enables collaboration processes. A critical property of this category is *accessibility*—the ability to search and discover that information is resident and the ability to gain access to that information.[10]

The activity of using external memory to augment individual memory to reason has been called *external cognition*.[11] It is the interaction between the internal (mental) model in the analyst's mind and external memory representations:

> *External cognition* is a phrase referring to ways that people augment their normal cognitive processes with external aids, such as external writings, visualizations, and work spaces. External cognition is human or cognitive information processing that combines internal cognition with perception and manipulation of external representations of information.[12]

The well-drafted intelligence report (in forms of discourse) is the primary external memory device and cognitive aid—allowing an analyst to build up a draft paper, add and refine details, check nuances of arguments and judgments, and review with others. In addition to the written piece, the analyst may use graphical depictions to represent evidence, arguments and hypotheses to expose their thought process, as well as their mental models of an event, situation, or a target system.

The increased use of computer-based interactive-visual graphics has introduced an entire discipline to enhance external cognition: *Visual analytics* is the term used for the science of analytical reasoning facilitated by interactive visual interfaces.[13] Card et al. have shown that visualization can be an external cognitive aid to enhance cognitive abilities in at least five fundamental ways:[14]

- Increasing human mental resources;
- Reducing the search time to locate information;
- Improving the recognition of patterns in information;
- Increasing the processes of inference making; and
- Increasing the scope of monitoring information.

Beyond these cognitive benefits, visual analytic *products* hold the potential to improve the clarity and comprehensibility of intelligence reporting, allowing an analyst to communicate evidence, arguments, and judgments more effectively to decision makers.

The National Visualization and Analytics Center (NVAC) has developed five principles for depicting information in visual form (figure 4.4). These visual depictions can represent: 1) a captured mental model that an analysts has formed by reviewing raw data or 2) information (structured and unstructured, qualitative and quantitative data) to enhance the ability to search, view, perceive, explore, and understand it. In both cases, the principles are focused on enhanced analytic reasoning. Notice that principles 2, 4, and 5 acknowledge the importance of making external representations of information correspond to mental model schemas, to enhance the natural cognitive process (not to confuse it with unnatural schemas).

Visual Analytic Principles for developing effective conceptual depictions

1. **Appropriateness Principle** – The visual representation should provide neither more nor less information than that needed for the task at hand. Additional information may be distracting and makes the task more difficult.
2. **Naturalness Principle** – Experiential cognition is most effective when the properties of the visual representation most closely match the information being represented. This principle supports the idea that new visual metaphors are only useful for representing information when they match the user's cognitive model of the information. Purely artificial visual metaphors can actually hinder understanding.
3. **Matching Principle** – Representations of information are most effective when they match the task to be performed by the user. Effective visual representations should present affordances suggestive of the appropriate action.
4. **Principle of Congruence** – The structure and content of a visualization should correspond to the structure and content of the desired mental representation. In other words, the visual representation should represent the important concepts in the domain of interest.
5. **Principle of Apprehension** - The structure and content of a visualization should be readily and accurately perceived and comprehended.

Source: Thomas J.J. and Cook, K.A. (eds) *Illuminating the Path: The Research and Development Agenda for Visual Analytics*, National Visualization and Analytics Center, Pacific Northwest National Laboratory, IEEE Press, 2005.,p.71.

Figure 4.4 Visual Analytic Principles for developing effective conceptual depictions

The preceding discussions have described the mental model capture process as if an analyst is informally capturing her own mental models or the aggregate model she learns by discussions with other subject matter experts informally. Ford and Sterman have described a more structured process for the analyst (or her supporting modelers) to elicit knowledge from multiple subject matter experts (SMEs) for model construction.[15] The more rigorous process includes three phases:

- *Positioning* (or *Framing*) establishes the context for the model by eliciting information on the model purpose, the major elements or subsystems and their interactions, and the boundaries of the model. Each subsystem is then described (inputs, outputs and internal functions) by each SME.
- *Description* is a phase of guided elicitation of each interconnecting relationship between modeled elements, depicting the relationship from four perspectives (visual, verbal, textual, and graphical), with a standard format for eliciting each.
- *Discussion* is the last phase that tests, understands, and refines the model by a facilitated discussion with all SMEs in a group setting, describing the different perspectives of the model across all SMEs. The purpose of this stage is not to achieve consensus but to understand the reasons for the diversity of views and the insight contributed by each.

Of course the collaborative process of sharing models across analysts allows the comparison of alternative competing models that represent different perspectives of a situation, different preferences for available evidence, and the different cognitive biases of their creators.

THE TACIT-EXPLICIT TRANSLATION PROCESS

So far, we have focused on the translation of tacit information to alternative explicit, codified forms. But the knowledge-creation process (including analysis, synthesis, discovery, and learning) includes all of the means of exchange between tacit and explicit of knowledge. Nonaka and Takeuchi have described a model of knowledge creation (figure 4.5) in which tacit-to-explicit (or, *externalization*) is but one of four modes of conversion.[16] The model proceeds in a clockwise spiral (of increasing knowledge) and can be illustrated by a hypothetical analytic modeling process, following the numbered stages in the figure. First, the analyst develops a concept for modeling an intelligence target or situation by discussions with subject-matter experts in other disciplines. This tacit-to-tacit *socialization* process (1) involves social interactions with other analysts, field personnel, and outside subject-matter experts to exchange experiences and mental models. The transfer involves discussions of experience (*storytelling*) to convey subjective understanding, to "re-experience" prior knowledge and explain context. Socialization includes the analyst's interactions with intelligence consumers, to share tacit knowledge about their own mental models (assumptions, preconceptions) and needs.

Externalization is the next stage (2) we have already discussed; the analyst articulates and expresses the mental model by choosing a representation method (metaphors, analogies or stories in text, graphics, spreadsheet, etc.) for explicit codification of the tacit models.

The third stage is the explicit-to-explicit *combination* process (3) where the codified models are characterized, indexed, correlated, and combined.

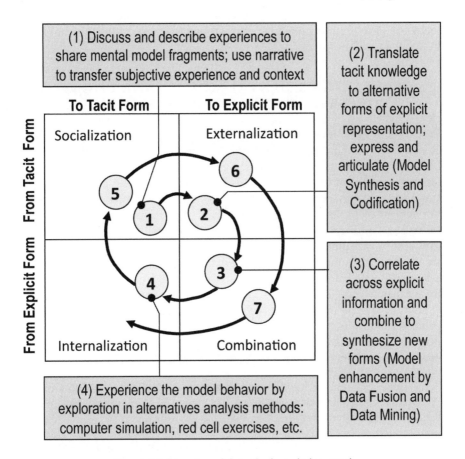

Figure 4.5 Use of models in the knowledge spiral

This can be performed by data fusion (deductive) or data mining (inductive) processes to locate related models, relevant information to support or refute the model, or other relevant sources of expertise.

Finally, to complete the first complete cycle of the spiral, the analyst experiences the combined knowledge in an exercise, simulation, or other method of engagement with the model to allow exploration of the consequences and effects beyond the initial context. In this explicit-to-tacit *internalization* step (4), the analyst is immersed in the model theory and behavior, experiencing and testing implications, and evaluating results in a new tacit experience. The internalization stage naturally leads to further socialization and process leads to further tacit sharing, creativity, and knowledge expansion. Of course, the model extends beyond the individual analyst; Nonaka and Takeuchi describe how these four stages of conversion represent an unending spiral—transferring knowledge throughout an ever-learning organization as intelligence analysts, in teams or in a common analytic environment, proceed through the steps together in collaboration.[17]

UNDERSTANDING MENTAL MODELS AND COGNITIVE PROCESSES TO ENHANCE ANALYTIC RIGOR

Researchers have long studied intelligence analysis to describe the processes involved, including the methods, procedures, and most significantly, the cognitive activities of the analyst. Efforts to describe the cognitive processes of intelligence analysis have tracked the progress in the cognitive sciences, seeking to describe system 1 and 2 processes and cognitive shortcomings, and to proscribe remedies to improve analytic performance.[18] More recent research in *sensemaking* (the cognitive processes that assign meaning to experience by placing information in context to create understanding) and *critical thinking* (the intellectual disciplines to arrive at belief from experience) has also focused on the processes and disciplines to increase the rigor in the analytic process.[19]

Beyond the theoretical analysis of analytic thinking in general, the process of studying a *particular* intelligence analysis task, to describe the process as a cognitive workflow and proscribe potential improvements applies the method of Cognitive Task Analysis.

> *Cognitive Task Analysis (CTA)* is the extension of traditional task analysis techniques to yield information about the knowledge, thought processes and goal structures that underlie observable task performance.[20]

The goal of CTA in intelligence is to understand how analysts perform cognitive tasks, capturing descriptions of the procedural activities and methods, reasoning processes, and decisions performed by analysts for *specific* tasks. The outcome of CTA studies include a description of the performance objectives, tools, conceptual knowledge, procedural knowledge, and performance standards used by analysts as they perform an analytic function to deliver a product.[21] The cognitive task-analysis process begins with a knowledge audit, conducted by reading prior analytic reports, interviewing analysts, observing analysts, and conducting interviews with consumers of the analytic products. Interview methods typically include standard approaches:

- Direct query to analysts for information to derive a description of the analytic process (abstract methods). Core questions to be answered include the representative items in table 4.2.
- Follow-up queries that ask for narrative descriptions of *specific* recent situations that illustrate the answer to the question (case method). The case answer is then followed up with deeper questions that enter more deeply into how the situation was handled and what rationale (thought process) was involved and what analytic judgments were made.

The knowledge audit is followed by an analysis to develop a model of the external procedural workflow as well as a description of the internal reasoning modes of the analyst, the explicit knowledge, and tacit knowledge (e.g., expertise expressed as the analyst's required knowledge, skills, and abilities) applied to the problem. The results of a CTA provide a baseline for evaluating current procedures, the analysts' use of mental models and cognitive processes, and analytic performance—and a basis to examine how external cognitive aids may improve performance. In the next chapter, we provide a very general analytic process that resulted from the CTA of a wide range of intelligence analysts, to distinguish the fundamental cognitive steps that move from source to intelligence product.

We have previously asserted that the process of explicitly capturing and representing models provides a level of discipline that can expose biases or errors introduced by mental shortcuts. This explicit representation process brings a rigor to the process—thoroughness that is inherent in the structured analytic methods promoted by Heuer's work (see notes 6 and 18) and subsequent analytic tradecraft methods taught within the Intelligence Community.[22]

Researchers D. J. Zelik, E. S. Patterson, and D. D. Woods at Ohio State University have studied the specific mechanisms that bring rigor to analytic processes in healthcare as well as intelligence.[23] The OSU team defined *rigor* as a depth of analysis that is achieved by analytic strategies that are opportunistically employed throughout the analysis process.

Table 4.2 Typical Questions to Be Answered in the CTA of an Analytic Task

Category	Representative Questions to Be Answered
Stakeholders and Context	1. Who are the primary consumers of intelligence products? How do they use it? What are the most important elements of products to consumers? How long does it take to produce the product? 2. What decisions are made as a result of products? 3. What gaps or shortfalls do consumers see in current products?
Inputs	4. What are the key questions that drive the analysis? 5. Do the questions change from analysis to analysis? 6. What are the primary sources used and their relative contribution?
Analytic Process	7. What are the analysts' educational and career backgrounds? 8. Are there any specialty analyst/analytic roles (e.g., geospatial, socio-cultural, targeting, source analysis, cryptanalysis, etc.)? 9. What are the forms of the products? What schemas are used to represent source information, analysis, and judgments? 10. How do the analysts find, use, and cite their data sources? 11. What is the notional workflow from source to finished product? Who is involved in each step? How are sources used, tracked, and cited? Are there standard metrics that are used in reporting? 12. How do analysts collaborate throughout the workflow? 13. What are the thinking processes that are employed in each stage of the workflow (e.g., foraging for information, checking sources, inferring causes, deducing effects, creating hypotheses, comparing evidence to arguments, making judgments, etc.)? 14. How do analysts use the forms of discourse, graphs, diagrams, or other visual analytic methods to support thinking or to supplement their reporting? 15. Does the production of final reporting proceed through a number of phases and reviews?
Automated Information Systems and Tools	16. How do the analysts manage their in-process work product? What tools are used to prepare the assessment? 17. How is each tool used in process? Are the tools linked in any way? How is in-process work stored? 18. Do analysts use any other form of collaborative software? 19. Do analysts represent their mental models? Do they consult any statistical data or theoretical models?

They further point out that these strategies are alternatively conceptualized as checks that "broaden" the analysis because they:

- tend to slow the analysis and production of an analytic product, and
- make the process of analysis more explicit, while
- both of these require with a conscious sacrifice of efficiency in pursuit of accuracy.

This emphasis on accuracy over efficiency is a key trait of rigor. The OSU team defined eight attributes that characterize rigor and established low, medium, and high degrees of rigor for each attribute. These degrees of rigor, measured across the eight attributes, provide a metric to assess the level of rigor applied in any analysis. The eight attributes, organized in the sequence from information acquisition and evidence marshaling to hypothesis evaluation, are summarized in table 4.3, with the contribution of explicit modeling to each attribute. In each case, the process of explicit modeling requires a conscious, structured approach to expose the analytic process itself and the underlying evidence and hypotheses.

Table 4.3 Role of Models in Supporting Analytic Rigor

Attribute	Rigor Attribute Description[1]	Contribution of Models to Rigor
1. Information Search	Measure breadth and coverage of search; estimate theoretical saturation where search reaches diminishing return.	Models of hypotheses provide a reference to quantitatively measure the contribution rate of new information obtained in search.
2. Stance Analysis	Analysis of backgrounds of sources of information to assess the stance (frame and bias) relative to particular issues.	Statistical analysis methods can provide data models that provide insight into *some biases* in quantitative and unstructured data sources.
3. Information Synthesis	Organize and place information in context to conceptualize appropriate schemas to fit evidence to hypotheses; provide traceability from evidence and inference to hypotheses.	Models of hypotheses and arguments explicitly reveal the relationships between evidence and alternative hypotheses.
4. Information Validation	Apply systematic processes to vet data and assumptions supporting key arguments.	Models require explicit exposure of assumptions, and the sources of data used for each modeled element.
5. Hypothesis Exploration	Explore broad range of hypotheses beyond the initial frame of the hypothesis space; expand range based on outlier and contradictory data that do not support strongest hypotheses.	Computational models and simulations allow analysts to efficiently examine and explore alternatives by changing structure or model parameters; they also allow rapid comparison of alternatives.
6. Sensitivity Analysis	Formal assessment of the sensitivity of hypotheses to the supporting evidence and assumptions.	Quantitative models provide measurement of sensitivity of hypothesis accuracy to available data; the models also allow analysis of how additional data can reduce uncertainty.
7. Specialist Collaboration	Analytic collaboration includes evaluation and contribution by key experts in the domain and sources to refine hypotheses.	Explicit models of hypotheses allow detailed and interactive examination by analytic teams.
8. Explanation Critique	Examination by peer and subject matter experts (SMEs) to examine framing and range of hypotheses, alternatives considered, and lines of reasoning in each hypothesis.	Models allow peer and SMEs to apply alternative and critical analyses of detailed, explicit explanations; simulations allow them to conduct analytic games to critique and explain the dynamics of hypotheses.

1. The "rigor metric" for any particular analysis measures the degree to which the analysis accomplishes the attribute. The OSU team defined high, medium, and low criteria for each of the eight attributes.

As analysts frame their problems, develop appropriate schemas to represent their mental models of their thinking and their subjects of analysis, and collaborate with others, they contribute greater rigor to their analysis—and increase the potential accuracy and clarity to their analysis. As analysts' mental models are captured, translated to explicit representations, and shared with others, there is also reduced potential for the errors of bias and mindset to remain hidden and influence analytic judgments without notice.

NOTES

1. For an elegant survey of graphical methods of capturing mental models and representing information, see Tufte, Edward R., *Envisioning Information* (Cheshire, CT: Graphics Press, 1990).

2. Kent, Sherman, "Words of Estimative Probability," *Studies in Intelligence* Vol.8, No. 4, (Washington, DC: Center for the Study of Intelligence) 49–64.

3. Berkeley, George, "For a Board of Definitions," *Studies in Intelligence* Vol. 9, No. 3, (Washington, DC: Center for the Study of Intelligence) 13.

4. U.S. Army TRADOC *Commander's Appreciation and Campaign Design*, TRADOC Pamphlet 525-5-500, Version 1.0, (January 28, 2008) 17.

5. *Framing effects* refers to the influence of frames on cognition in decision making; people make different choices depending upon how an option is expressed when presented to the decision maker. Tversky and Kahneman's *prospect theory* (1981) posits that decisions are based more on the decider's prospect of potential value (losses and gains), rather than on the final outcome. The way an option is expressed (framed) influences how decision makers perceive gains and losses; they tend to avoid risk when an option is framed positively but accept risk when framed negatively.

6. The framing process develops the mental schema structures that Richards Heuer refers to as "lenses" in his work because they direct, screen, and focus (and sometimes distort) the information used in our cognitive processes.

7. We noted earlier in this chapter that our academic training influences our choice of preferred schemas to represent situations (and our skepticism of other schemas); these preferences can readily be seen in intelligence reports from different agencies. It is no wonder that analysts trained in the liberal arts prefer the nuance of careful forms of discourse, while analysts with science and mathematical training will supplement discourse with charts, graphs, and quantitative depictions.

8. For a summary of the research in cognitive models of the author's revision process, see chapter 3, Becker, Anne, "A Review of Writing Model Research Based on Cognitive Processes," in Alice Horning and Anne Becker, *Rhetoric and Composition, Revision: History, Theory, and Practice*, (West Lafayette, IN: Parlor Press, 2006). Conceptual models of the writer's revision process can be directly mapped to the intelligence model synthesis- revision process (e.g., see the process revision model, page 29).

9. Wegner, D. M. "Transactive Memory: A Contemporary Analysis of the Group Mind" in B. Mullen, and G. R. Goethals (eds.), *Theories of Group Behavior* (New York: Springer-Verlag, 1986), 185–208.

10. Note that Wegner includes external memory *within* transactive memory; the external memory of colleagues, as well as the individual memory of colleagues is included within this broad category. Wegner, D. M., "Transactive Memory: A Contemporary Analysis of the Group Mind," in B. Mullen and G. R. Goethals, (eds.), *Theories of Group Behaviour*, (New York: Springer-Verlag, 1986) 185–208. Also see Wegner, D. M., T. Giuliano, and P. Hertel, "Cognitive Interdependence in Close Relationships" in W. J. Ickes (ed.) *Compatible and Incompatible Relationships*, (New York: Springer-Verlag 1985) 253–76.

11. Scaife, M. and Y. Rogers, "External Cognition: How Do Graphical Representations Work?" *International Journal of Human-Computer Studies*, 45, (1996) 185–213.

12. Palo Alto Research Center (PARC) Glossary of Sensmaking Terms, accessed online March 29, 2011, http://www2.parc.com/istl/groups/hdi/sensemaking/glossary.htm.

13. Thomas, J. J. and K.A. Cook, (eds.), *Illuminating the Path: The Research and Development Agenda for Visual Analytics*, National Visualization and Analytics Center (Joint publication of Pacific Northwest National Laboratory and IEEE Press, 2005).

14. Card, Stuart K., Jock D. Mackinlay, and Ben Shneiderman, *Readings in Information Visualization: Using Information to Think*, (New York: Morgan Kaufman,1999) 15–17. For another view of these benefits, see Hegarty, Mary, "Mental Visualizations and External Visualizations" in *Proc. of the 24th Annual Conference of the Cognitive Science Society*, CogSci'02, (Mahwah, NJ: Lawrence Erlbaum Associates, 2002) and Hegarty, Mary, "Diagrams in the Mind and in the World: Relations Between Internal and External Visualizations," *in Proc. Diagrams 2004—Diagrammatic Representation and Inference—Third International Conference*, Cambridge, UK, (March 2004).

15. Ford, David N. and John D. Sterman, , "Expert Knowledge Elicitation to Improve Mental and Formal Models", Report D-4686, (Cambridge: MIT Sloan School of Management, May 1997).

16. Nonaka, Ikujiro and Hirotaka Takeuchi, *The Knowledge-Creating Company: How Japanese Companies Create the Dynamics of Innovation* (New York: Oxford University Press, 1995).

17. A more abstract model of the information creation and diffusion process is presented by Max Boisot in a three dimensional Information Space (I-Space). The knowledge creation cycle moves from 1) *personal knowledge* (experience that is concrete, not codified, and undiffused to others) to 2) *proprietary knowledge* (codified and abstracted, but undiffused) as it is explicitly represented, then 3) it can be diffused to others and it becomes *public knowledge* that can be applied by many. The cycle continues as 4) the abstract knowledge is applied and individuals experience *common sense* knowledge in their own applications domains, leading back to 1) *personal knowledge* as they discover nuances and refinements about the general knowledge. This forms a learning cycle in the I-space framed by three dimensions: the degree of diffusion, degree of codification, and degree of abstraction of the

knowledge. See Boisot, M. H., *Knowledge Assets: Securing Competitive Advantage in the Information Economy* (New York: Oxford University Press, 1998), and Boisot, M. H., *Information Space: A Framework for Learning in Organizations, Institutions and Culture* (London: Routledge, 1995).

18. The Army Research Institute has published a series of reports that document its research over three decades to apply emerging cognitive science research to intelligence analysis and military decision making. See: 1) Katter, Robert, Christine Montgomery and John Thompson, "Cognitive Processes in Intelligence Analysis: Descriptive Model and Review of the Literature," ADA-086451 (U.S. Army Research Institute for the Behavioral and Social Sciences, December 1979); 2) Katter, R., C. Montgomery, and J. Thompson, "Human Processes in Intelligence Analysis: Phase I Overview," ARI Research Report No. 1237, (U.S. Army Research Institute for the Behavioral and Social Sciences, February 1980); 3) Thompson, J.R., R. Hopf-Weichel and G.E. Geiselman, "The Cognitive Bases of Intelligence Analysis," AD-A146132, (U.S. Army Research Institute for the Behavioral and Social Sciences, January 1984); and 4) Cohen, Marvin S., Bryan B. Thompson, Leonard Adelman, Terry A. Bresnick, and Lokendra Shastri, "Training Critical Thinking for The Battlefield Volume I: Basis in Cognitive Theory and Research," (Ft. Leavenworth, KS: U.S. Army Research Institute Field Unit-Leavenworth, June 2000). Richards Heuer's work focused on cognitive biases in *The Psychology of Intelligence Analysis*, (Washington, DC: Sherman Kent School, 1999) and Thomas Gilovich provided a popular presentation of the cognitive shortcomings in, *How We Know What Isn't So: The Fallibility of Human Reason in Everyday Life* (New York: Free Press, 1991).

19. Two texts in the National Defense Intelligence College series provide comprehensive introductions to these areas. See Moore, David T., *Critical Thinking and Intelligence Analysis*, Occasional Paper Number 14, (Washington, DC: National Defense Intelligence College, March 2007), and Moore, David T., *Sensemaking: A Structure for an Intelligence Revolution*, (Washington, DC: National Defense Intelligence College, March 2011).

20. Schraagen, J. M., S. F. Chipman and V. L. Shalin (eds.), *Cognitive Task Analysis*, (Mahwah, NJ: Lawrence Erlbaum Associates, 2000), 3.

21. Crandall, Beth, Gary Klein, and Robert R. Hoffman, *Working Minds: A Practitioner's Guide to Cognitive Task Analysis*, (Cambridge, MA: MIT Press, 2006).

22. U.S. Government, *A Tradecraft Primer: Structured Analytic Techniques for Improving Intelligence Analysis*, Unclassified unlimited distribution, Released March 2009, accessed July 15, 2009, at the CIA website: https://www.cia.gov/library/publications/publications-rss-updates/tradecraft-primer-may-4-2009.html.

23. Zelik, D. J., E. S. Patterson, and D. D. Woods, "Measuring Attributes of Rigor in Information Analysis" in E. S. Patterson and J. E. Miller (eds.), *Macrocognition Metrics and Scenarios: Design and Evaluation for Real-World Teams* (Aldershot, UK: Ashgate, 2010). For an example application of the rigor metric assessment applied to healthcare, see Patterson, E. S., D. Zelik, S. McNee, and D. D. Woods, "Insights from Applying Rigor Metric to Healthcare Incident Investigation," in *Proceedings of the Human Factors and Ergonomics Society Annual Meeting*, Vol. 52, No. 21 (September 2008) 1766–70.

5

Explicit Models in Structured and Quantitative Analysis

Detailed and rigorous analytic methods are those that follow a process that is *structured* and *systematic*: an objective and organized process that records the context of the problem, the evidence used, and the thought processes involved. In addition, they are *transparent*—with the transparency provided by *explicit representations* of the analyst's understanding about a complex situation. Explicit representations, especially in the form of conceptual models (logical and mathematical) and computational models or simulations (that implement the mathematics and logic), are supportive of traditional narrative descriptions, and provide a unique ability to achieve the structure, systematic and transparency properties.

The characteristics of analysis that is explicitly structured, systematic, and transparent include:

- *It Demands Rigor*—Logic and mathematics demand a level of formality that requires complete expression of an intelligence problem to allow for consistency, proof, and solution. This formality imposes a level of rigor on the expression of a problem and the approach to development of a solution.
- *It Enables Sharing and Is Open to Examination*—As a result of the rigorous effort to formally express a problem, the results are inherently shareable and the explanation is provided with the shared product.
- *It Promotes Alternatives*—Once the formal expression (or model) of the intelligence problem is developed, the model may be modified to consider alternative versions or entirely different explanations.

STRUCTURED AND QUANTITATIVE ANALYSIS

Structured Analysis is a mechanism by which internal thought processes are externalized in a systematic and transparent manner so they can be shared, built upon, and easily critiqued by others.[1] Structured analytic techniques are based on the premise that analysts must expose their mental models in a way that will allow them to be scrutinized by the analyst and by others in order to mitigate the effects of cognitive shortfalls.

The Intelligence Community identifies specific characteristics of structured analytic methods intended to assist in making mental models more explicit and exposing their key assumptions:[2]

1. Instilling more structure into the analysis process.
2. Making analytic arguments more transparent by articulating them and challenging key assumptions.
3. Stimulating more creative, "out-of-the-box" thinking and examining alternative outcomes, even those with low probability, to see if available data might support these outcomes.
4. Identifying indicators of change (or signposts) that can reduce the chances of surprise.
5. Highlighting to intelligence consumers the potential changes that would alter key assessments or predictions.
6. Identifying to consumers key assumptions, uncertainties, intelligence gaps, and disagreements that might illuminate risks and costs associated with policy choices.
7. Exploring for consumers the alternative outcomes for which policy actions might be necessary.

While IC descriptions of structured analytic methods are relatively broad, experienced analysts Richards Heuer and Randolph Pherson developed a taxonomy of analytic methods that distinguishes four methodology categories:[3]

1. *Expert Judgment*—Intelligence analysis performed by analysts who are experts in the subject matter; these subject matter experts (SMEs) rely on their familiarity with the evidence and context and the application of critical thinking skills and analyst-unique methods. Analysts apply their experience and mental models formed by examination of the information available. Any explicit representations of the problem or the analyst's thinking are for the analyst's personal use.
2. *Structured Analysis*—A set of methods that provide procedural methods to organize and represent information and the critical thinking process used in analysis. Structured methods use *conceptual models* to

organize and represent the information. While none of the methods require computational tools, some may benefit from such tools to manage the data bring represented conceptually.[4]

3. *Quantitative Methods Using Expert-Generated Data*—In many intelligence problems the target is difficult to observe and empirical measurement data are sparse. For example, underground facilities, activities covered by denial and deception, covert organizations, and social systems are among the classes of intelligence subjects that defy the collection of abundant empirical data. In these cases, SMEs are called upon to estimate the structural characteristics (for example, organization structure, underground facility tunnel configuration, etc.) and parametric properties (for example, number of organization members and recruitment rates, facility electrical power consumption and feed water supply pressure, etc.). These estimates are based on contextual knowledge (e.g., about terrorist organization operations or about facility operations) and inferred from the limited information about the target. The contextual knowledge provides a hypothesis about the target system, and expert-generated data instantiate a hypothetical model of the system. SMEs model alternative theories about a target system, and generate synthetic data that would be observed empirically if that hypothesis were true of the observed target. For example, an analyst studying a protected foreign nuclear program may develop *hypothetical models* of two nuclear processing methods used in weaponization: Method A (Uranium U-238 enrichment) and B (Plutonium Pu-239 made from U-238 in reactors) as candidates. The models, tailored to the limited information collected, are instantiated with parameters to produce data that can be compared to observations to test the method A and method B hypotheses, and guide what data should be collected (see chapters 7 and 9 for examples of this use of hypothetical models).

4. *Quantitative Methods Using Empirical Data*—Some intelligence problems focus on target systems that produce measureable empirical data. Social systems (e.g., individuals, organizations, or populations), communication systems, traffic systems, and financial systems are examples of targets that produce empirical data sets that may be collected by intelligence. The empirical data are statistically analyzed and a *data model* is generated to estimate the internal behavior of the system producing the data. For example, an analyst studying narcotics systems and their flows may compare crop acreage data and production data to create a data model that relates acreage (input) to production (output) to understand the factors that can support counternarcotics operations.[5]

In chapter 7 the distinction between empirical data models and theoretical models is further described in the context of target system modeling, and the characteristics and appropriate applications of each for intelligence analysis are described.

Table 5.1 Role of Models in Categories of Analytic Methods

Analytic Category	Description and Representative Methods	Role of Models
Expert Judgment (Qualitative)	Subject matter expert (SME) applies critical thinking methods to precede analytic judgment on the basis of evidence: • Historical and case study methods that rigorously collect and organize evidence to develop explanatory hypotheses; • Evidentiary reasoning methods that move logically from evidence and inference to propositions and judgment; • Analogous reasoning methods that make inferences about an unknown subject based on analogies to known subjects, distinguishing similar and dissimilar characteristics.	**Mental models** hold the expertise (experience, knowledge, perspective) of the SME, and the SME's conception of a particular situation.
Structured Analytic Methods (Qualitative)	Procedural analytic methods externalize mental models and the analytic procedures themselves in conceptual, explicit representations. Methods include: • Problem decomposition and representation visually • Methods to generate and organize ideas (concepts) • Scenario representation and identification of indicators that distinguish between scenarios, or indicate the emergence of a particular scenario • Methods to generate hypotheses, to evaluate alternatives and reason about diagnostic evidence • Causality assessment (Key assumption checking, reasoning by analogy, role playing, etc. to represent cause-effect) • Methods to challenge established hypotheses (alternative analysis methods) • Conflict management methods to coordinate analysis of conflicting points of view • Decision analysis methods to represent options, decision spaces, and factors that influence outcomes	**Conceptual models** capture the representation of mental models explicitly—adding structure and visibility to the reasoning process, assumptions, evidence, hypotheses, and basis of judgments.
Quantitative Methods	Hypothetical (expert-generated) models are based on hypotheses of the structure and parametric data representing target systems. SME models alternative theories about a target system; *theoretical models* produce data that can be compared to observations and guide what data should be collected (see chapter 9 for examples)	**Computational models, simulations and games** represent situations quantitatively to enable dynamic exploration of the behavior of a target system to understand causality.

All of the categories rely on models; the three categories of models introduced in this text map readily to the categories of Heuer and Pherson's taxonomy (table 5.1). Expert judgment relies on the *mental models* of the experts making judgments. Structured analysis utilizes a variety of *conceptual models* to provide an objective and procedural structure to organize the intelligence problem, to marshal evidence, and evaluate candidate hypotheses.

Quantitative methods apply *computational models* and *simulations*, as well as *games* that are instantiated with the numerical parameters generated by SMEs or from collected data sets. While structured methods generally use conceptual, qualitative models, quantitative computational models can be applied. In chapter 6, for example, we illustrate a computational implementation of the structured method of Alternative Competing Hypotheses (ACH), where the computational tool aids in organizing evidence and hypotheses, and computing hypothesis scores.

Heuer and Pherson note that the most common criticism of structured techniques is that analysts claim they do not have enough time in their hectic schedules to apply the methods.[6] While this complaint is characteristic of structured analytic methods—the complaint is also true of quantitative modeling methods, perhaps with twice the emphasis, because computational methods demand a higher level of rigor, data, and validation. Quantitative methods generally require significant time and discipline to implement, and the Intelligence Community has introduced analytic methodolologists to support analysts in applying these methods.

FIRST, A CAUTION

While promoting the virtues of models in structured and quantitative analysis, we are careful to note that such analysis is not *in itself* the analytic panacea; indeed, the approach may tempt the analyst to place greater confidence in the results than they should. Consider for example, the case of analytic estimates of munitions traffic to lower South Vietnam through Sihanoukville, Cambodia, during the Vietnam War. A recently declassified study has described the competition between a sophisticated (structured and explicit, as we are recommending in this chapter) CIA analysis of munitions traffic and a Pentagon analysis based on empirical field reporting. The contentions between the deductive (deductions from a theoretical model) and empirical approaches, respectively, were severe throughout 1960–1970 until the CIA analysis was proven wrong. This was a major failure, because it denied U.S. forces a necessary threat understanding, particularly in the months leading up to the 1968 Tet offensive. The declassified study of this failure provides us a stern warning:

The effort to make sense out of ambiguous, inconsistent, even contradictory data is a fundamental human impulse. Clarity, certitude, or just escape
from the discomfort of not knowing—the urge is to bring order out of chaos,
to eliminate uncertainty. The order in things that this effort discovers—or
imposes—is taken to be the truth. Certitude has, of course, no necessary
connection with truth. Partly responsible for this is what might be called
the paradox of belief. That is, the level of emotional attachment to a given
interpretation tends to vary inversely with the amount of empirical evidence
supporting it. The more a hypothesis rests on *a priori* argument or circum-
stantial evidence, the more intensely its proponents defend it. But the less the
direct evidence, on an issue of empirical fact, the greater the probability that
it is flawed or simply false. Intelligence analysis approaches the truly objective only to the extent that its practitioners recognize and compensate for the
subjective factors that so easily corrupt professional judgment. But even the
most professional of analysts is vulnerable to the influence of unexamined
preconceptions and values.[7]

Here, the author of the study is emphasizing that the use of analytic
models (with rigor, openness to examination, shared, and open to alternatives) does not trump the flaws of subjective human bias and judgment.
Indeed, the study showed the failure of analysts who simply preferred
the elegance of their "deductions from an academic model over inferences
from incomplete and inconsistent clandestine reporting."[8]

While some drew the conclusion that even spotty reporting is always to
be preferred to analytic models, it was recognized that individual reports
of fact acquire meaning only when integrated into a hypothesis, which
demands an overall conceptual model.[9] In the end, the study concluded
that "assumptions and biases most strongly held are those most in need of
examination. Accepting as a general principle the danger of unexamined
premises may open the analyst, if not always to proactive self-criticism, at
least to respectful attention to divergent views. Absent that openness, the
universal human desire for the comfort of certitude may overwhelm the
spirit of neutral inquiry that remains the ideal of professional analysis."[10]

EXPLICIT MODELS IN THE ANALYTIC PROCESS

Explicit modeling fits within a larger intelligence analysis process that
moves from empirical evidence to intelligence judgments contained in
formal intelligence reports.[11] Pirolli and Card describe the intelligence
analysis process in a model of *sensemaking* (the cognitive processes that
assign meaning to experience by placing information in context to create
understanding). The model identifies the stages of reasoning between
empirical data and presentation of an analytic judgment (figure 5.1).[12]

The model distinguishes the bottom-up (driven by data) process of foraging, then organizing, data and the top-down process (driven by hypothesis) of refining and testing hypotheses against data, and conceptualizing alternatives. Of course, in practice, analysts perform this process in both directions concurrently, driven down to data by the critical questions and guiding hypotheses, and upward toward new or refined hypotheses by the discovery of new insights revealed from data.

From the bottom-up perspective, the analyst forages through data, searching for information relevant to the issue, storing that data in a "shoe box" (local repository of information, so named after the historical use of shoe-box sized containers for imagery analysts' reference images) and then, from that corpus, selecting subsets of data (e.g., text *snippets*, annotated image *chips*, map *chips*, or other data subsets). These directly relevant items are maintained in an evidence file that can be used to instantiate a conceptual model (based on some schematic format or schema in step 10) and subsequently to support a specific hypothesis (in step 13).

The explicit modeling process occurs in stages 10 and 13 in the sense-making model—the process of developing a schema and hypothesis:

- Schematize (Step 10)—The analyst develops one or more schemas— or frameworks—into which the data may fit (or correspond); typical schemas include: a logical proposition, a map of spatial relationships, a timeline that implies causal relationships, a network of social relations, etc. Even with sparse or incomplete data, the analyst may begin to lay out concurrent schemas (e.g., a timeline of phone calls and the network of callers) to better understand a situation.
- Hypothesize (Step 13)—This stage is the formal placement of data into the schema and explanation of gaps to assemble a working hypothesis (gaps may be completed by inference or assumption—and require further collection). The hypothesis may be used to deduce expected observations—thus driving collection to focus on information that may support or refute a hypothesis. (In the Center for the Study of Intelligence report cited earlier, this is the process of "deduction from an academic model.")

The analyst iterates between these stages: building, examining, refining, discarding, and finally adopting hypotheses as the basis for analytic judgments when reporting to decision makers.

The modes of this iteration (figure 5.2) describe the analyst's initial interaction with raw data, conceptual models, and computational models. In the empirical data-driven mode (1), the analyst is foraging for data, scanning and then drilling down into the content to search for relevant evidence (e.g., collecting snippets in the shoe box). In this process, the analyst forms tentative mental models of possible explanations of the data.

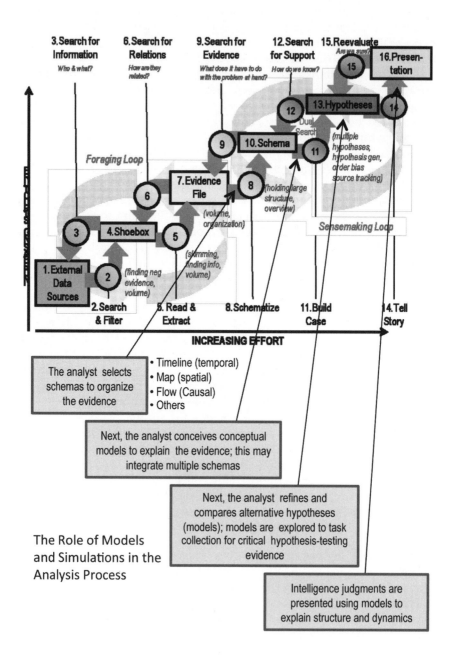

Figure 5.1 Analytic Sensemaking Model (Pirelli and Card 2005)

In the next mode (2), as the mental models develop, the analyst may explicitly represent the data in an explanatory schema, an explicit conceptual model that is shareable with others as a working hypothesis. The hypothesis describes how the evidence fits the models, where it does not (potential inconsistency and refutation), and the gaps in information to confirm the model (incompleteness). At this point the foraging and collection processes may become more driven by the hypothesis as the analyst seeks additional data to develop and test the hypothesis; data may confirm or refute the hypothesis.[13] At this stage, the analyst may develop alternative hypotheses to account for all of the available data and the gaps in information.

Depending upon the difficulty, importance, and the enduring nature of the issue, it may be appropriate to build a computational model that represents the dynamic behavior of the target system. (For example, a foreign WMD facility may have the properties of difficulty, importance, and endurance; on the other hand a small criminal organization may not.) This model applies the data in the conceptual model and represents the behavior to explore the dynamics of the hypothesis and seeks temporal data to further refine (refute-support) the hypothesis. The model may also be used to predict the expected behaviors of the target system and test against actual data to refute-refine the dynamic hypothesis.

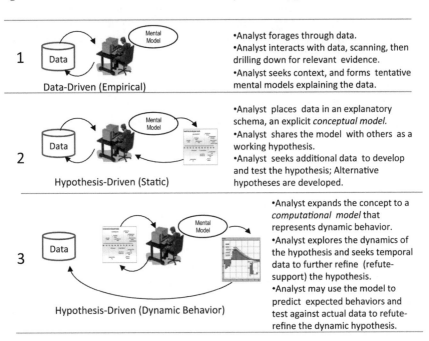

1	Data — Data-Driven (Empirical)	•Analyst forages through data. •Analyst interacts with data, scanning, then drilling down for relevant evidence. •Analyst seeks context, and forms tentative mental models explaining the data.
2	Data — Hypothesis-Driven (Static)	•Analyst places data in an explanatory schema, an explicit *conceptual model.* •Analyst shares the model with others as a working hypothesis. •Analyst seeks additional data to develop and test the hypothesis; Alternative hypotheses are developed.
3	Data — Hypothesis-Driven (Dynamic Behavior)	•Analyst expands the concept to a *computational model* that represents dynamic behavior. •Analyst explores the dynamics of the hypothesis and seeks temporal data to further refine (refute-support) the hypothesis. •Analyst may use the model to predict expected behaviors and test against actual data to refute-refine the dynamic hypothesis.

Figure 5.2 Stages of schema and hypothesis development

THE EXPLICIT MODELING PROCESS

Following our own emphasis on explicit representations, we describe the explicit modeling process in a *concept map* that links the relationships among a set of related concepts. The mapping process is an informal method for organizing and representing knowledge and precedes more formal methods of ontology development. The concept map of the explicit intelligence modeling process (figure 5.3) distinguishes three high-level concepts and the relationships between them:

- Real-world systems and their characteristics—Systems in the real world of interest to intelligence (the intelligence target or target system) include those activities that produce threats or problems that create critical analytic questions for policy makers. These systems (e.g., a terrorist organization, a foreign military weapon system, a narcotics distribution network, etc.) are characterized by a structure and behavior that must be understood to estimate the threat potential, and identify approaches to mitigate the threat.
- Analytic Framework—The approach to analyze (i.e., to decompose or separate into constituent elements) the situation and explain it is performed in this framework. This framework distinguishes the analytic methodology from the method to explicitly represent the problem in conceptual models and from the method to synthesize a computational model.
- Documentation—The analytic process must be documented, as well as the results of the analysis in the intelligence reports that describe analytic judgments. When the analyst chooses explicit models, the burden for documentation is higher (it is a part of the rigor) because the models, their rationale for use, and validity must be documented.

Notice that the process includes a critical validation element that compares the real world system and the models of that system to determine the degree to which the models correspond to the real world, for the intended purpose of analysis. This effort is essential to support claims of model utility, and to develop confidence in the modeling process.[14] The analytic framework, at the center of the figure, includes three aspects or perspectives of the analysis that must be described (table 5.2).[15] The first perspective is a description of the *analytic method*—the approach to decompose the problem, acquire data, and create hypotheses that answer (or most completely address with the information at hand) the critical analytic questions. This perspective provides a rationale for the methodology and justifies the use of conceptual and computational models, as well as the roles that models contribute to analysis. The purpose for each

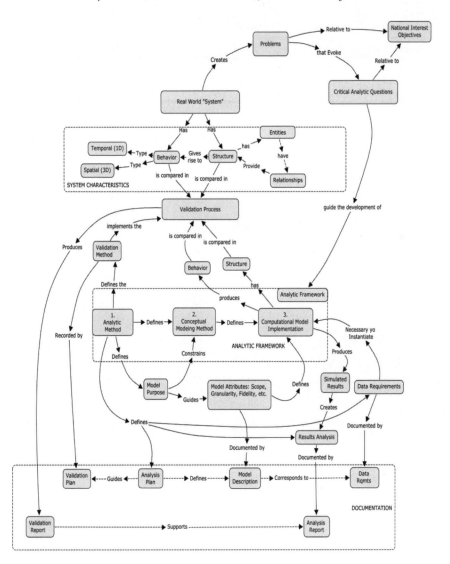

Figure 5.3 Elements of the analytic framework

model should be clearly described, as well as the method to validate the model for that purpose.

The second perspective is the *conceptual model*. This is the temporal, spatial, logical, relational, or other frameworks, against which evidence will be marshaled to create hypothetical explanations of the target system. From this perspective, the analyst must describe any conceptual models

Table 5.2 Analysis Framework Perspectives

Perspective	Description	Typical Products
Analytic Approach	Describes the overall analytic approach, rationale, and expected form of solutions to the critical analytic questions. Defines the information needed to perform analysis and the expected sources of that information. Justifies the use of models and the role that models contribute to analysis, and limitations. Defines the purpose of each model and the method to validate the model for that purpose.	• Objective, key issues and analytic purpose • Analytic workflow • Information requirements • Uses of models in the analysis • Validation approach to meet intended purpose
Conceptual Modeling Method	Describes the conceptual models used in analysis, the schema for each, and the data required to instantiate each schema. Identifies the theoretical basis for each model and the uncertainty in the theory, the data, and the effect on modeling results.	• Model schema • Empirical and theoretical basis for the model • Instantiated conceptual models • Data requirements
Computational Modeling Implementation	Describes the approach to implement computational models and the basis for translating the concept to computation. Identifies data inputs and input requirements, internal model processes, empirical and theoretical basis, and outputs.	• Functional description • Software description • Data model • Data files (input data, results)

used in analysis, the schema for each, and the data required to instantiate each schema. (The process of accumulating evidence around a hypothesis often referred to as *marshalling*; the process of explaining the hypothesis is referred to as *argumentation*, where the hypothesis provides a means of structuring the argument for presentation to decision makers. This process is described in detail in chapter 6.) There exists a number of classical approaches to representing hypotheses, marshalling evidence to them, and arguing for their validity. The validity of this process rests on the critical and objective testing of those hypotheses by either or both of two means: confirmation of a hypothesis to a degree, or disconfirmation (or falsification).[16] The theoretical basis for each model must be carefully justified (i.e., prior experience with similar targets, an academic theory of behavior, an accredited and widely adopted commercial model, etc.).

Where appropriate, the analysis may require a *computational model*. This third perspective of the analysis describes the implementation of the model and the basis for translating the conceptual model to a computational version. The required data, functional processes, and outputs must be described, as well as the specific means to perform validation for the purpose it is intended for.

CASE STUDY: AN EXAMPLE OF THE EXPLICIT MODELING PROCESS

To illustrate the process of developing an analytic framework and implementing a simple computational model, consider the development stages that might be taken by an analytic team studying a particularly thorny problem—the growth processes that influence terrorist activities in a foreign country. In this situation, the analysts have available data on the number of terrorist activities (e.g., violent acts and criminal activities to provide financial support) and a limited understanding of the groups themselves, based on information from captured terrorists.[17]

Policy makers define the key critical question: *What are the recruitment rates of this growing threat?* and *What mechanisms account for the growth?*

Analytic Method—The team moves from these questions to define an approach to use available data and identify gaps in data to task collection. The focus is to provide two answers:

- an estimate of growth rates over the past year, and a projection of continued rates under alternative circumstances; and
- a description of the recruitment mechanisms contributing to growth in the number of terrorists, and the likely actions that may impact the growth rate.

The method involves organization of the active participant data and the activities data in a spreadsheet to identify gaps and needs for collection. From the spreadsheet, the team identifies two organizing schema to structure the data: a timeline of estimated census and activities, and a geospatial map on which census and activity can be located. The analytic concept identifies several theories of recruitment and radicalization; the organization of data in these conceptual models of time-behavior and geospatial locations may allow testing of the hypotheses that relate growth to societal mechanisms. For this reason, the team also identifies and requests additional demographic data in terrorist operating areas that may help assess the correlation of actual data with hypotheses to determine the validity of alternative hypotheses.

Conceptual Model—Next, the team develops an approach to implement the analytic approach, explicitly representing the raw data, temporally smoothed data to estimate terrorist census growth, and its geospatial distribution. The organization of these conceptual models (figure 5.4) includes the structure of analytic activities, focused on three models:

- *Data organization model* is a simple spreadsheet such as Microsoft Excel™ that organizes available data in weekly columns over the past year; this includes estimated population, and activities of different categories. Analysts also organize geographic location data on activities, events, and areas where suspected terrorist groups operate.
- *GIS spatial model* places the activity and residing area data in GIS map layers in a tool such as ESRI ArcGIS™ to visualize terrorist operations and activities relative to other map layers of demographic data (income, ethic patterns, locations of political sites, etc.).
- *Dynamic organization model* includes alternative simple growth models based on the alternative recruitment theories, each estimating group population (the dependent variable) as a function of candidate contributors (independent variables) defined in the theories (e.g., demographics, economics, crime rate, sentiment of population toward government and toward terrorist appeals, etc.).

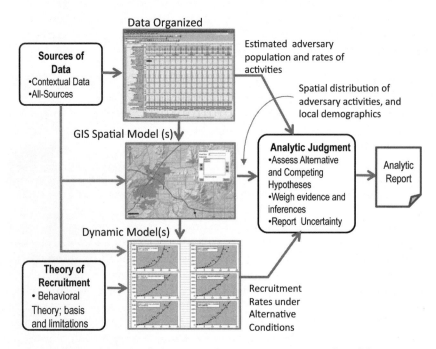

Figure 5.4 Example terrorist analysis using computational models

Computational Model—For this analytic method, and the conceptual models defined by the analytic team, three computational models are required. First, the Excel™ spreadsheet requires a definition of the simple schema (spreadsheet time-based layout of data) and the identification of data to populate the sheet. Often these data are available, and a data model is required to show the data are mapped from collection formats to the spreadsheet format. Second, the ArcGIS™ data layers and spatial analysis approach must be described. Because both the spreadsheet and GIS tools are commonplace, and the approaches are intuitive, the computational description is relatively straightforward and easily justifiable. The third computational model of recruitment rates requires description of the translation of two alternative recruitment theories into computable models.

Depending on the complexity of the theories, these models may be implemented in a spreadsheet such as Excel™, or a more sophisticated continuous-time model, such as system dynamics using tools such as VenSim™ or iThink™. The behaviors produced by these models are evaluated by comparison of the previous year's actual data against model predictions based solely on the independent variables for that period.

All models are quantitative in nature—the data-organization and spatial model are based on empirical data sources, while the dynamic-organization model is based on a theoretical model of organization dynamics and uses SME-generated data. The three models may be compared and even functionally linked (e.g., observed event location data can be used to estimate organization event capacities). The implementation of the conceptual models in computational forms allows the analyst to explore the relationships between organization data, locations, and dynamics—and identify the needs for collection to enhance the models and understand relationships between organization size, capacity, finances, and recruitment and locations of operation.

SUMMARY

Explicit models, especially formal models that provide a logical and mathematical basis to marshal evidence and argue for a hypothesis, provide a degree of analytic rigor that exceeds that of less formal methods and narrative argumentation. The formal modeling concepts introduced here provide an explicit representation that allows sharing (for analytic collaboration) and critical examination (for analytic criticism), while revealing supporting and refuting data. But rigor comes with a price—the necessity for documentation and validation that peels away the mystique of sophisticated approaches and creates confidence in users who are skeptical of elegance and complexity.

NOTES

1. This definition is provided in Heuer, Richards J. Jr. and Randolph H. Pherson, *Structured Analytic Techniques*, (Washington, D.C.: CQ Press 2011) 4. The text is a handbook of structured methods and provides a comprehensive and helpful taxonomy of methods that we adopt in this and following chapters.

2. U.S. Government, *A Tradecraft Primer: Structured Analytic Techniques for Improving Intelligence Analysis*, 2.

3. Heuer and Pherson, *Structured Analytic Techniques*, chapter 2. See also Heuer, Richards J. Jr, "Taxonomy of Structured Analytic Techniques," *Proceedings of the International Studies Association 2008 Annual Convention*, (March 26–29, 2008).

4. Perhaps the most well-known structured techniques, the method of Alternative Competing Hypotheses (ACH), is illustrated in chapter 6 using a simple computational tool to organize information.

5. See, for example, a narcotics empirical quantitative analysis that also applies a theoretical model of production operations in: Blanchard, Christopher M., "Afghanistan: Narcotics and U.S. Policy," Congressional Research Service Report RL 32686, (updated June 19, 2007).

6. Heuer and Pherson, *Structured Analytic Techniques*, 7.

7. Ahern, Thomas L. Jr., *Good Questions, Wrong Answers: CIA Estimates of Arms Traffic through Sihanoukville, Cambodia during the Vietnam War*, (Washington, DC: Center for the Study of Intelligence, February 2004), vii. Declassified and Approved for Release February 19, 2009, CaseCOS260S26.

8. Ibid., 41.

9. Ibid., 48.

10. Ibid., 48–49; the study acknowledged the limitations described in Richards Heuer's, *The Psychology of Intelligence Analysis* (Washington: Center for the Study of Intelligence, 1999).

11. For a more detailed description of this process, see the author's text, *Knowledge Management in the Intelligence Enterprise*, (Boston: Artech House, 2003).

12. Pirolli, Peter and Stuart Card, "The Sensemaking Process and Leverage Points for Analyst Technology as Identified through Cognitive Task Analysis," in *Proceedings of the 2005 International Conference on Intelligence Analysis*, (Washington, DC: Office of the Assistant Director of Central Intelligence for Analysis and Production, 2005).

13. The cognitive shortcoming at this point in analysis, described by Richards Heuer (*Psychology of Intelligence Analysis*, 1999), is the *confirmation bias*—the tendency of the analyst to seek confirming information and discount conflicting information that refutes the hypothesis. See also Davis, Jack, "Combatting Mind-Set" (*Studies in Intelligence*, 1992).

14. *Validation* is the process of determining the degree to which a model or simulation is an accurate representation of the real world from the perspective of the intended uses of the model or simulation (DoD definition). A more general definition that applies to the entire analytic process is provided by ISO 9000 standards: Confirmation by examination and through provision of objective evidence that the requirements for a specific intended use or application have been fulfilled.

15. The three perspectives of the framework introduced here are similar to the DoD Architecture Framework perspectives used to develop and describe enterprise architectures; see "DoD Architecture Framework" Version 1.5, Volume I: Definitions and Guidelines (Department of Defense: April 23, 2007).

16. In practical intelligence analysis, efforts to both confirm and refute are important methods of comparing, evaluating, and selecting hypotheses. It is important to note, however, that the philosophy of science has hotly debated these methods, with some viewing either one or the other as valid means of obtaining objective knowledge, but not both. Philosopher Karl Popper (1902–1994) applied the term "falsification" to the process of gaining certain knowledge by disconfirming conjectures. Popper rejected the traditional logic of induction and confirmation as the basis for scientific discovery, asserting that certain knowledge is gained only through falsification.

17. A description of just such an analysis was published in Waltz, Ed, and Jeffrey White, "Exploratory Intelligence Analysis of Insurgencies: Analytic Methods and Tools for Large-Scale Dynamic Assessment," *BAE Systems EI&S Fellows Journal* 7 (September 2006) (unclassified, limited distribution).

6

Explicit Models of Analytic Thinking

Earlier, in chapter 2, we introduced the distinction between representations of our thinking about a problem, and representations of the real-world problem itself (or the intelligence target). The distinction is subtle but important; one is a model of our reasoning process to allow us to reason about our reasoning, the other is a model of what that reasoning leads us to believe about reality. One is a model of abstract things; the other is a model of concrete things in the real world.

Models of analytic thinking represent our assumptions, rationale, argument, logic, assessments, and judgments regarding an object; they are models of a situation or target that explicitly reveal the basis of our belief about the object itself.

The 2007 Intelligence Community Directive (ICD) 203 on analytic standards specifically notes that the explicit presentation of the basis for analytic assessments and judgments is required to meet proper standards of analytic tradecraft (see figure 6.1).[1] The standards emphasize explicit description of the following elements of analysis:

- underlying sources and their effect on conclusions;
- assumptions (implicit or explicit hypotheses) and information gaps (assumptions may be used to bridge these gaps);
- distinctions between source information, inferences to hypotheses, and resulting judgments, and the logical argumentation that proceeds from source evidence to judgments or assessments.

Intelligence Community Analytic Standards
For Explicit Representation of Analytic Thinking

The following selected subparagraphs from ICD 203 specifically establish the necessity for describing the elements of thought that lead to intelligence assessments and judgments.

4. c (1) *Properly describes quality and reliability of underlying sources* – Analytic products should accurately characterize the information in the underlying sources and explain which information proved key to analytic judgments and why. ...

4. c (2) *Properly caveats and expresses uncertainties or confidence in analytic judgments* – Analytic products should indicate both the level of confidence in analytic judgments and explain explain the basis for ascribing it. ...

4. c (3) *Properly distinguishes between underlying intelligence and assumptions and judgments* – For the purposes of this standard, assumptions are defined as explicit or implicit hypotheses that may affect outcomes or the way in which information is interpreted or weighed. They deal with identifying underlying causes and/or behavior of systems, people, organizations, states, or conditions. Assumptions comprise the foundational premises on which information and logical argumentation build to reach analytic conclusions. Assumptions may also Span information gaps that would otherwise inhibit the analysis from reaching defensible judgments. Judgments are defined as logical inferences from the available information or the results of explicit tests of hypotheses. They comprise the conclusions of the analysis.

4. c (6) *Uses Logical Argumentation* – Analytic presentation should facilitate clear understanding of the information and reasoning underlying analytic judgments. Key points should be effectively supported by information or, for more speculative or "think pieces," by coherent reasoning. Language and syntax should convey meaning unambiguously. Products should be internally consistent and acknowledge significant supporting and contrary information affecting key judgments. Graphics and images should be readily understandable and should illustrate, support, or summarize key information on analytic judgments.

4. c (8) *Makes accurate judgments and assessments* – Analytic elements should apply expertise and logic to make the most accurate judgments and assessments possible given the information available to the analytic element and known information gaps. Where products are estimative, the analysis should anticipate and correctly characterize the impact and significance of key factors affecting outcomes or situations. Accuracy is sometimes difficult to establish and can only be evaluated retrospectively if necessary information is collected and available.

Figure 6.1 Explicit representation of analytic thinking

Explicit structural and quantitative models described in this chapter provide three potential benefits to the analytic process. First, these methods allow analysts to conceive, structure, evaluate, and articulate their reasoning about an intelligence problem. They allow the analyst to examine and challenge their own thinking, clarifying the representation before exposing it to the scrutiny of others. These methods also allow the analysts to track the changes in their reasoning over time—as new evidence is obtained (and as old evidence may be proven false). It allows the analyst to explain how arguments are dependent upon certain evidence, inferences, and assumptions—and how judgments will change if some of these elements are faulty.

Second, collaborative development of an argument and intelligence judgment can be facilitated by explicit models, whether on a whiteboard or by using a computer-based model to represent group contributions. The process, called *participatory modeling*, seeks to benefit from collaborative multiple-perspective thinking and group ownership in the model. Sticha et al., have demonstrated, for example, the use of a visual modeling tool to facilitate collaborative reasoning by a team about an intelligence situation to arrive at a group judgment. The facilitator guides subject matter experts (SMEs) to develop the problem and then elicits estimates of model parameters. The model in this case was a Bayesian network that estimated probabilities of alternative hypotheses for a situation, based on SME estimated probabilities for root conditions and an SME-developed structure of intermediate inferences from the root conditions to the terminal hypothesis to be judged. The group-developed model is projected onto a screen and the participants visualize the structure of the argument and the probabilities being jointly assigned.[2]

Third, and perhaps the most advanced use of explicit models of thinking, is the ability for computational tracking and scrutiny of the analyst's reasoning. Just as word processors are now expected to check spelling and grammar, in the future analytic reasoning expressed explicitly may be checked computationally for coherency and correspondence, and changing arguments may be tracked over time to aid the analyst in argument refinement.

In this chapter we describe and illustrate common modes of thinking and the methods that can be applied to explicitly capture and describe the analytic thinking to support appropriate analytic standards. We will move from informal and loosely structured concepts to more formal tightly structured representations that follow the analyst's move from a creative problem conception phase to a more logical characterization of hypotheses to explain a problem. Throughout, we illustrate the analytic modeling process using a progressive development of models that support the analysis of a notional foreign chemical weapons (CW) capability.[3]

EXPRESSING ANALYTIC THOUGHT
IN EXPLICIT MODELS

Earlier, in chapter 3, the fundamental modes of intuitive and deliberate thought were described, and in chapter 5 we introduced a conceptual model of the general sensemaking process followed by analysts as they move from data to analytic judgments. Between these fine-grain and top-level abstractions are the reasoning processes that analysts apply to scan data, discriminate relevant information (evidence), develop hypotheses, and then test and refine them into intelligence assessments and judgments.

Consider how the flow of this process (figure 6.2) integrates several forms of reasoning to move from intelligence sources to an intelligence judgment:

- *Problem Decomposition*—Of course, the first step of the model-based approach to analysis, introduced earlier in chapter 2, includes a decomposition of the intelligence problem to derive the specific knowledge required to satisfy the need, identify current information available and gaps.
- *Information Scanning*—The analyst reviews incoming data and forages through data in holdings to gain context and locate directly relevant information. This largely intuitive (system 1) process relies on existing mental models to associate new information and determine relevance to the analytic problem. Relevant information is generally filed in the analyst's local holdings ("shoebox")—and organized by a taxonomy that will allow it to be easily recalled. In some cases, key "snippets" (extracted paragraphs with source citations) or "chips" (extracted and annotated imagery selections) are selected for integration into a written argument or a model of the line of reasoning. Evidential science professor David Schum describes the importance of this process and its need for guidance from the more deliberate hypothesis generation process:

> Having expectations, in the form of initial or preliminary hypotheses, is commonly recognized as a necessary prerequisite for efficient and productive data search. Alas, in this matter, the eminent sage Sherlock Holmes may have given poor advice. He is reported to have told Dr. Watson: "It is a capital mistake to theorize before you have all the evidence." Without at least some hypothesis or guess, Holmes could never have decided where to begin his search for clues. There is, of course, absolutely no requirement that preliminary hypotheses be "final" in any sense or that they require lasting commitment; they serve to initiate the investigative or discovery process, are tentative in nature, and are subject to refinement or revision in light of new data. Of course, entirely new hypotheses may come to mind as work proceeds on an inference problem. The generation of hypotheses is, like problem definition, a creative process resting upon the analyst's substantive expertise.[4]

- *Deliberate Analytic Reasoning*—The deliberate and conscious process includes interactions between at least three basic forms of thinking (next bullets); and these thought processes rely on existing mental models (beliefs) to generate and express new lines of reasoning, tentative beliefs (hypotheses), and judgments.

- *Abductive and Retroductive Reasoning*—These less formal (but more immediate and common) forms bring imaginative or creative thought to synthesize alternative explanations of evidence and then to assess their feasibility. By abductive reasoning, the analyst conceives alternate (even hypotheses yet unsupported by the evidence) explanations and seeks to "reason to the best explanation." By retroduction, the analyst returns to the pool of information to seek evidence to match (or test) a newly conjectured hypothesis.

- *Inductive Reasoning*—In the process of reviewing many specific cases, the analyst may *induce* a general pattern from the many particular cases. The analyst scanning a foreign country's chemical-weapon intelligence data may, for example, notice similarity in structure (e.g., of covert chemical purchasing networks) or of causality (e.g., of weapon testing sequences). By inductive inference, the analyst may assert a new conditional hypothesis describing a general theory for how *this class* of CW developers operating *under these conditions* will structure their purchasing processes and conduct testing.

- *Deductive Reasoning*—When the analyst is focusing on a specific target or situation, relevant evidence may be assembled and linked together to form a hypothesis that explains the evidence. By deductive inference, the analyst may assert a hypothesis and the linkage that connects evidence via deductions to the hypothesis. Logical syllogisms often provide the linkages; the most basic form (*modus ponens*) is the primary example: "We know that if A then B; because we have evidence of A, then B."

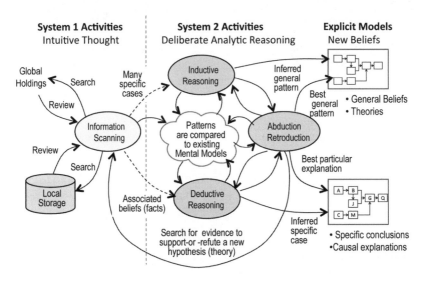

Figure 6.2 Representative flow of reasoning in intelligence analysis

Notice that all three processes synthesize models and draw on mental models that represent currently held beliefs. This entire process fits within the sensemaking model described earlier (figure 5.1); the information scanning and selection for relevance occurs within the foraging loop, and the deliberate reasoning processes occur within the sensemaking loop that applies schemas to frame information and then conceives hypotheses.

The following four subsections introduce four fundamental modes of thought involved as individuals or collaborating teams work on an intelligence problem, identified as four activities summarized in table 6.1:

- *Conceptualize the Problem*—First, the analyst associates, organizes, sorts, and clusters information to develop a conceptual framework to understand a domain (context), the available intelligence data, or the issues associated with arriving at judgments. Outlines, tables, or graphical tools may be used to explicitly represent the frameworks.
- *Reasoning to Converge on a Conclusion*—The analyst may also review the accumulated information to associate the evidence, assumptions, and contextual knowledge to place the evidence in a framework for reasoning to an explanation of the evidence or a solution. This process is inherently convergent—seeking to explain by moving toward hypotheses and judgments. In this process, the analyst develops

Table 6.1 Four Roles of Thinking in Analysis

Role of Thinking	Functional Purpose in Intelligence Analysis	Modeling Tools
Conceptual Thinking [p. 100–106]	*Conceptualize*—associate, organize, sort, and cluster information to develop conceptual frameworks to understand a domain (context) or a problem.	• Concept and mind mapping tools • Formal semantic modeling
Counterfactual Thinking [p. 107–110]	*Create*—explore counterfactuals— conditional claims about alternate possibilities and their consequences; examine feasibility, impacts, and indicators if the alternatives were to occur.	• Structured methods • Models and simulations • Analytic games
Convergent Thinking [p. 111–116]	*Converge*—associate evidence, assumptions, and contextual knowledge to place the evidence in a framework (e.g., argument) to synthesize hypothetical explanations that may be confirmed or refuted.	• Logical, structured argument forms • Logical argument diagrams • Probabilistic networks
Comparative Thinking [p. 117–121]	*Compare*—evaluate alternative hypotheses and diagnose the value of contributing evidence and sensitivities of conclusions.	• Spreadsheet • Alternative competing hypothesis tools

arguments to infer hypothetical explanations; these hypotheses expose assumptions, information gaps and provide tests that could refute, support, or confirm a belief in the hypothesis. Lists, tables, graphical, and quantitative tools can be applied to represent the arguments that make up the hypotheses.

- *Counterfactual Reasoning to Explore Alternative Possibilities*—While the previous thought processes converge toward explanations and solutions, this process diverges even beyond the current evidence as the analyst considers counterfactuals—conditional claims about alternate possibilities and their consequences. For example, the previous process focused on what *may be* the state of a foreign CW program, but counterfactual thinking focuses on what *would or might occur* because

---

Terminology of the Forms of Human Reasoning

1. *Critical thinking* – the conscious style of thinking that improves the quality of thinking by applying skillful disciplines of reasoning that conform to critical intellectual standards.

2. *Sensemaking* – the thinking process by which people assign meaning to experience by by placing information in context to create understanding and develop beliefs about things, associations, and causality.

3. *Reasoning* – deliberate thought processes that seeks a solution by applying logic, argumentation, imagination, creativity, and evaluation. A *line of reasoning* is the specific framework or path that is used to move from evidence, via argument to a conclusion or judgment.

4. *Hypothesis* - a proposition or tentative explanation that is asserted with supporting reasoning; tests may be deduced from the hypothesis to determine if belief in the hypothesis is justified.

5. *Judgment* – the result of a logical inference from available information or the result of explicit tests of hypotheses.

6. *Assessment* - evaluation or estimation of the nature, characteristics, or properties of an intelligence subject.

7. *Convergent forms of reasoning* – thinking processes that marshal information to converge on a solution or belief.

8. *Divergent forms of reasoning* - thinking processes that are stimulated to explore a wide range of perspectives, lines of thinking, and alternatives to search for novel or creative solutions not immediately apparent.

9. *Inductive Reasoning* – the inferential process that moves from particular beliefs, general principles or hypotheses; a more general or more abstract belief is developed by observing a limited set of observations or instances.

10. *Deductive reasoning* – the inferential process that moves from general beliefs to particular beliefs (or from cause to effect); a conclusion is inferred by applying the rules of a logical system to manipulate statements of belief to form new logically consistent statements of belief.

11. *Abductive reasoning* – the informal or pragmatic mode of reasoning that synthesizes alternative explanations and then assesses their feasibility to identify the "best explanation"; abduction is the imaginative or creative process that extends a belief *beyond the original premises.*

12. *Retroductive Reasoning* – the feedback process that occurs when a new conceptual hypothesis is conjectured that causes a return to the pool of information to seek evidence to match (or test) this new hypothesis.

13. *Counterfactual (Hypothetical) Reasoning* – the thinking processes that conceives conditional claims about alternate possibilities (*hypotheticals*) and their consequences.

Figure 6.3 Terminology of the forms of human reasoning

of the country employing those CW capabilities under a particular set of conditions. Such thinking can provide indicators (variables that measure changes in a phenomenon or process, and that may warn of a change of state) that could precede the alternate possibilities. Tools supporting, and extending such divergent thought processes include simulations and analytic games to explore the span of possible trajectories of causes, effects, and consequences.

- *Comparative Thinking*—Finally, the analyst must perform comparative thinking to objectively evaluate alternative hypotheses, and diagnose the value of contributing evidence and sensitivity to assumptions, inferences, and evidence.

MODELING THE CONCEPTS THAT
PRECEDE ANALYSIS

Given a new assignment or confronted with a new intelligence problem, the analyst must conceptualize the problem and establish a framework to conduct the analysis. The analyst asks: *What do we already know? Where can I find it? What are the key issues? What is the current situation? How did we get to this situation, and how did it unfold? What are the dynamics of the situation and the drivers? Who are the key actors in the situation, and what are their relationships? What unknowns could possibly surprise me? What do I need to understand? What questions should I be asking? What sources are providing information? How do I task them? What other analysts in this or other agencies have expertise on this problem?*

All of these questions will provide answers that must be placed in a framework (an external structure to capture knowledge) that will help the analysts build mental models (comparable cognitive structures) that represent the analyst's learned knowledge on the subject. The analyst performs these kinds of conceptualizing functions:

- Conceptualize the problem—Enumerate and organize the many aspects of the problem. This includes specifying the particular aspects of the *Who, What, Why, When, How,* and *Where* questions about the problem.
- Associate, sort clusters, and organize information—Based on the issues identified above, begin assembling relevant sources of information, and
- Conceive schemas—Identify the schemas that most effectively can be used to structure information and hypotheses.
- Hypothesize Explanations—Conceive possible explanations or outcomes and the kinds of information needed to confirm or disconfirm the hypothesis.

Each of these steps builds the framework for representing what the analyst is learning. The process includes divergent thinking that stimulates the consideration of many possible hypotheses and convergent thinking to marshal information toward a specific hypothesis. The conceptualizing process alternates between convergent and divergent thinking, exploring broad areas of thought, followed by focusing to gather information to develop (or discard) one of the more promising thoughts.[5] Lists, outlines, tables, or graphical tools may be used to explicitly represent these frameworks.

We illustrate here, three graphical modeling approaches that can be used to capture the analyst's thoughts or "cognitive structures" while building the initial basis for analysis. The models are introduced in order of increasing detail and structure.

The first method, *mind mapping*, allows the analysts to quickly capture, structure, and refine a representation of the intelligence topic, questions, sources, and required judgments. The method is a basic method of capturing concepts and a relationship between concepts—effectively capturing a mental model in its most basic form. The method may be used to explicitly represent the structure of knowledge of a subject-matter expert (in a narrow area) or to develop a knowledge structure used by an intelligence analyst learning about a situation. The map organizes information spatially, to support spatial thinking, reduce cognitive load, and enhance visual recall. A mind map focuses on a single central topic (the "conceptual hub") and presents hierarchically associated subjects in a radial tree-structured arrangement that distinguishes group, branches, or groups concepts (by enveloping them in a cloud).[6]

The CW analyst's mind map (figure 6.4) illustrates an initial capture of the considerations for developing collection and analyzing a suspect chemical weapons program. The map can be entered in a variety of computer tools that enable simple entry, editing and export in a variety of formats.[7]

The second method, *concept mapping*, allows multiple hubs and clusters of concepts, represented as circles that are connected with labeled arrows in a downward-branching hierarchical structure. Concept maps are less constrained than mind maps; while mind maps have a single conceptual center, multiple hubs and clusters can be created in concept maps. The concept map does require the analyst to identify the relationship between concepts on the lines between them. In figure 6.5, the analyst has structured the necessary elements of the suspected CW program and the relationships to scant evidence that supports or refutes four candidate production sites. In this example, the analyst is focusing on the considerations to support a comprehensive collection and analysis plan to monitor the procurement of precursor materials for suspected dual-use CW facilities.

Figure 6.4 An analyst's initial mind map organizing the key concepts related to intelligence collection and analysis for a CW situation

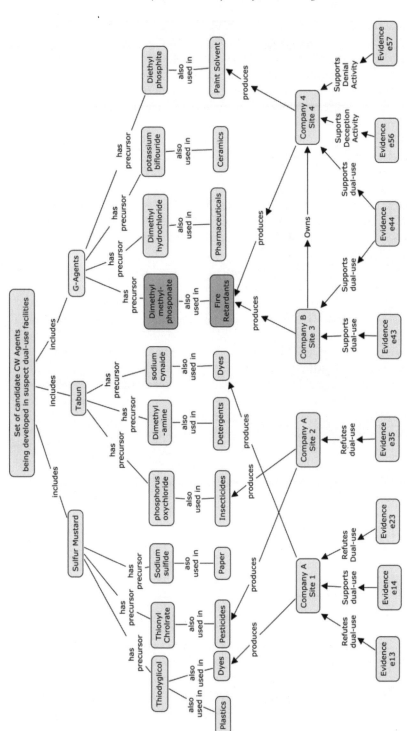

Figure 6.5 Analyst's concept map of the alternatives considered for a foreign suspect dual-use CW capability[8]

More extensive concepts maps can be developed in the Oculus nSpace SandBox® tool that enables concept maps to be created with integrated graphics, maps, timelines, video, assertions, and text. In addition, the tool allows the analyst to link source information to the concept map (figure 6.6). In our CW example, the analyst could link accumulating evidence to the initial concept map developed earlier. nSpace provides a zoomable mental model to increase an analyst's cognitive span. It provides a flexible "blank slate" for informal and formal analytical thinking: from brainstorming to evidence marshalling to evidence-based concept mapping, to asynchronous and synchronous collaboration. As the conceptual models mature, the analyst can translate them into structured arguments and alternative competing hypotheses that logically represent alternative explanations of the data (this is described in the next section). All references are preserved and endnotes are automatically generated when exported to a MS Word or Wiki report.[9]

These models place few restrictions on the analyst, providing the freedom of creativity to rapidly capture, extend, and refine concepts in graphical forms, yet they are basic forms of knowledge representation and are a step away from a more formal semantic representation (one that allows interpretation of a word or sentence linguistically or logically to derive meaning) that is computational—and can be used for computer-based reasoning to support the analyst.

The resource description framework (RDF) representation is a semantic basis for encoding knowledge more richly than tables (relational databases) or hierarchies (e.g., eXtensible markup language, XML). RDF uses a labeled, directed graph expression that is similar to, but more formal than the concept map. Each vertex represents an entity; each edge represents a fact, or a relation between two entities. Statements of fact are expressed as a Subject-Predicate-Object "RDF triple," for example, consider these CW facts:

<Diethyl Phosphite> <is_precursor_to> <G Agent>
<Diethyl Phosphite> <is_precursor_to> <paint_solvent>
<G Agent> <is_a_kind_of> <Nerve Agent>
<Diethyl Phosphite> <is_precursor_to> <G Agent>

The entity <Diethyl Phosphite> can be given as text (literal values), or can represent more abstract things (e.g., a person, place, or an abstract state.) The predicates provide the type of relationship between entities. A small segment of the knowledge about G-agent production processes is represented in the directed graph, figure 6.7, and example RDF concepts in the CW domain are illustrated in table 6.2.

Visible Mental Models

The analyst builds mental models using graphical and text objects to convey key entities and their relationships.

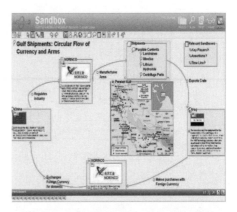

Evidence Marshalling

Next, the analyst builds alternative hypotheses, and organizes the evidence for each case in a chosen structure. Evidence is linked to mental model sandboxes

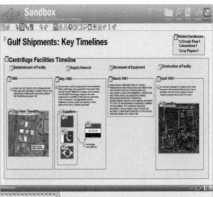

Automatic Report Generation

The contents of any of the sandboxes may be directly exported to support text reports, or media wiki discussions on intelligence social media.

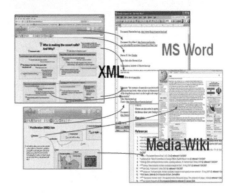

Figure 6.6 Oculus nSpace conceptual modeling tool (Wright et al., 2006) Images © and courtesy Oculus Info, Inc.

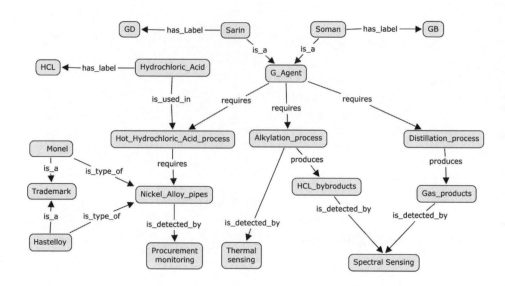

Figure 6.7 A formal RDF description of the CW G-type agent production processes and indicators

Table 6.2 Example Elements of a Chemical Weapon (CW) Ontology

Ontology Concept	Examples from the general domain of Chemical Weapon (CW) Development
Entity Classes (general categories of things)	CW Facilities, CW Agents, CW Skills, CW Organizations, CW Production processes, CW Weapons, CW Munitions, etc.
Instances (particular cases of entities)	CW Agent Class: <H-Agent Sulfur Mustard>, <G-Agent Tabun (GA)>, <G-Agent Sarin (GB)>, <G-Agent soman (GD)>, <V-Agent VX>, etc.
Relations: is_a, subclass_ of, (kind_of), instance_of, part_of, etc.	<VX> is_ a_ kind_ of <nerve agent> <VX> contains_not <fluoride> <VX>requires <alkylation process> <hydrochloric acid>is_byproduct_of<alkylation process>
Properties	<Munition>: Agent fill, Purity, Shelf life
Values (for properties)	Fill: VX; Purity: 60%; Shelf life: 30 days.
Rules (axioms) for reasoning	IF <hydrochloric acid>AND NOT<fluoride> THEN <VX> production likely

Using a formal model of these CW concepts enables machine reasoning about this domain, to support the analysts in searches for relevant information, to associate relevant relationships across data, and to reason about the implications of those associations. For example, using a formal model of CW precursor purchasing processes, the analyst could be supported by computational processes that:[10]

- *Search* for terms in collected reports related to precursor purchases, transit paths, and deliveries.
- *Associate* patterns across supply chains to identify abnormal and inefficient paths that may indicate suspect or intended covert purchases.
- *Reason* about those supply chains that are inconsistent in declared purpose and actual products produced at delivery facilities.

MODELING IN COUNTERFACTUAL REASONING

The analyst may be called upon to address questions of possibility— "what if" questions that require the analyst to consider what "might" happen or "would" happen (with an estimated probability of occurrence) under various circumstances. These conditional circumstances require the analyst to perform *counterfactual thinking*—the exploration of counterfactual scenarios that are conditional claims about alternate possibilities and their consequences. These claims are *conditional* because they are conditioned on specified circumstances (independent conditions) expressed as a consequence of some prior (or antecedent) scenario and intermediates states that transition to the consequent scenario.[11]

Consider three kinds of counterfactual scenarios that analysts may be asked to consider:

- *Past (historical)*—What might have happened to the adversary's CW program if [condition: economic sanctions and a surgical military action had been conducted at time x]? (This case is counter to historical facts);
- *Present*—What would we estimate the present CW capability to be if [condition: the adversary was able to sustain production yields at level y for the past three years?] (This case may actually be factual, but the facts are not known) ;
- *Future*—If [condition: the adversary actually deploys their CW capability], what would their deployment tactics look like and how effective would they be? (This case is counter to facts because it is in the future and has not, in fact, occurred).

The purpose of these kinds of questions is to understand causal relationships and examine feasibility, impacts, and indicators if the scenarios were to occur under the conditions stated. At the outset, we should distinguish between informal methods of counterfactual analysis (e.g., brainstorming, Delphi methods, etc.) that elicit imaginative consideration of alternatives, counterfactual games (approaches described in chapter 8 that use competitive play to follow a single or small set of counterfactual trajectories) and formal counterfactual analysis that applies a more analytic discipline to explicitly develop and analyze counterfactual scenarios. Noel Hendrickson, author of *Counterfactual Reasoning: A Basic Guide for Analysts, Strategists, and Decision Makers*,[12] describes approaches to increase the formal structure of the process and offers four specific purposes for conducting rigorous counterfactual analysis:

- *To facilitate causal analysis.* Counterfactual thinking necessarily requires deep and rigorous consideration of causal dependence between the intermediate transition states that proceed from antecedent to consequent situations.
- *To overcome deterministic biases.* Explicit considerations of alternative causal scenarios can mitigate common cognitive biases: 1) hindsight bias that regards past events (factuals) as having been more probable than they were, and 2) foresight bias that regards future events as more probable than they are. Both biases fail to consider the potential or likelihood of counterfactuals.
- *To incorporate analytic creativity.* Counterfactual thinking provides a disciplined method to explore alternative possibilities, with a focus on causal dependency, and the sensitivity of these dependencies to external conditions (context).
- *To ground strategic assessment.* Strategic intelligence by its very nature considers counterfactual scenarios, and any estimation of the effects of alternative policies (courses of action) necessitates an understanding of causal dependencies.

The formal analysis of counterfactuals requires the consideration of an initial situation (antecedent state or scenario) and the specific intermediate states that transition to a consequent scenario (figure 6.8). In addition, the analyst must define the conditions that exist during the transitions. The figure illustrates an antecedent scenario A for country X, defined by specific political, economic, and technical states in the country. The transitions are conditioned on the independent political, military, and economic conditions (C1 . . . C4) that are also specified. From this initial state and conditions, the analyst must specify and justify the specific states that transition the CW program through intermediate states of CW R&D (S1, a set of states that represent active R&D), then testing and production (S2) and deployment of CW munitions to storage (S3).

These states must be specific (*What kinds of agents? What precursors and indigenous production or covert purchasing? What kinds of munitions and delivery systems?*, etc.) and the conditions must be detailed (*What drives the political commitment to CW? How is the program funded? What is the deployment risk calculus?*, etc.). The analysts must explicitly define the causal dependencies between antecedents, intermediate states, and consequents—exposing them to critical analysis. Notice that in the figure, the analyst has considered two possible consequents from the state of CW deployment:

- Consequent scenario B1 (e.g., disarmament), occurs under conditions C5, moving the country through intermediate state S4 to B1; and
- Consequent scenario B2 (e.g., breakout and employment) occurs under conditions C6, moving the country through intermediate state S6 to B2 (e.g., engagement and use of CW).

Preceding any counterfactual analysis, the analyst must define the scope of analysis, the expected results and their intended use. There are a number of methods that analysts apply to develop counterfactual models (table 6.3), including methods that *forecast* antecedent scenarios and a method that *backcasts* from consequent scenarios backwards to an antecedent to identify what conditions and triggers would be required.[13]

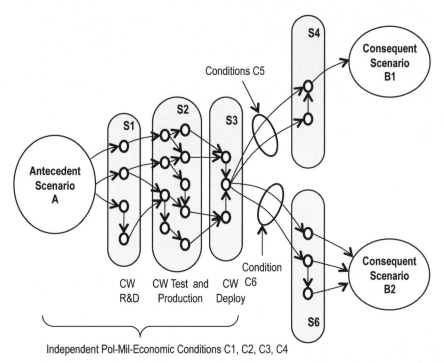

Figure 6.8 Graphical representation of counterfactual scenario analysis

Table 6.3 Typical Analytic Methods Employed in Counterfactual Analysis

Counterfactual Focus	Alternative Analysis Method	Approach
Causal Analysis of conditions (assumptions, drivers) and trigger events	Contingency "What-If" Analyses	Perform counterfactual analysis on plausible trajectories to alternative contingency consequent scenarios. Beginning with an antecedent scenario, *forecast* to estimate the trajectory of states and events that would lead to alternative consequent scenarios.
	Contingency High-Impact/Low-Probability (HI/LP)	Perform counterfactual analysis of specific large-consequence (and low-probability) scenarios. Beginning with the high-consequence scenario, *backcast* to estimate the trajectory of states and events that would lead to the consequence. Identify the potential factors and indicators if the scenario were to develop.
	Alternative Future Scenario Development	Identify factors and drivers associated with a key issue, and then develop a range of future scenarios that encompass the option space created by the factors-drivers.[1]
	Formal Counterfactual Analysis	Apply a set of formal counterfactual reasoning principles in three stages: 1) define antecedent scenario and its preceding conditions, 2) identify intermediate conditions and states that proceed from antecedent to consequent, and 3) select consequent scenario based on steps 1 and 2.[2]
	Red Cell Exercise	Conduct an exercise in which the red cell role-plays adversary actors with cultural perspective, norms, and decision making style to produce results that approximate the adversary behavior.[3]
	Analytic Gaming	Conduct a competitive game to replicate a situation to consider uncertainties, alternative explanations, internal processes, and outcomes of intelligence and policy activities.
Causal Analysis to develop integrated forecast from independent forecasts	Cross Impact Analysis	Identify and evaluate sensitivities of the interrelationships between events and developments (cross-impacts) in independently developed forecasts; adjust probabilities of consequent states based on judgments about potential interactions.[4]
	Scenario Fusion	Apply series of logical principles to integrate multiple independent estimates into a single projection; structure intermediate states, identify conditionals, and logically combine.[5]

1. See Schwartz, Peter, *The Art of the Long View: Planning for the Future in an Uncertain World*, (NY: Currency Doubleday, 1991).

2. Hendrickson, Noel, *Counterfactual Reasoning: A Basic Guide for Analysts, Strategists, and Decision Makers*, Proteus Monograph Series, Vol. 2, No. 5, National Intelligence University and the Center for Strategic Leadership, U.S. Army War College (October 2008).

3. For an example of an adversary perspective analysis, see Kent, Sherman, "A Crucial Estimate Relived," *Studies in Intelligence*, Vol. 36, No. 5 (Washington, DC: Center for the Study of Intelligence Analysis, Spring 1964), 117–18.

4. Moritz, Frank, "Cross Impact Analysis and Forecasting the Future of Rhodesia," in Richards J. Heuer, Jr. (ed.), *Quantitative Approaches to Political Intelligence: The CIA Experience*, (Boulder, CO: Westview Press, 1978).

5. Hendrickson, Noel, "Counterfactual Reasoning, Structured Scenario Fusion, and Futures Analysis," in Auger, John and William Wimbish (eds.), *Proteus Futures Digest: A Compilation of Selected Works Derived from the 2007 Proteus Workshop*, (The National Intelligence University, 2007), 181–98.

In all cases, the focus of analysis is on causality arguments about the inter-mediate states—considering the sensitivity of causal arguments to the contextual conditions. Within the alternative analysis, these conditions include:

- *Drivers*—key variables and unknown factors that analysts judge most likely to determine the outcome of a complex situation
- *Linchpin assumptions*—working assumptions about the drivers
- *Triggering events*—occurrences that cause another event or a change of state to occur

Notice that the table also summarizes two methods that allow a causal analysis to be conducted between a set of independent forecasts, even when the conditions and interactions may not have been taken into consideration when the individual forecasts were produced. This is often the case when strategic assessments are required, and the most thorough set of information to draw on is more detailed counterfactual analyses conducted independently and without the intention of being considered in combination.

MODELING IN CONVERGENT REASONING FROM EVIDENCE TO INFERENCE

Once the analyst has defined the characteristics of the problem or situation—the evidence at hand, context, and subject matter expertise are used to develop hypothetical explanations. This is the result of the reasoning processes introduced at the beginning of this chapter (abduction to the best explanation, deduction to a specific explanation based on evidence, or induction to a general belief or theory.) Inspired by the screening of data and contextual knowledge, relevant data (evidence) are identified that can be assembled (or marshaled) into hypotheses, to affirm or refute them. The convergent form of thinking occurs when the analyst focuses on developing a hypothesis, seeking to discredit it as a viable option, or to confirm that it may represent reality. Critical or rigorous reasoning can be aided by an explicit representation of the argument or proposition that moves from evidence, through logical inferences to the hypothesis they assert. If the analyst seeks confirming evidence at the expense of an objective equal effort to consider disconfirming evidence, the analysis exhibits the well-known *confirmation bias*—the tendency to selectively search for and favor confirming information, while discounting information that discredits the hypothesis.

Argumentation refers to the process of explaining the rationale and basis for a hypothesis. *Argument structure* is the configuration of relationships between evidence, inferences, and the assertion of the hypothesis. The structure reveals the propositions that move from premises to conclusions, and can be represented as an explicit model. Of course, each alternative (or competing) hypothesis that an analyst creates to explain a pool of evidence may have a different argument structure. As in any explicit model, these structures support visual cognition to aid the analyst in constructing and evaluating complex arguments that are difficult to manage in mental models alone, as well as helping the analyst explain the argument to decision makers.

A variety of similar representation methods have been put forth to represent arguments in philosophy, law, and analysis. In the following paragraphs, we introduce three methods of modeling arguments, presented in increasing order of sophistication and development. In each case, we consider models of the argument used in the intelligence assessment of Iraq's CW program in a declassified 2002 U.S. National Intelligence Estimate (NIE) on the Iraq WMD program. The assessment (a hypothesis believed and asserted as an intelligence judgment) is based on an argument that includes three lines of evidence and inference identified as supporting bullet points (figure 6.9).[14]

Argument Map—The first argument-modeling method develops an informal representation of an argument that is elaborated in a graphical freeform tree structure, which proceeds from "claim" nodes to a main conclusion (e.g., the intelligence assessment) via supporting "reason" nodes or opposing "objection" nodes. A reason is a collection of supporting claims; claim nodes contain a concise sentence asserting the claim; reason nodes represent the conjunction of claim nodes that precede it. The

---

We assess that Baghdad has begun renewed production of mustard, sarin, GF (cyclosarin), and VX; its capability probably is more limited now than it was at the time of the Gulf war, although VX production and agent storage life probably have been improved.

- *An array of clandestine reporting reveals that Baghdad has procured covertly the types and quantities of chemicals and equipment sufficient to allow limited CW [chemical weapons] agent production hidden within Iraq's legitimate chemical industry.*
- *Although we have little specific information on Iraq's CW stockpile, Saddam probably has stocked at least 100 metric tons (MT) and possibly as much as 500 MT of CW agents—much of it added in the last year.*
- *The Iraqis have experience in manufacturing CW bombs, artillery rockets, and projectiles. We assess that they possess CW bulk fills for SRBM [short-range ballistic missile] warheads, including for a limited number of covertly stored Scuds, possibly a few with extended ranges.*

Source: *Key Judgments from the National Intelligence Estimate on Iraq's Continuing Programs for Weapons of Mass Destruction*, October 2002, Director of Central Intelligence, available at: http://www.ceip.org/fi les/projects/npp/pdf/Iraq/declassifiedintellreport.pdf (accessed October 22, 2003).

Figure 6.9 Excerpt from NIE Iraq WMD 2002

nodes can be colored to distinguish claims that are supporting (green), opposing (red) or neutral (white) to the conclusion.

The argument map for the NIE argument for Iraq CW capabilities (figure 6.10) clearly shows the assessment and the three contributing bullet points (claims); the colors of the claims distinguish those that support (white) or oppose (shaded) the claim. The benefit of this informal map is that it reveals the structure and common errors of argumentation, moving one important step toward formal evaluation. Van Gelder has demonstrated software tools to enable users to construct maps for complex arguments and has articulated the potential benefits to achieve substantial gains in reasoning.[15] Some empirical studies have shown that this easy-to-use method of visual argument structuring (external cognition) can substantially improve measures of critical thinking.[16] Other mapping tools have been used to enable graphical creation of maps from existing textual arguments; elements of text are highlighted and designated as conclusion, premise, co-premise or assumption, and the graphical argument map is created to show the structure of the argument.[17]

Toulmin Argument Form—The next model is a more structured but practical argument structure that distinguishes six different elements of all arguments that should be explicitly defined, and that proceed from data or evidence (D) to the Claim (C):[18]

- Claim (C) is the assertion of the hypothesis supported by the argument.
- Qualifiers (Q) are conditional statements that specify the degree or limits to the claim, warrant, and backing.

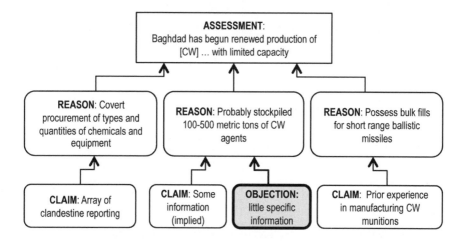

Figure 6.10 A basic argument map of the NIE argument for Iraq CW capabilities

- Rebuttals (R) are those conditions that may refute the claim, if they are true; this specifies any caveats to the Claim (C).
- Warrants (W) are the implicit propositions (rules, principles) that permit inference from data to claim.
- Backing, (B) are assurances that provide authority and currency to the warrants.
- Evidence or data (D) are the observations in the real world.

This method, like the last, requires the analyst to carefully distinguish between evidence and the basis for making inferences to the claim; it also requires explicit recognition of rebuttals. Notice that because this method has a standard structure for all arguments, an outline format can be used to list the supporting elements for each claim, and a graphical representation is not required to preserve the structure. This approach also requires the argument to be placed in a standard form exposing the six elements. Like the argument map, this is not a formal method, and it lacks logical rigor and a method to quantify the strength or support for arguments. Figure 6.11 illustrates the same NIE argument expressed in a graphical Toulmin form, distinguishing the six elements of argument.

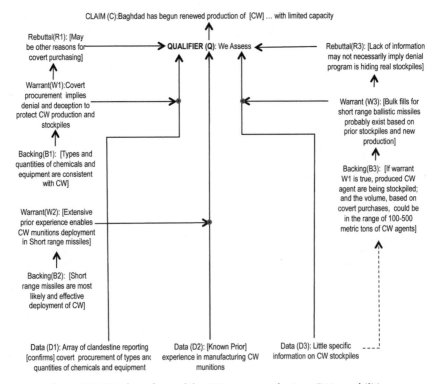

Figure 6.11 Toulmin form of the NIE argument for Iraq CW capabilities

Conforming to the structure compels the analyst to explicitly articulate each element of argument—requiring careful thought and examination. Notice that the Toulmin form requires us to add text that is shown in brackets; this text goes beyond what is provided in the NIE assessment (our best estimate of the rationale not explicitly provided in the declassified NIE) and forces us to distinguish data and the warrants for using the data to support the claim. The structure also shows us that the claim is not qualified (other than "we assess" meaning, it was a judgment), but we do see that the bulk fill estimate was qualified with the word "probably."[19] We do not imply that intelligence assessments should conform to the argument format, but such a form can help in the development and evaluation of structure before preparing the textual argument to check for the desired clarity, coherence of logic, and correspondence to supporting data.

Structured Argument Form—The third model of argumentation is the *Structured Argument* form described by David Schum. This is a more formal representation than the prior two and uses a directed acyclic graph format that provides a basis for logical consistency and a mathematical basis (graph theory) to allow the propagation of the "strength" of arguments through a chain of inferences in the graph.[20] The graph is *directed* because the lines connecting nodes include a single arrow indicating the single direction of inference; it is *acyclic* because the directions of all arrows move from evidence, through intermediate inferences to hypothesis, but not back again: there are no closed-loop cycles.

Again, we illustrate this method with a depiction of the NIE argument in figure 6.12. The directed graph proceeds from evidence (E) at the bottom and proceeds upward through a series of inferences (graph edges—represented by arrows) to intermediate hypotheses ($i_1, i_2, i_3 \ldots i_n$) and then to the final hypotheses (H). The inferences and final hypothesis are graph vertices (represented as circles).

This diagram goes beyond the prior two argument structures by expanding the sequence of inferences that proceed from evidence to the terminal hypothesis. For illustrative purposes, the figure has again extrapolated beyond the words in the assessment above to illustrate the following kinds of information that are found in the structure to support the argument:[21]

1. *Evidence*—(data that are relevant) is at the root of the graph, and is arbitrarily assumed, for this example, to be ten specific elements of data (E1 to E10) that form the basis for subsequent inferences. E9 and E10 are corroborative evidence that support the credibility of E8 and enhance the force of the inference i_{32}.

2. *Linchpin assumptions*—are the key factors underlying the argument; these are factors that are likely to drive the inference, especially where there is little hard information available, such as in knowledge of intentions and specific plans.[22]
3. *Deception factors*—are the factors related to evidence or inferences that are vulnerable to denial or deception, the potential methods of deception, and vulnerabilities in channels of information.
4. *Inference structure*—Proceeding from the evidence at the roots of the graph are the inferences (arrows) that lead to propositions (circles); the terminal proposition is the summary hypothesis. Each proposition is numbered (e.g., i_{23}); propositions and the top hypotheses are summarized in text. Note that the structure shows the three major lines of inference and the convergent nature of the three propositions that enhance the final proposition when they all occur together.

The graph structure provides a means of propagating the accumulated weight of evidence in an argument, if the evidence is quantified (e.g., conditional probabilities are provided that quantify the probability that a hypothesis is true given the evidence is present). This argument structure provides a degree of formality and insight into the basis for the hypothesis and the relative roles of linchpin assumptions, evidence, and inference. The structure provides a means for explanation, examination, and the development of metrics for use in the next stage of hypothesis comparison. It also illustrates the complexity of the argument structure for even a relatively simple set of propositions asserted as judgments in an actual high-level intelligence judgment.

Tecuci, Schum, and Boicu et al. have progressively refined a comprehensive reasoning support tool to model structured arguments for intelligence analysis and training. The TIACRITIS tool develops an explicit model of evidential and idea inferential chains of reasoning to allow the development and evaluation of defensible and persuasive arguments.[23] The tool aids the analyst in decomposing a problem and creation of very large reasoning trees (even with thousands of nodes) to distinguish evidence and inferential chains. The analyst can browse and review the trees to evaluate the structure of arguments, as well as to "drill down" to individual components to evaluate the strength of its elements. In the next section, we illustrate how quantitative argument structures can be implemented in Bayesian network tools to propagate probability estimates to derive aggregate estimates of the likelihood of a candidate hypothesis, given a set of evidence available.

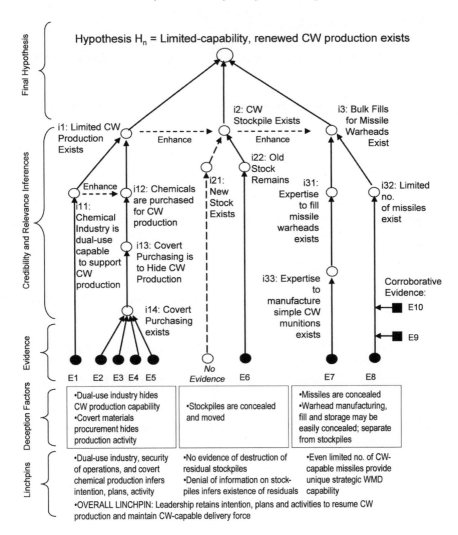

Figure 6.12 National Intelligence Estimate CW argument in structured argument form (Reproduced by permission from Michael Bennett and Edward Waltz, *Counterdeception Principles and Applications for National Security*. Norwood, MA: Artech House, Inc, 2007. ©2007 by Artech House, Inc.)

MODELING COMPARATIVE REASONING ABOUT ALTERNATIVE HYPOTHESES

Hypotheses are conjectures of possible realities, synthesized as candidate explanations, estimations, assessments, or forecasts that address an intelligence issue. Each hypothesis is an *alternative,* a possible reality competing with others to best describe past, current, or future reality. Best, in the epistemological sense, means that it most effectively corresponds to available empirical evidence and remains logically coherent. In this section, we briefly consider complementary qualitative and quantitative methods to compare alternative hypotheses.

Qualitative comparison provides a structured method to objectively evaluate the relative attributes of each hypothesis, focusing on the contribution of evidence to each hypothesis. Remember that each hypothesis should have an argument structure developed and evaluated for coherence, and that the comparison can focus on the strength of each element of evidence and its contribution to the argument. The well-known method of Alternative Competing Hypothesis Analysis (ACH) assembles a matrix of evidence (rows) and hypotheses (columns) to describe the relationship between evidence and alternative hypotheses. The method intentionally focuses on explicitly showing the contribution, significance, and relationships of each item of evidence to all hypotheses, rather than on building a case for a single most plausible hypothesis; the method also requires the assessment of evidence contribution to inference (horizontal assessment across the rows) before evaluating the relative strength of hypotheses (vertical assessment down the columns.

The sequence of the ACH process to create and assess alternative hypotheses follows eight steps. The first two steps include synthesis of a complete set of mutually exclusive hypotheses and development of the arguments and evidence for (and against) each, as described in the previous subsections, to explicitly represent the assumptions regarding evidence and the arguments of inference. The remaining six steps deal with the comparative and judgment process:[24]

1. *Matrix Construction and Analysis*—Construct an ACH matrix that arrays evidence in rows and hypotheses in columns. Proceed across each row, considering the implication of each item of evidence (and inferences required) for each hypothesis. A judgment is made in each evidence-hypothesis cell to judge if the evidence would be observed if the hypothesis were true. Evidence may be judged supporting (consistent with), refuting (inconsistent with), or irrelevant (not applicable) to a hypothesis (each cell is marked with appropriate notation, e.g., +, −, or N/A, respectively).[25] Once a row is complete, the analyst can assess the diagnostic value of each evidence-inference component to each hypothesis.[26]

2. *Matrix Refinement*—Return and synoptically review the entire matrix; refine evidence and inference assignments (step 1 may require rethinking inferential chains, and may reveal new inferential possibilities. Eliminate evidence and inferences that have no diagnostic value.

3. *Hypotheses Likelihood Analysis* — The analyst now proceeds to evaluate the likelihood of each hypothesis, by evaluating entries *down* the columns. The analyst focuses on refutation of hypotheses by reviewing the characteristics of supporting and refuting evidence. At this point the analyst should be very aware of hypothesis distinctions and evidence gaps and may identify critical collection gaps that provide highly diagnostic information.

4. *Hypotheses Sensitivity Analysis* — The sensitivity of the hypotheses to contributing assumptions, evidence, and the inferences is considered and explicitly enumerated. Again, at this step, the analysts should become acutely aware of any critical information that could enhance confidence in a hypothesis.

5. *Decision Synthesis (Judgment)* — The analyst now applies judgment to report the analysis, the alternatives considered, and the basis for judging the most likely. Models of assumptions, evidence, and inferential chains should be available to explain the judgment; gaps, inconsistencies, and their consequences on the any judgments should be made explicit.

6. *Monitor Indicators* — The analyst also identifies critical indicators that should be monitored, to determine if a situation changes from the current judgment. These indicators, usually identified in the sensitivity analysis, provide a means to warn intelligence consumers if the judgment has changed.

The sample ACH matrix illustrated in figure 6.13 (top) is implemented in the ACH modeling tool developed by Palo Alto Research Center (PARC).[27] Elements of evidence, assumed independent, are numbered and arrayed in the first column of the spreadsheet format; the consistence ("I") or inconsistence ("C") with each hypothesis is entered in each corresponding cell under the Hypothesis (H_n) columns. A heuristic weighting may be assigned to evidence to grade the relative credibility and relevance of each item to the hypothesis, and summary inconsistency value is computed for each hypothesis and reported at the top of each column.

Quantitative comparison can be applied when numerical values are assigned to compute the relative strength of each hypothesis, in a rigorous and formal mathematical manner. The analysis is framed by considering a mutually exclusive and exhaustive set of hypotheses ($H_0, \ldots H_N$) and presuming that the observations (and therefore the evidence they provide) are independent (this is required to assure that the conditional probabilities are independent.)

The formal mathematical method that uses probabilities to express uncertainty, requiring the analyst to enumerate and quantify the following for each hypothesis, H_0 is described as follows:

- *Define* each element of evidence E_i that is related to the belief in the hypotheses $H(H_0 \ldots H_N)$.
- *Estimate* the prior probability for the occurrence of each hypothesis, P_j *for all* $(H_0 \ldots H_N)$; this is called the *a priori probability* that *each hypothesis* is true, independent of the evidence.
- *Define* for each element of evidence, $P(E_i \mid H_j)$, the *conditional probability*; of observing the evidence E_i conditioned on (given that) hypothesis H_j is true. This of course requires an analysis of the inference structure that proceeds from evidence through the chain of inferences to the hypothesis.
- *Estimate* $P(E_j)$, the *marginal probability* that each E_i will be observed at any time; given no other information.

Based on this information, enumerated for each element of evidence and each hypothesis, the *a posteriori probability* for each hypothesis, $P(H_0 \mid E)$, may be computed using the method of Bayesian inference. The probability is a function of the prior probability of H_0 and the *conditional probability*, normalized by the marginal probability:

$$P(H_O|E) = \frac{P(E|H_O)\,P(H_O)}{P(E)}$$

The posterior probabilities for each hypothesis, H_N represent the probability that H_N is true, conditioned on (given that) the evidence E is present. The Bayesian method provides a relative measure of belief in each of the mutually exclusive hypotheses $(H_0 \ldots H_N)$.[28]

Notice that conditional probabilities are required to move from evidence, through intermediate hypotheses, to terminal hypotheses; the structured arguments described in the prior subsection on arguments are translated into a graphical Bayesian belief net structure. The practical application of this method can be achieved by directly describing the hypotheses and estimating probabilities in a Bayesian analysis tool that propagates probabilities. We illustrate this approach using the Norsys Netica™ tool (figure 6.13 [bottom]). The graphical display provides the argument structure and bar graph representations of probabilities at the intermediate nodes and top-level posteriori probabilities. Conditional probabilities are entered in a matrix form, where conditional probability cells are defined across all possible input states (e.g., states of evidence) versus the node output states (e.g., inferred beliefs as a result of the evidence). As new evidence is obtained and the argument refined, the network can be modified to enter the evidence at root nodes, the overall argument structure, as well as the conditional probabilities at nodes.

Alternative Competing Hypothesis matrix

Alternative Hypotheses in Columns (H1, H2,...)

Summary score

Elements of evidence in Rows (e1, E2,...)

Evidence type

Evidence characteristics

Cell: Assessment of evidence contribution or refutation of hypothesis

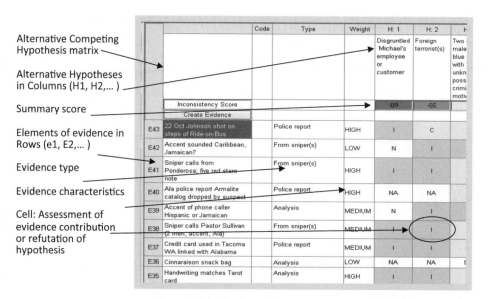

Solution: Posteriori probabilities in bar-graph format for each alternative hypothesis

Argument structure and intermediate nodes with probabilities for inferences

Root nodes provide elements of evidence

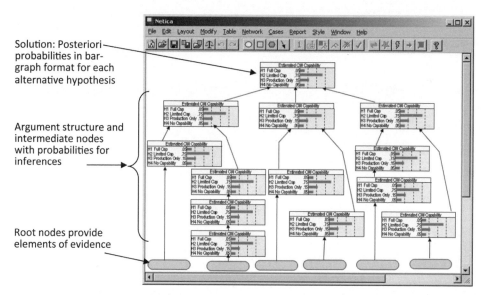

Figure 6.13 Qualitative and quantitative methods to explicitly represent hypothesis comparison, illustrated in two modeling tools

INTEGRATING TARGET AND ANALYSIS MODELS

The prior subsections have described explicit models of analytic thinking without regard to the type of models of the targets of analysis (tacit mental models in the heads of experts, or explicit conceptual or computational models). Before proceeding to the next chapter that describes target system modeling, we illustrate how analysis integrates these models in this chapter, with the target system models of the next.

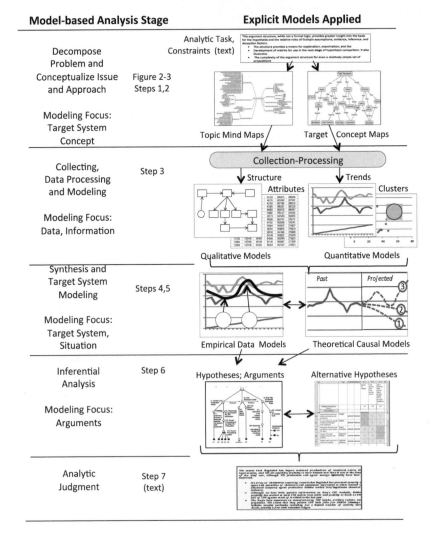

Figure 6.14 Explicit models used throughout the stages of model-based analysis

If we consider the steps in the sensemaking process described earlier, the analysis task description begins with a high-level, abstract description of the issue (in text), then proceeds to increasing levels of "concrete" depth and detail of analysis and synthesis, before returning to a high-level more abstract judgment. Figure 6.11 shows the typical progression of models from a statement of the intelligence issue and analytic task to the reported judgment.[29] As in most analytic-synthetic problems, not just in intelligence, the process moves from an abstract high-level task description to a detailed and very concrete problem-solving activity, and then back to a high-level answer (judgment, recommendation, assessment, or design) that can be supported by the detail developed in the middle phase.

The methods described here also provide an audit trail for analysts and a means to back up analytic judgments for decision makers.

NOTES

1. United States Government, Office of the Director of National Intelligence, *Intelligence Community Directive 203* (effective June 21, 2007). We distinguish between an assessment (an evaluation or estimation of the nature, characteristics, or properties of an intelligence subject) and a judgment (a logical inference from available information or the result of explicit tests of hypotheses).

2. Sticha, Paul, Dennis Buede, and Richard L. Rees, "APOLLO: An Analytical Tool for Predicting a Subject's Decision Making," in *Proceedings of the 2005 International Conference on Intelligence Analysis* (Washington, DC: Office of the Assistant Director of Central Intelligence for Analysis and Production, 2005). The author participated in a two-hour demonstration analysis of the alternatives for North Korean nuclear testing at the conference, where the APOLLO team used the Netica™ tool to capture and project the discussion.

3. All examples in this and subsequent chapters are based on information provided in U.S. Congress, Office of Technology Assessment, *Technologies Underlying Weapons of Mass Destruction, OTA-BP-ISC-115* (Washington, DC: U.S. Government Printing Office, December 1993); the examples are based on chapter 2, "Technical Aspects of Chemical Weapon Proliferation."

4. Schum, David A., *Evidence and Inference for the Intelligence Analyst*, Vols. I and II (Lanham MD: University Press of America, 1987), 16. This text was authored while Schum was a scholar in residence at the CIA. The quote from Sherlock Holmes is from Sir Arthur Conan Doyle's first novel, *A Study in Scarlet* (published in 1887).

5. Cropley, Arthur, "In Praise of Convergent Thinking," *Creativity Research Journal* 18, no. 3 (2006), 391–404. Cropley warns against unfettered convergent thinking, recommending approaches that combine novelty generation (divergence) and careful evaluation (convergence). The explicit modeling methods described here provide a method to support evaluation and guidance of divergent thought.

6. For the basis of mind maps as spatial representations of knowledge that map mental models, see O'Keefe, John, and Lynn Nadel, *The Hippocampus as a Cognitive Map* (Oxford: Oxford University Press, 1978).

7. The example was implemented in Freemind, a basic mind mapping tool available at http://freemind.sourceforge.net/wiki/index.php/Main_Page; more capable mind mapping tools are available with more extensive networking, graphical, import-export, and linking features that allow concepts to be hyperlinked to external objects (documents, images, maps, etc.)

8. This concept map was developed in the CMAP tool, http://cmap.ihmc.us, See Novak, Joseph and Alberto Canas, "The Theory Underlying Concept Maps and How to Construct and Use Them", Technical Report IHMC Cmap Tools 2006-01 Rev 01-2008, (Pensacola FL: Institute for Human and Machine Cognition, 2008).

9. Wright W., D. Schroh, P. Proulx, A. Skaburskis, and B. Cort, "The Sandbox for Analysis—Concepts and Methods" *Proceedings of the SIGCHI 06 conference on Human Factors in Computing Systems*, ACM Press (2006) 801–10. See also William Wright, David Schroh, Pascale Proulx, Alex Skaburskis and Brian Cort "Information Triage with TRIST" in *Proceedings of the 2005 International Conference on Intelligence Analysis* (Washington, DC: Office of the Assistant Director of Central Intelligence for Analysis and Production, 2005), and Proulx, P., L. Chien, R. Harper, D. Schroh, T. Kapler, D. Jonker, and W. Wright, "nSpace and GeoTime—VAST 2006 Case Study," *IEEE Computer Graphics and Applications*, Vol. 27, No. 5, (September 2007), 46–56.

10. For an example of a tool to support intelligence analysts, see Tecuci, Gheorghe et al., "Cognitive Assistants for Analysts," in Auger, John and William Wimbish (eds.), *Proteus Futures Digest: A Compilation of Selected Works Derived from the 2006 Proteus Workshop*, (Joint publication of the National Intelligence University, Office of the Director of National Intelligence, and U.S. Army War College Center for Strategic Leadership, 2007).

11. Counterfactual statements occur in the English subjunctive mood to express conditions of possibility (would, could, might, should, etc.) or desires about past, present, or future events.

12. Hendrickson, Noel, *Counterfactual Reasoning: A Basic Guide for Analysts, Strategists, and Decision Makers*, Proteus Monograph Series, Vol. 2, No. 5, National Intelligence University and the Center for Strategic Leadership, U.S. Army War College (October 2008). This is an excellent introduction to formal counterfactual analysis for intelligence, applying a rigorous methodology that conforms to logical and causal reasoning principles. See also Hendrickson, Noel, "Applied Counterfactual Reasoning" in Argamon, Shlomo and Newton Howard, *Computational Methods for Counterterrorism* (New York: Springer, 2009) 249–62.

13. For a description of the principal techniques to practically implement alternative analysis, see George, Roger Z. "Fixing the Problem of Analytical Mind-Sets: Alternative Analysis," *International Journal of Intelligence and Counterintelligence*, Vol. 17, No. 3 (Autumn 2004) 385–404.

14. U.S. Government, *The Commission on the Intelligence Capabilities of the United States Regarding Weapons of Mass Destruction*, (Washington, DC, March 31, 2005). The commission noted: After the war, the [Iraq Survey Group] concluded—contrary to the Intelligence Community's pre-war assessments—that Iraq had unilaterally destroyed its undeclared CW stockpile in 1991 and that there were no credible indications that Baghdad had resumed production of CW thereafter. The ISG further found that Iraq had not regained its pre-1991 CW technical

sophistication or production capabilities. . . . Finally, the ISG noted that the only CW it recovered were weapons manufactured before the first Gulf War, and that after 1991 only small, covert labs were maintained to research chemicals and poisons, primarily for intelligence operations. The ISG did conclude, however, that "Saddam never abandoned his intentions to resume a CW effort when sanctions were lifted and conditions were judged favorable," and that Iraq's post-1995 infrastructure improvements "would have enhanced Iraq's ability to produce CW" if it chose to do so. (p. 112).

15. For descriptions of the progressive capabilities of Reason!able™ and Rationale™ argument mapping software tools, see van Gelder, Tim, "How to Improve Critical Thinking Using Educational Technology," in *Proceedings of the ASCILITE 2001 Conference, 2001,* 539–48 and van Gelder, Tim, "The rationale for Rationale™," *Law, Probability and Risk* 6: (1–4) (2007) 23–42.

16. See van Gelder, Tim, Melanie Bissett, and Geoff Cumming, "Cultivating Expertise in Informal Reasoning," *Canadian Journal of Experimental Psychology* 58 (2004) 142–52.

17. Butchart, Sam, et al. "Improving Critical Thinking Using Web Based Argument Mapping Exercises with Automated Feedback," *Australasian Journal of Educational Technology,* Vol. 25, No. 2 (2009) 268–91.

18. Toulmin, Stephen Edelson, *The Uses of Argument,* (Cambridge: Cambridge University Press, 1958).

19. Current NIE judgments are qualified on a five-step scale of "remote, unlikely, even chance, probably or likely, and almost certainly" to indicate judgments on degrees of likelihood; confidence in a judgment are qualified as "high," "moderate," or "low" levels based on the scope and quality of information that supports the judgment.

20. Schum, David A., *The Evidential Foundations for Probabilistic Reasoning,* (Evanston IL: Northwestern University Press, 2001). The brief introduction to inferential networks in this section is based on Schum's exhaustive treatment but does not approach the many critical nuances of the theory developed by Schum.

21. This paragraph and associated figure adopted from Bennett, Michael and Edward Waltz, *Counterdeception Principles and Applications* (Boston: Artech, 2007) 260–61.

22. For an overview of linchpin analysis process, see Krizan, Lisa, *Intelligence Essentials for Everyone,* Occasional Paper 6, Joint Military Intelligence College, June 1999, page 34. In the case of the Iraq WMD example, a major analytic shortcoming was the linchpin assumptions about Iraq's leadership intentions and the reliance on old assumptions and inferences drawn from Iraq's previous behavior and intentions (see U.S. Government, *The Commission on the Intelligence Capabilities of the United States Regarding Weapons of Mass Destruction,* pages 3 and 9).

23. For the development of this software tool, with screenshots of the argument models, see the series of papers: Schum, David A., Gheorghe Tecuci, and Mihai Boicu, "Analyzing Evidence and Its Chain of Custody: A Mixed-Initiative Computational Approach" *International Journal of Intelligence and Counterintelligence,* Vol. 22, No. 2 (2009) 298–319; Tecuci, Gheorghe, et al. "Cognitive Assistants for Analysts," in John Auger, and William Wimbish (eds.), *Proteus Futures Digest: A Compilation of Selected Works Derived from the 2006 Proteus Workshop,* (Joint

publication of the National Intelligence University, Office of the Director of National Intelligence, and U.S. Army War College Center for Strategic Leadership, 2007) 303–29; Tecuci, Gheorghe, Mihai Boicu, Dorin Marcu, David Schum, and Benjamin Hamilton, "TIACRITIS System and Textbook: Learning Intelligence Analysis through Practice," *in Proceedings of the Fifth International Conference on Semantic Technologies for Intelligence, Defense, and Security—STIDS 2010,* and Tecuci, G., D. Schum, M. Boicu, D. Marcu, B. Hamilton and B. Wible, "Teaching Intelligence Analysis with TIACRITIS," *American Intelligence Journal,* Vol. 28, No. 2 (December 2010).

24. This process is adapted from the 8-step process introduced in Heuer, Richards J. Jr., *Psychology of Intelligence Analysis,* Chapter 8 "Analysis of Competing Hypotheses"; See also Sawka, Kenneth, "Competing Hypothesis Analysis," *Competitive Intelligence,* Vol. 2, No. 3, (July–September 1999) 37–38.

25. In some ACH methods or tools, the analysts may annotate a quantitative likelihood value (or probability) value that this evidence would be observed if the hypothesis were true.

26. *Diagnosticity* refers to the significance or diagnostic value to support, refute, or distinguish between hypotheses; evidence that uniquely supports a single hypothesis is more diagnostic that evidence that supports multiple hypotheses. Evidence has no diagnostic contribution when it supports to any degree, all hypotheses.

27. For an overview of the ACH tool, see Section 2, "Evaluation of a Computer Support Tool for Analysis of Competing Hypotheses" in Pirolli, Peter "Assisting People to Become Independent Learners in the Analysis of Intelligence" Office of Naval Research Contract N00014-02-C-0203, (Palo Alto, CA: Palo Alto Research Center, 2006). The ACH software may be downloaded from PARC online at http://www2.parc.com/istl/projects/ach/ach.html.

28. The brief description here only introduces the basic concept of Bayesian inference; for more complete descriptions of the application to analysis, see the author's description in chapter 7 of Bennett, Michael and Edward Waltz, *Counterdeception Principles and Applications for National Security,* (Boston: Artech, 2006). Also for example applications of this method to intelligence problems, see Sticha, Paul, Dennis Buede, and Richard L. Rees, "APOLLO: An Analytical Tool for Predicting a Subject's Decision Making," in *Proceedings of the 2005 International Conference on Intelligence Analysis* (Washington, DC: Office of the Assistant Director of Central Intelligence for Analysis and Production, 2005) and Nixon, Mark, "Inference to the Best Next Observation in Probabilistic Expert Systems," *Technology Review Journal,* Northrop Grumman, Vol. 13, No. 1 (Spring/Summer 2005) 81–101.

29. This figure is synchronized with Figure 2.3 and illustrates the categories of explicit models used throughout analysis.

7

+

Explicit Models of the Targets of Analysis

While the models in the last chapter explicitly describe *how* the analyst thinks about a problem, this chapter describes the models that represent what the analyst is thinking about—the intelligence target itself. We use the word "target" to refer to the subject of study, which can be as general as a "situation" or as specific as "the activities at a specific facility."

Analysts maintain and grow an understanding of their targets in the form of models—mental models that are synthesized from scant evidence and prior experience about the context and target subject. As targets grow more complex, these mental models may be externalized to enable greater scrutiny, refinement, and sharing. Tacit mental models represent something physical or concrete as an abstraction (a concept or idea without concrete form) in the mind, and then the target model represents that mental model explicitly.

Up front, we should recognize that the overarching purpose of target system modeling is to help the analyst understand the target, and this requires confidence in the analytic method and the model itself. In the best of conditions, the models can be validated by comparing to real-world target observations; analysts can confidently use these models to understand their observations and relate external observations to internal behaviors. But in many intelligence problems, the target is hidden, the data are sparse and highly uncertain, and models are based on "best estimates" of what the target may be. In these cases, one may reasonably ask "Of what use could such hypothetical models possibly be to the analyst?" In a classic RAND paper entitled, "Six (or so) Things You Can Do with a Bad Model," James Hodges addressed this question:

Many models used in policy or systems analysis either cannot be validated in any fully adequate sense, such as by comparing them with actual data. . . . Nevertheless, such models are often used and can be used fruitfully, even though they have no theory for how to use them or how to place value on the results they produce.[1]

Hodges's six legitimate uses of inaccurate models of target systems can be related to intelligence analysis:

1. The model may be used as a *bookkeeping device to organize data,* providing an incentive to improve data quality; for the analyst this means the model provides an explicit descriptive framework around which evidence can be marshaled and organized.
2. The model may be used in an *automatic management system,* in those cases where model usefulness is not determined by accuracy. For example, multiple hypothesized alternative models of a target system may be used to guide collection against the target; though accuracies are not known, the models provide a rigorous means to guide resources.
3. The model may be used as a *vehicle for* a fortiori *(with greater reason) arguments* that assert:

   - If the modeled condition X were true, then COA A would be preferable to other candidates;
   - But reality deviates from condition X in a way that favors A even more;
   - Therefore, a *fortiori*, A is preferred.

   While uncertainties exist in models, the model can be constructed such that estimated parameters are conservative and the model, though inaccurate, provides an *a fortiori* basis for COA comparison; subsequent discussion about development of robust strategies address *a fortiori* methods in a quantitative manner.
4. The model may be used as an *aid to thinking and hypothesizing* for intellectual exploration, providing a tool to conduct computational experiments about the target systems, allowing a bad model to be compared to reality and refined.
5. The model may be used as an *aid to present an idea* where the model is but an illustration; the analysts can use models to illustrate the expected effects of low probability, high consequence situations for which there may be no prior data (e.g., simulating large-scale biological weapon effects).
6. The model may be used as a *training aid* to induce a particular behavior, enabling the analyst to train others on how targets behave

and their responses to alternative courses of action (e.g., training analysts to deal with denial and deception (D&D) by exposing them to hypothetical D&D situations).

In subsequent sections, we address validation of models and their potential uses in each of the areas that Hodges has enumerated. In this chapter we introduce the methods of computational modeling and simulation to describe, explore, and even anticipate a range of potential behaviors of analysts' targets. To illustrate the methods, we provide several examples that show how models are applied to intelligence problems.[2]

MODELS OF DATA AND MODELS OF THEORY

Before we proceed to develop target system models, we distinguish two major model categories that may be selected to address a problem or be applied jointly. The two model categories are:

- *Empirical Data models* of a situation or system are mathematically derived functions that relate dependent output variables to independent variables; the mathematical derivation of the model function is based on the analysis of empirical data sets, and these models are also referred to as *empirical models*. The models are inherently quantitative; the modeling process applies inferential *statistical* methods to infer a general function from a population of data, such that given a set of input variables, the dependent output variables can be predicted with a specified confidence. The validation of these models is based on a measure of the "goodness of fit," a measure of how well model-predicted outputs fit a set of real-world observations.
- *Theoretical Models* represent the internal elements and functions of a situation or system, based on some theory of how the system operates. The model is referred to as a *causal model* because it attempts to explicitly represent causality—the relationship between external driving causes and the effects (or outputs) of the system. In some cases the functional operation is well-known (e.g., operation of integrated air defenses, manufacturing processes, etc.), but in other areas the functional operation is based on much less deterministic theories (e.g., social science theories of human behavior).

Within the physical and social sciences (and within the Intelligence Community) data and theoretical modeling disciplines are distinct specialties. Because modeling in science, as in intelligence, is a challenging effort to represent reality, the two disciplines often compete for viability and acceptance to provide knowledge about very difficult problems. Albert Einstein recognized the tension between the empirical approach of the experimenter, and the theoretical approach vying for acceptance of a valid representation of reality; he humorously commented, "A theory is something nobody believes, except the person who made it. An experiment is something everybody believes, except the person who made it."[3] The tension is as old as the divide between the early empiricists who believed truth came only by observation and description of reality (e.g., David Hume, Francis Bacon, Robert Boyle, and Lord Kelvin) and the theoretical idealists who developed mathematically rigorous causal theories that could be compared to observations (Rene Descartes, Isaac Newton, Laplace, and Robert Maxwell). The divide is more than practical, it is epistemological.[4]

Of course, as in science, both of these modeling approaches provide valuable contributions, and the intelligence analyst is not confronted with an either/or choice; an analyst may apply both methods to obtain two perspectives. Data modeling approaches are favored where data exist—and in many areas of intelligence, data are plentiful (e.g., in areas of SIGINT, cyber forensics, social behavior analysis, etc.). In other areas, observations are limited, but subject matter experts have functional theories that can be modeled and tested against observations to gain insight to a target system. The two methods approach a problem from different perspectives.

Data modeling is "driven" by and dependent on accumulated empirical data that measure independent variables and system output variables external to the system; the focus of these methods is on the functional relationship between a relatively small number of critical variables. Data modeling methods are statistical and measure the correlation between independent and dependent variables.

Theoretical modeling is "driven" by the development of a core theory of behavior; the emphasis is not on correlation of variables, but on the causal relationships between external causes (inputs) and model outputs (effects). Theoretical models attempt to capture and represent even intangible variables of causation that are not easily measured or represented in empirical models. Table 7.1 compares these contrasts in approach. While an in-depth treatment of these modeling methods is beyond the scope of this book, we provide a brief introduction appropriate for the intelligence analyst and methodologist to select and apply appropriate methods to intelligence problems and references to study more deeply in each area.[5]

Table 7.1 Comparison of Empirical Data Models and Theoretical Models

Approach	Empirical Data Model	Theoretical Causal Modeling
Description	The **data model** is a mathematical relationship between output and inputs derived solely from prior data; internal operation of the system need not be known.	The **causal model** is a functional representation that produces output as a causal consequence of inputs based on a theory of the inner causality of the system.
Analytic Approach to Develop the Model	 ***Derive,*** *by mathematical methods (e.g., regression, causal induction), the dependent variable, z, as a function F, of independent variables x and y.*	 ***Theorize,*** *by logical induction, the inner elements of the system and the causal relationships between elements to produce z from variables x and y.*
Character-istics of the Approach	***Empirical***—Model equations are determined by statistical derivation from prior data sets that empirically measure the system output, z, as function of observed variations in x and y. ***External Observed Behavior***—*The system, S, is a black box knowable only by outward behaviors. Internal causality is not known, only outward behavior.*	***Theoretical***—Model equations are based on a causal theory of how the system internally operates; it represents the causal chain from (causes) x and y to the dependent system output (effect), z. **Internal Causal Hypothesis**—A theory of internal operation is hypothesized and represented in a quantitative model to produce results that can be tested against empirical data.
Evaluation Criteria	Correlation of model predictions to observations by goodness of fit measures.	Explanation of relationships between causes and effects; plausibility, explanatory and descriptive adequacy, fit, and parsimony.
Focus Issue addressed	How does the system behave the way we observe it?	Why does the system behave the way we observe it?

Empirical Data Modeling Methods—The objective of empirical modeling is to create a mathematical model (a function) that most accurately represents the relationship between multivariate inputs $\mathbf{X}=(x_1, x_2, \ldots x_N)$ and output variables $\mathbf{Y}=(y_1, y_2, \ldots y_M)$ of a target system; generally $N \gg M$. The model may include assumptions about the system behavior, placing constraints on the estimated mathematical function. The validity of such a model is measured by its ability to replicate the aggregate relationship between x and y variables. The criterion to measure this is generally a "goodness of fit" statistical measure of how well a model-predicted output compares to empirical data used to derive the model function and to examine the residual errors between predictions and observations.[6] A model function that accounts for the most variance in the empirical data set will achieve the highest fit when compared to empirical data.

Descriptive statistical methods can be applied to empirical data sets to measure aggregate properties of the associations between the most significant independent (or "predictor") variables $X=(x_1, x_2, \ldots x_N)$ and dependent variables $Y=(y_1, y_2, \ldots y_M)$, such as correlation (scatter diagrams) and covariance, but these methods do not produce models. Inferential statistical methods are required to derive the relationships between X and Y, allowing the user to then "predict" a value of X, given Y. Consider the most basic linear regression that assumes linear relationships between x and y variables and normally distributed error, ε. In this most basic empirical model, Y is represented as a function of X with the parameters α_i, β_i, and the error ε:

$$Y = \sum_{i=1}^{n} \alpha_i X_i^{\beta_i} + \varepsilon$$

Given a set of empirical data, the values of α_i and β_i are derived to minimize ε. Once the model is derived from *past* empirical data, it allows us to "regress on X" for future values of X to "predict" the values of Y. The correlation of the model to the data is measured by the general coefficient of determination (R^2). Spreadsheet tools, as well as comprehensive statistical packages, enable users to array input data sets and develop regression solutions. Of course, beyond the basic multiple regression methods, a wide range of empirically based analytic methods have been applied to intelligence and related problems (table 7.2). These empirical-based modeling methods have been widely applied to intelligence warning problems at strategic and operational levels, using multivariate analysis of many indicators of state stability.[7]

Theoretical or Functional Modeling Methods—The objective of this approach to modeling is to create a mathematical representation of the structural and functional properties of a system, inferring from external empirical data generated by the system, the internal operation of the system. This modeler attempts to understand and represent a theory about the causal nature of the target system. Key terms in this domain include:

Table 7.2 Categories of Empirical Analysis Applied to Intelligence Problems

Modeling Methods	Estimation and Modeling Approach	Example Applications
Statistical Regression Analysis	Apply linear or logistic regression methods to derive the functions that relate dependent variables to independent ("predictor") variables, then estimate current or future dependent variables based on predictor values.	• Estimate weapons production rates based in observed activities that are predictor variables.
Statistical Response Surface Analysis	Using observed data from a target response to stimuli, create a response surface with a high-order polynomial to represent the relationships between M predictor variables and N dependent (response) variables.	• Identify target system behavior surface; locate vulnerabilities and instabilities to support planning.
Statistical Time Series Analysis and Forecast	Characterize the properties of a process that produces a sequence of observations by estimating functional parameters and then forecast future values of the time series variable. Common methods include Auto-Regressive Integrated Moving Average ARIMA, exponential smoothing, or Fourier analysis.	• Identify trends or "seasonal" variations in narcotics growth and production. • Forecast terrorist recruitment based on prior trends.
Pattern Classification Analysis	Apply a supervised pattern classifier, trained on prior indicator data vectors for conflict/no-conflict conditions; forecast future feature vectors using time series analysis and classify using classifier.	• Estimate nation-state conflict potential based on statistical distance from prior feature vectors trained on reference vectors.[1]
Causal Inference	Apply graphical probabilistic models to reason about the actual cause of an event based on non-experimental data; apply causal effect analyses to support conterfactual reasoning, to estimate the outcome of events that did not happen.	• Estimate the causal behavior of partially observed foreign targets, to estimate unobserved variables.[2]

1. Shearer, Robert and Marvin, Brett, "Anticipating Terrorist Safe Havens from Instability Induced Conflict," in Argamon, Shlomo and Newton Howard, *Computational Methods for Counterterrorism* (New York: Springer, 2009) 2229–48.
2. The key text in this area is Pearl, J., *Causality: Models, Reasoning and Inference* (Cambridge: Cambridge University Press, 2000). For a thorough statistical treatment, see Spirtes, P., C. Glymour, and R. Scheines, *Causation, Prediction, and Search*, 2nd edition (Cambridge, MA: MIT Press, 2000).

- *Causal Explanation* refers to a hypothesis about the causes and effects associated with a single or multiple events.
- *Causal Inference* is the process of developing and testing a general causal explanation using the method of inference by first positing

conceptual models (conceptual hypotheses), then deduction of specific, operational hypotheses using the model to predict effects, then testing the hypotheses against similar conditions in the real-world system. Analysis of the hypothesis tests will lead to refinements in the conceptual hypotheses, to achieve a model that adequately explains the target system, for the model's intended purpose.

- *Causal Modeling* is the process of developing a computational model that instantiates a causal hypothesis within the context of the domain, to compute output effects from input conditions and causes.
- *Theoretical Modeling* is the process of developing a hypothesized structural or causal model of a process to explain or explore the hypothesis or to conduct hypothesis testing to falsify or confirm aspects of the hypothesis based on empirically collected data.

While data-modeling methods may choose from alternative forms of regression to improve the goodness of fit, alternative theoretical models may differ significantly as competing hypotheses to explain a system. Choosing among alternative hypotheses was discussed in the last chapter, and theoretical modelers must choose among theoretical models that best explain data. Besides goodness of fit measures, additional criteria used to evaluate theoretical models include:[8]

- Model plausibility — Are the assumptions and behavioral theory reasonable and consistent? Are they credible as a hypothesis?
- Explanatory adequacy — Is the theoretical explanation reasonable and consistent with accepted knowledge in the domain?
- Interpretability — Does the model, its structure, components, and parameters make sense to a subject-matter expert in the domain, and are they understandable?
- Descriptive adequacy — Does the model sufficiently describe the behavior of the observed data (this includes quantitative goodness of fit measures)?
- Generalizability — This is a criterion that assesses the generality of the theory. Is the model sufficiently robust to produce accurate data for conditions that goes beyond the limited conditions (empirical data sets) used to test the model?
- Parsimony (least complexity) — Does the model represent the system and its behavior the most succinct way and with the least assumptions?[9]

Models and their underlying theories are *underdetermined* if the empirical data also support an alternative and competing theory.

Data modeling methods are widely applicable to many disciplines, and the statistical methods are applicable to intelligence data sets and just as well to medical, political, economic, or other domain data sets. The methods do not distinguish the domain in which the modeled system exists; they only develop mathematical functions of the data sets. Theoretical modeling methods, on the other hand, develop application-unique models, and for that reason, the remaining sections of this chapter are dedicated to developing the methods for implementing functional or theoretical models for intelligence applications.

Integrating Empirical and Theoretical Models—Hybrid modeling methods can integrate empirical and theoretical models to apply the strengths of each approach to address applications such as warning and planning. Two forms of integration illustrate the alternatives (figure 7.1).

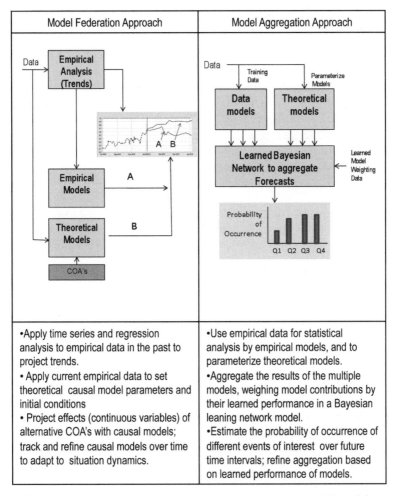

Figure 7.1 Two methods of integrating empirical and theoretical models

The model federation approach applies empirical models to track prior behavior to develop statistical models that can estimate future outcomes based on current conditions (e.g., regression) and time series models that can project some variables (e.g., auto-regressive methods). Current conditions and regression-derived variables are used to set initial conditions and parameters in theoretical models to project future behavior under alternative course of action (e.g., do nothing, COA1, COA2, . . .). The model aggregation approach combines the predicted results of multiple models (both empirical and theoretical) into an aggregate estimate of the probability of occurrence of different events of interest over future time intervals; the combination process is refined over time based on the learned performance of models.[10]

MODELS AND MODEL PREDICTION IN INTELLIGENCE

In a 1994 *Foreign Affairs* article entitled "Peering into the Future," former chairman of the National Intelligence Council (NIC) Joseph Nye asked, "Like all kinds of intelligence, estimative intelligence starts with the available facts, but then it trespasses into the unknown and the unknowable— the regions where we simply lack facts. Is it any wonder that national intelligence estimates are sometimes wrong?"[11] Succeeding chairman of the NIC John Gannon wisely noted,

> I want to make a small digression and address a widely held but incorrect perception that the job of intelligence officers is to predict the future. That is not the case. Only God is omniscient, and only the Pope is infallible; intelligence officers are too savvy to compete in that league. Rather, the function of intelligence is to help US decisionmakers better understand the forces at work in any situation, the other fellow's perspective, and the opportunities and consequences of any course of action so that US policymakers can make informed decisions.[12]

The role of "predictive" models in complex geopolitical situations is just this—to provide decision makers with improved understanding of the factors, dynamics, and possible effects of complex systems. But what can we expect from empirical models (properly validated by empirical data) and theoretical models (not validated with prior data, but with the potential power to explain causal mechanisms)?

- *Empirical models* provide a strong, statistically validated, approach to detect or predict events in steady-state systems with regular, statistically measured data. But these models will not detect or foresee events that lie far from the statistical norm, occurring in the narrow "tails" of a statistical distribution (these "low base rate" events have also been called "black swan" events[13]).

- *Theoretical models* provide a means of hypothesizing the underlying causal mechanisms of complex processes that are not statistically understandable. They do provide a means to explore the behavior of such systems and foresee possibilities of never-before-observed outcomes. These models can provide *anticipation*—the ability to see possible futures—even high consequence, low base rate ones—to help analysts anticipate such events.

We can illustrate the potential value of each model type by considering the complex social mechanisms and underlying context that led to the Arab Spring phenomena that began across North Africa and the Middle East in 2011 (see figure 7.2).

ABSTRACTING REAL TARGET SYSTEMS

Because a model is an abstract representation (also called an "abstraction"—something that exists conceptually) of a literal ("real," "physical," or "concrete") target in the real world, a process of *abstraction* is required to translate the properties of the real target into its abstract representation. This translation process is entirely dependent on the analytic purpose, for which the model is intended to be used.

Any modeling effort must begin with a concise statement of the analytic purpose or intended application—as well as the limits or constraints on the model use. In addition to the statement of purpose, an application-use case that illustrates how the model will be used is also very useful. The explicit purpose description provides a clear understanding between the modeler-methodologist and the analyst-user to guide all development. The broad categories of model purposes useful to intelligence analysts (table 7.3) include Hodges's "six, or so" uses of models (except for use in automated management systems). The three major categories distinguish the objectives of describing a situation or target, providing a means to explore the situation to improve understanding, or enabling some degree of prediction of aspects of the future state of the systems involved. Within each purpose category, the table distinguishes specific application objectives (e.g., to support presentation, warning, training, collection, operations planning). Descriptive and exploratory model purposes generally provide support to "thinking"—providing rigor, explanation, and anticipation to the analytic process.

The Arab Spring, Social Media, and Modeling

The "Arab Spring" of rebellions against autocratic regimes across North Africa and the Middle East opposed state corruption and repression, seeking to overthrow regimes to gain freedom, reform and democratic governments. The dramatic speed of the cascade of activities across the Arab world occurred with little warning to leaders. Foreign policy articles asked, *Why did we not predict?* and *What was the cause?* Several hypotheses have been offered, including the effects of demographics (high percentage of mid-20's youth bulge), the introduction of widely available social communication capabilities (e.g. blogs, microblogs, smart phones) that raised the "collective consciousness about both shared grievances and opportunities for action", empowering populations in way never before possible [i]. The National Intelligence Council considered the questions: *What role did social media play? Are there limitations to what social media can accomplish? How will regimes respond to social media?* [ii]

This example enables us to consider the potential contribution of each form of model to address this issue:

- Empirical models – Structural stability indictors of Arab societies leading up to the events of 2011 (e.g. political, socio-economic, public attitudes, social movements, etc.) could be compared to empirical data for prior state instability and conflict. Although social media enabled social mobilization has not been seen before, such validated models may indentify instability, although occurring at a rate and by a mechanism not in prior empirical data.
- Theoretical models – Social models of Arab societies would be based on empirical data, but would represent the theorized causal relationships between exogenous economic conditions, political repression, social behaviors, and the effects of attitudes toward the government and willingness to revolt. In addition such a model could represent the theorized mechanisms by which social media empowers social mobilization - the hypothesized effects of increased communication on a population's willingness and ability to mobilize opposition to the government. This model, though not validated by prior empirical data (because social media, smart phones, etc. did not exist in any prior data) could explore the potential for protest, violence, and government overthrow, and the impact of new technologies on societal mobilization in forms not before observed.

---

[i] Howard, Philip N. and Muzammil M. Hussain, "The Role of Digital Media: Upheavals in Egypt and Tunisia", *Journal of Democracy*, Vol. 22, No. 3, (July 2011) 35-48.
[ii] Berg, CDR Heidi, Deputy National Intelligence Officer for Military Issues, "Middle Eastern Unrest and the Role of Social Media," National Intelligence Council, Office of Director of National Intelligence, Unclassified Presentation (15 March 2011).

Figure 7.2 The Arab Spring, social media, and modeling

Predictive models, on the other hand, are expected to provide support to decision making and action. Often called "action models," these support collection and operations planners who demand greater confidence in the models and the implications of the results they predict, forecast, or project. These users seek guidance in choosing alternative course of action and the potential consequences of each alternative.

Table 7.3 Model-Based Analysis Purpose Categories

Analytic Purpose	Description	Specific Intelligence Purposes and Examples
Description and Explanation	The target system is modeled to organize information, develop hypotheses, and support argumentation.	Strategic target development for a physical site, cyber system, or social situation to support analysis or threat assessment.
		Operational target system modeling to support targeting or functional battle damage assessment.
		Analytic support for hypothesis representation and argument creation and assessment.
		Training support for target system analysis.
Exploration	The target system is modeled to gain new insights in potential behaviors and emergence.	Dynamic analysis of a target system to explore potential sensitivities, dynamic modes, phase shifts (tipping points), vulnerabilities, etc.
		Robustness and resilience analysis to assess sensitivities of COAs to modeled uncertainties.
		Support to counterfactual analysis to enable alternative chains of causality to be explored.
		Modeling of component systems to support analytic wargaming (see chapter 8).
Prediction	The target system is modeled (in an "action model") to predict effects to support decision making.	General prediction of trends using data models (statistical regression), or theoretical models.
		Prediction of hypothetical behaviors to support hypothesis testing by active stimulation of targets (see chapter 9).
		Systems effects analysis; e.g., Kinetic munitions effects and non-kinetic action effects.
		Prediction with and without a course of action (intervention) to assess.

Lustick and Miodownik have further distinguished three categories of analytic scope that distinguish the purpose of models.[14] The categories are applied to agent-based social system models of interacting actors for exploration and prediction, but they can be applied more generally to distinguish other types of system models as well:

- *Abstraction Models* are theoretically justifiable models that represent the most general processes of a general population of actors. The model is generative in that it models very simple relationships and allows analysis of the impact of changes at the micro level on behavior at the macro level, as the actors interact to generate macro effects.

- *Ensemble Models* are theoretically justifiable models that are based on data aggregated from a wide number of cases of a specified problem. The model is hypothesized to have important isomorphisms with the causal relations in the specified set of problems. The set (or envelope) of behaviors represented by the model may include situations that occur in the specified set of problems.
- *Virtualization Models* are based on specific data for particular situations; the model represents the actors, relationship structure, patterns of behavior, etc., of the particular case to virtually represent the situation in appropriate detail for a problem being solved. The model is theoretically justifiable AND documented with reference to data drawn from the actual case.

The distinctions are helpful to further specify the focus of analysis, expected results, and the degree of complexity and dependence on real-world data for implementation and validation. The exploratory or predictive purposes of these models and examples are provided in table 7.4.

Table 7.4 Three Categories of Exploration-Prediction Models

Category	Model Purpose	Example Uses to Support Intelligence and Planning
Abstraction Models	Explore dynamics of a fundamental theory of behavior of a *general* problem.	Analyst uses an abstraction model to explore the effects of a new kind of social media influence on unstable population groups, and the mechanisms by which threatening messages may incite violence.
Ensemble Models	Explore dynamics of a specified class of situations or systems.	Analyst uses an ensemble model to assess the range of population responses to incitement messages over social media channels; the model is isomorphic to the characteristics of a specific country situation.
Virtualization Models	Explore or predict the potential behavior of a specific real-world situation of people, in a context at a point in time.	Analysts use a virtual model to assess the potential effects of a specific plan of action to mitigate the effects of incitement messages against a specific real-world population group at a specific period of time.

The abstraction process reduces or compresses the detail of the real-world target, retaining in the model only the information that is relevant for its representation, requiring the modeler to define a required level of the following model properties appropriate for the intended purpose of the model:[15]

- *Model Fidelity*—The degree to which a model or simulation reproduces the state and behavior of a real-world object or the perception of a real-world object, feature, condition, or chosen standard in a measurable or perceivable manner; a measure of the realism of a model or simulation; faithfulness. Fidelity should generally be described with respect to the measures, standards, or perceptions used in assessing or stating it.
- *Model Granularity or Resolution*—The degree of detail and precision used in the representation of real-world aspects in a model or simulation. It defines how the target system is subdivided into and represented by component parts or behaviors. Granularity can refer to spatial, temporal, behavioral, causal, or other attributes of the model. Fine grained models (high resolution) have more components than coarse-grained models. Multi-resolution models include mutually consistent components of a target system that are represented at different levels of resolution.
- *Model Accuracy*—The degree to which a parameter or variable, or a set of parameters or variables, within a model or simulation conforms exactly to reality or to some chosen standard or reference.

Besides fidelity, accuracy, and granularity, the modeler must define these additional properties of the model (figure 7.3):

- *Model Boundaries*—The distinction between what behaviors, functions, and elements are included in the model and what are excluded (because they are not relevant for the model's purpose).
- *Exogenous Variables*—External variables that develop or originate from without provide the context for the model; the model is influenced by these key variables, but they are not a part of the model.
- *Endogenous, Internal Modeled Components and Variables*—The specific internal modeled entities and functions are specified, as well as their interrelations, and the necessary variables that represent interactions. Endogenous variables develop or originate from within the model; the output variables are endogenous.
- *Time Horizon and Time Granularity*—The period over which a model is expected to operate (e.g., forecast possible outcomes for six months) and the time granularity (e.g., simulation steps are updated every week) are determined by the purpose.

Intelligence analysts model a wide variety of target system types (table 7.5) that distinguish the role of physical and technical processes, cyber (computer automated or networked) processes, and human (social) behavior. The abstraction process requires decisions on the degree to which

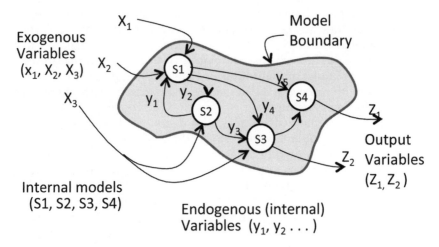

Figure 7.3 Top-level properties of a model

Table 7.5 System Categories

System Category	Definition	Example Intelligence Target Systems
Physical Systems	Natural or engineered systems whose operations are dominated by physical laws; role of human activity is minor.	Narcotics growth and production, low-tech manufacturing
Cyber Systems or Physical-Cyber Systems	Engineered computer-mediated physical systems that integrate computational and physical components. Computational systems and networks that perform collection, processing, use, sharing, maintenance, or dissemination of information.	Weapon systems, autonomous systems, supervisory control SCADA systems (e.g., electrical power, telecommunications, manufacturing), computer networks
Human (Social) Systems	Natural systems of human-social activity dominated by human behavior and interaction within a cultural context.	Political-military organizations, social groups, economies, nation-states
Socio-Technical Systems	Engineered and interacting human, cyber and physical systems that integrate social and technology systems to perform a mission. Social interaction and human decision making are important aspects of the system operation.	Command and control systems, network-centric ISR and weapon systems

each of these elements is represented. Most systems of interest have human elements of management and control (decision making), and are operated by individual humans (labor); the abstraction must define to what degree human behavior must be represented in the model.

Of course the abstraction process that defines the boundaries and degree of fidelity, granularity, and accuracy is dependent on the reason for which the model is being used. The model design process generally proceeds in the sequence (table 7.6) that broadly requires three steps.

Table 7.6 Three Broad Phases of Model Implementation[1]

Phase	1 Enumeration	2 Relation	3 Simulation
	Descriptive Models		Exploratory and Predictive Models
Description	*Enumerate* the elements of the models; characterize the properties of the elements.	*Model the structure* of relationships between the elements, identifying exogenous and endogenous variables.	*Simulate the behavior* of the system and the dynamics of interaction among system elements.
Analytic Focus	**SIZE:** Scope, size of system; boundary and functional elements	**STRUCTURE:** Functional relationships and transfer functions between elements	**BEHAVIOR:** Function and performance of interacting elements; characteristics of dynamics
Modeling Tools	• Organized data sets in spread-sheets, databases	• Relational Databases • Network graphs • System or Functional Diagrams • Statistical analysis	• Computational experiments conducted in simulations
Typical Products Developed in Each Phase	• Lists of human actors • List of functional elements • Timelines of observed activities	• Social Network Graphs (nodes and links—relations) • Functional system diagrams of sub-model components • Integrated model functional relationship diagrams	• Simulation experiment plan • Simulation validation plan and results • Simulation results and analysis
Example Modeling Tools Used in Each Phase	• Spreadsheet or database • Statistical analysis tools	• Link Analysis and modeling tools • Mathematical modeling tools; Causal inference tools • Data Mining (automated induction of nets)	• System Dynamics, Discrete event, Discrete time simulation tools • Bayesian Net modeling tools • Agent-based modeling tools

1. Table adapted from Waltz, Ed, "Practical Approaches to Impact Adversary Decision-Making Processes" (Reproduced by permission from Alexander Kott, editor, *Information Warfare and Organizational Decision-Making*. Norwood, MA: Artech House, Inc, 2007. ©2007 by Artech House, Inc.)

In the first phase of model development, the analysts must *enumerate* the elements within the model boundary that make up the target system. If the model is of a narcotics organization, the elements are human actors; if the model is of a narcotics production system, the elements may include crops, laborers, transport channels to production, production processes, and channels to deliver products. In the enumerations step, the analyst accumulates the entities and their properties using a spreadsheet, database, or other tool.

The second phase of model implementation is to *relate* the entities and develop a model of the interaction among entities. If the model is of a narcotics threat, the relations between the organization and production submodels described above must be defined (e.g., how key actors in roles in the organization model control production activities). In this stage, the analyst also introduces the functional (theoretical) processes that describe how the actors interact (e.g., rational man, game theoretic, etc.) and how the production processes work (e.g., standard model of poppy-to-morphine refinement by boiling water precipitation, filtering, and drying for packaging as a paste). At this point a *dynamic hypothesis* is developed to explicitly theorize and explain the causal behavior of the system and the interaction of its elements.[16] The analyst may choose a high-dimensional, fine-grain (microscale) agent-based model to capture many detailed features of a system to understand complex behaviors or may choose a low-dimensional (macro-scale) system dynamics model that is more abstract and looks at the system at a more aggregate behavior level. The analyst also distinguishes between the *generic model* of a theorized system (e.g., a narcotics organization with crops, production facilities, distribution channels, etc.) and an *instantiated model* of a particular process that has been instantiated with specific properties (e.g., a specific narcotics organization in Country X, when operating at half capacity, distributing by the southern route, while using production units A, C, and G, version 4.05).

The analyst must also choose the appropriate schema(s) to represent the target system. (In chapter 4 we introduced problem framing and the concept of *schemas* to represent information in models, and in chapter 5 we applied schema description in structured analysis and model building.) The target system and analytic purpose guide the selection of schema(s) to represent the target system. Consider typical choices analysts make from the common schemas (table 7.7):

- A narcotics production activity is modeled using a spreadsheet (structured data) to estimate monthly production as a function of crop acreage observed in satellite imagery (input) and information on deliveries provided by HUMINT sources (output). This is coupled with an operational model (system schema) to understand the dynamics of the seasonal production delivery process and evaluate methods to disrupt the process.

Table 7.7 Common Modeling Schemas for Representing Target Systems

Schema Category	Common Representations Methods	Example Modeling Tools
Argument	Logical argument structures that reason from evidence and inference to hypotheses or premises	See chapter 6
Entity-Relationship	Concepts—Informal representation of relationships between ideas, concepts	See chapter 6
	Social Network—Directed graph representations of relationships between actors to model organization structure, and structural metrics	ORA, UCINET, DyNet
	Formal Entity-Relationship Structures—Formal knowledge representation in directed graph forms (e.g., RDF, OWL, etc.)	Formal ontology modeling tools (e.g., Protégé)
Spatial	Geographic Information System (GIS)—Geospatial mapping and creation of registered map layers (e.g., Shape files)	ArcGIS
	3D—Detailed representation of engineered objects (e.g., weapons, buildings, etc.) and their properties	Computer aided design (CAD) tools
	4D—Three dimensional space plus time dynamic visualization- a synthetic video or movie presentation of hypothesized behavior.	4D modeling tools (e.g., STK™)
Timeline	Chronological ordering of events in annotated time-sequential timelines (often to support causal inference)	Analyst Notebook, Timeline Maker
Structured Data	Time Structured—Data organized in time series with supporting statistical analysis tools to perform trend analyses and forecast future values.	Spreadsheets, databases, and statistical analysis packages (e.g., R, SAS, SPSS, etc.)
	Domain Structured—Data organized by domain category, type, time, or other categories, supported by tools to perform regression and causal inference analyses.	
Causal Structures	Directed graph representation of structures leading from causes to effects; Event trees that begin with undesired initiator event and represent effects thru sequence of events; Fault trees that begin with effect of interest and decomposition backward to root causes	Bayesian Net tools that represent causal chains with associated probabilities
Systems	Discrete event—Event-ordered representation of system activities to model process interactions, synchronization, and scheduling of discrete events.	Simulation Modeling tools (See table 7.10)
	System Dynamics—Macro-level simulation of the flow of abstract and real resources in systems, and the feedback (balancing) loops that represent natural and management controls	
	Micro-Granularity—Agent-based models that model large-scale systems with actor interaction at the micro (individual) level of granularity to produce emergent, complex behaviors.	

- A military garrison is modeled in a geographic information system (geospatial schema) to overlay layers of information about buildings, road networks, estimated capacities, and operations. This model may be supported by a 4D (dynamic spatial schema) model that estimates the operations of the garrison under alternative deployment conditions.

The final phase of model implementation is to *simulate* the model by stepping through time, conducting computational experiments for purposes of model evaluation and validation, exploration, and prediction. The analyst runs these experiments following a plan or analytic framework that includes the following elements:

1. The rationale for translating analytic purpose to model and selected schemas.
2. Model data and structure information to instantiate models; basis and representation of uncertainties.
3. Simulation cases to be run, defined by: 1) Exogenous conditions over which simulations are to be run, 2) data collection methods and basis for statistical sampling of cases, 3) procedures to conduct sensitivity analyses, 4) procedures to conduct specific test cases to support analysis.
4. Additional testing procedures (e.g., procedures to run and compare alternative models that represent alternative hypotheses).

THE VALIDITY OF MODELS

Explicit modelers like to quote George Box's famous observation that "All models are wrong; some are useful."[17] Of course this adage applies to the mental models of experts, the conceptual models they create and explicitly represent, as well as to the computational models we have introduced in previous sections of this chapter. But users want a measure of just *how useful* a model is—and they innately know that usefulness is related to how faithfully a model represents aspects of reality. The fundamental question that must be answered for data and theoretical-based models alike is, *"How valid is the model?"*

Validity is the measure of how appropriate the model is for its intended use, and *validation* is the process of determining the degree to which a model or simulation is an accurate representation of the real world *from the perspective of the intended uses of the model or simulation* (emphasis added).[18] This is distinguished from *verification*, the process that precedes validation, to evaluate the correctness of a computational model with respect to a certain formal specification of a theory (e.g., a conceptual model), using the formal methods of testing, inspection, and review. The literature of verification is robust in the domain of computer science; we focus here on the challenge of verifying that a model appropriately represents the real world for the analytic process that it supports.

Among the greatest challenges to modelers that attempt to faithfully represent real world systems is the process of providing users with confidence in the validity of the model. Two aspects of validity that must be considered, each being related to the correspondence or coherence criteria we introduced earlier for evaluating belief (table 7.8):

- Internal criteria—This evaluates if the internal behavior of the model is consistent with a theory or understanding of phenomena or causality (i.e., the model is internally consistent with a coherent explanation of a system and its observed phenomena; this theory should be an accepted general theory of structure and behavior). These tests often include verification that the computational model represents the conceptual model, but more importantly confirming that the conceptual model itself is consistent in its representation of a coherent theory.
- External criteria—This evaluates if the model output is consistent with corresponding observed measurements of real-world behavior. The model should be consistent with at least one relevant instance of such a system observed in the real world. Of course, a model should be shown to be consistent over a wide range of conditions to be generally applicable, if such data are available. The informal evaluation methods are often called "face validity" tests because they measure the degree to which the model "on the face" appears to represent the real world in the opinions of subject-matter experts.

The criteria for model fidelity, accuracy, and granularity and the appropriate validity tests in the table are based on the defined purpose for the model in an analytic process. The analyst and modeler-methodologist must explicitly describe the translation from purpose to validation criteria; this is generally provided in a model-definition document or specification that: 1) defines analytic purpose, 2) establishes model fidelity, accuracy, and granularity based on purpose, and 3) derives the level of validity required to achieve model purpose, and the validation methodology to be applied.

As we noted earlier, the validation process and the criteria for an abstraction model intended to explore fundamental behaviors of a class of systems is quite different from the process and criterion for the virtualization model of a specific system—for the purpose of predicting its response to a very specific set of conditions.

Table 7.8 Two Perspectives of Validity

Aspect	Internal Validity	External Validity
Standard of validity	Structure and behavior of the model is consistent with a theory or understanding of phenomena or causality over all conditions (even beyond those observed in the real world).	Behavior of the model output is consistent with the finite set of observed real-world behaviors and conditions
Aspect of belief criteria emphasized	Coherence—degree to which model behavior coheres (is consistent) with theory	Correspondence—degree to which model behavior corresponds to observed reality
Model is based on	A coherent and general theory or functional explanation of a system and its phenomena	This particular instance of a system in the real world as revealed by data across as broad a set of conditions as possible
Validation Focus	Theoretical—evaluate by assessing model principles with coherent theory	Empirical—evaluate by assessing model performance against real world data
Common Validity Tests	• Informal inspection of theory, conceptual model • Formal comparison theory-to-conceptual model for completeness and consistency (Correctness of Content and Structure)	• Regression test comparing model output to empirical data • Sensitivity testing of model over a range of conditions • Boundary condition testing • SME evaluation of model behavior over a range of conditions • Blind evaluation of model and empirical data by SMEs (Turing Test)

The Validation Process—Validation is not limited to a "final test and evaluation" process; rather, it is an ongoing process throughout model development, test, and use, requiring documentation, reporting, and refinement. Averill Law describes techniques for developing valid and credible models for a typical model with multiple model components. The seven-step procedure addresses each component, before conducting an evaluation of the combined multi-model. Applied to intelligence analytic support, the steps are summarized:[19]

1. *Formulate Problem Precisely*—Define and fully document the purpose of the model, its contribution to solving the analytic problem, and the translation to model attributes, validation process, and validation criteria. Define the analytic methodology that will apply the model to the analytic problem, and the expected use of results and

their contribution to the methodology. Establish a set of SMEs in the modeled domain to provide oversight through the development process and to support independent validation. Collaborate with appropriate stakeholders (decision makers, analytic units, operations planners) in the analysis frequently; review model purpose, approach, and implementation to assure joint agreement on the model and the methodology.

2. *Document Assumptions, Model and Collect Data*—Document the conceptual model and basis for translating it to a computational model; describe the theoretical and functional basis, assumptions, boundary conditions and constraints. Identify the sources of data required to instantiate the model and the period for which the data will remain valid or must be updated. Identify the quantitative methods to validate model components (e.g., use regression tests to compare model output to empirical data over a range of conditions). Acquire the data to support the model and identify gaps and the approach to deal with uncertainty.

3. *Evaluate Validity of the Assumptions*—Conduct a structured walk-through of the model that is a comprehensive analysis of the conceptual model and computational implementation; the structure includes a step-by-step documented review of each element, relationship, variable, and boundary.

4. *Implement the Computational Model*—and perform verification to ensure the computational model properly and completely represents the theory or functions in the conceptual model.

5. *Perform Results Validation*—Perform a sensitivity analysis to evaluate each component model over a sample of the range of combinations of exogenous variables to determine sensitivities to variables; compare and refine the model functions to validation criteria using empirical reference data. Identify which model factors have a significant impact on the identified measures of model performance. Evaluate the integrated model over a sample of the range of combinations of exogenous variables; compare and refine the integrated model to validation criteria using empirical reference data.

6. *Conduct Analytic Experiments*—Once validated, apply the model according to the previously documented analytic methodology.

7. *Document and Present the Results*—Document results and support the overall intelligence analysis with information on model results, use of data, uncertainties, and gaps.

While we have focused on the verification of a model for a specific intelligence analytic problem, the model may be adopted for broader application. In this case the analyst may seek *accreditation*, the official certification by an appropriate authority, that a model or simulation and its associated data are acceptable for use for a specific purpose.[20] For example, a model for planning an operational mission may in high-consequence environments require formal accreditation for wider operational use.

These organized procedures are appropriate for many physical target system models where physical laws are known, remain constant, and constrain system behaviors, but models of more complex human systems (e.g., political, social, and economic systems) that exhibit highly nonlinear behavior and are plagued by uncertainties require a more cautious approach. Even the concept of validation of such models requires rethinking, where profound uncertainties exist in the model, in its underlying social or human behavior theories, and in the empirical data itself. Bigelow and Davis have noted the challenge in validation of such models:

> [Our conclusions] apply when the models or their data are more afflicted with uncertainty. For example, no one has a "correct" model of war with all its notorious complications, and, even if such a model existed, it would have large numbers of uncertain inputs. . . . In such cases, we believe that model validation should be construed quite differently than might be suggested by the usual definition of validity. A validation process might reasonably conclude by assessing the model and its associated databases as "valid for exploratory analysis" or "valid, subject to the principal assumptions underlying the model, for exploratory analysis."[21]

The authors recommended that *comprehensibility, explainability,* and *uncertainty-representation* criteria were critical for addressing validity in these models. Similarly, the National Research Council (NRC) has recognized that the techniques used to validate models in the physical sciences are not appropriate for modeling the behavior of human target systems:

> Current verification, validation, and accreditation (VV&A) concepts and practices were developed for the physical sciences, and we argue that different approaches are needed for IOS [individuals, organizations, and societies] models. . . . Basing model validation on the usefulness of the model for specific problems requires that model purposes be clearly stated by model users and clearly understood by model developers.[22]

In these cases, the NRC notes that such models cannot be validated in a general sense but must be validated for specifically defined uses, using methods such as triangulation approaches that combine expert judgment, qualitative and theoretical analysis, as well as quantitative analysis. In addition, the NRC report recommended the use of hybrid models and model docking to support comparative analysis. NRC distinctions for the descriptive, exploratory, and predictive purposes are summarized in table 7.9.

Table 7.9 Distinguishing Model Purposes and Application

Model Purpose	Modeling Approach

Description and Exploration Exploration model represents a dynamic hypothesis about a system in order to gain new insights.	• Primary Application: Description, exploration, and the generation of non-obvious insights into complex phenomena that could not have been obtained without the model.
	 • Three optional use situations:
	   ○ A—(Limited explanation) Model of a given phenomenon is incomplete in the sense that it is not capable of explaining all aspects of the phenomenon deemed to be important for an intended purpose.
	   ○ B—(Generative sufficiency) Intermediate possibility is that a model has been constructed that is capable of reliably generating a particular phenomenon of interest; it can be compared to empirical data.
	   ○ C—(Observational equivalence) Multiple distinct models offer alternative competing hypotheses (explanations) for a given phenomenon, none of which can reliably be eliminated on the basis of currently available empirical evidence.

Prediction for the Purpose of Action (to support decision making to take action) Action model relates actions of interest to outcomes of interest; model does not necessarily need to reveal deep understanding.	• Primary Application: Prediction of effects without and with intervention; model includes action choices, and modeled effects must show with and without interventions.
	 • Two key considerations:
	   ○ Action model must include the full range of action options in the action domains of decision makers to permit them to display a realistic degree of flexibility in the face of changing and possibly unanticipated conditions.
	   ○ Validation process for action models cannot provide general validation, but narrowly defined validity for a specific decision-making use case and context, with usability conditions well defined.

A pioneer of social modeling, Robert Axelrod distinguished classical mathematical analysis (formal deductive models and closed form solutions derived for use in operational analysis) and empirical data models (inductive models) used in studying social systems phenomena. He referred to the exploratory use of models as "a third way of doing science" because computational models empower synthetic conceptual experiments. Axelrod wisely noted that for exploratory analysis (generally in abstraction and ensemble models), "The moral of the story is that models that aim to explore fundamental processes *should be judged by their fruitfulness, not by their accuracy. For this purpose, realistic representation of many details is unnecessary and even counterproductive. . . . The intention is to explore fundamental social processes. . . . The interactions of adaptive agents typically lead to nonlinear effects that are not amenable to the deductive tools of formal mathematics.*"[23]

DESCRIPTIVE MODELS IN ANALYSIS

Descriptive models are the result of the first phase of model development that enumerates entities and the second phase that relates the entities (model development process introduced in a previous section). They are often the precursor to exploratory and predictive models that examine target dynamics. Descriptive modeling tools generally fall into three categories:

- *Data Organization Tools* that enable the analyst to import, categorize, and structure qualitative and quantitative data to prepare it for visualization and analysis. Databases and spreadsheets organize data in some structuring schema (described by a *data model* that describes how data are represented in a database or software program) that enables patterns of causal behavior to be revealed and examined. Spreadsheet tools are perhaps the most flexible modeling and analysis environment, enabling the analysts to accumulate and structure quantitative data sets (data and parameters), then compute output data (e.g., aggregate or statistical values), or even use "Solver" tools to optimize objective functions under some constraints. Spreadsheets are suitable for data entry, graphing, and first-order analysis prior to commitment to more refined methods and tools.
- Models that process and visualize structure in data against a temporal-timeline, causal, relationship, or geospatial schemas. Widely used general relation-data tools (e.g., i2 Analysts Notebook™, Palantir™, FMS Sentiel Visualizer™, etc.) and Geospatial Information System (GIS) tools (e.g., ESRI ArcGIS™ and ArcView™, Intergraph Auto-CAD Map 3D™, MapGuide Open Source, etc.) are in this category.[24] Satellite Toolkit (STK™) by Analytic Graphics, Inc. (AGI) is a 3D descriptive modeling tool used by analysts to describe 4D kinematics, trajectories, sensor coverage of ground, air, and space objects; to the degree that the physics-based motion of objects holds (e.g., satellite ephemeris governed by Kepler's laws), these models are predictive. Computer network modeling tools to support information-operations analysts include OPNET Technologies Modeler®, the VINT Project NS2 Network Simulator, OMNeT++, and the Georgia Tech Network Simulator (GTNetS).
- Models that provide a higher degree of quantitative modeling that includes uncertainty representation and graphical representation of the models that convert input data to solutions. (e.g., Lumian Analytica™, MatLab™, etc.)

A Crime Mapping Descriptive Model Example—We can illustrate geospatial and statistical modeling used in crime mapping analysis. The analytic modeling method in this criminal activity example can be directly applied to military intelligence applications to identify threat behaviors (e.g., improvised explosive device IED placement hot spots or terrorist activity locations). For example, these methods can identify "hot spots" to support planning, to guide surveillance, and sensor ambushes.[25] The objective of crime mapping analysis is to place geocoded crime data in a geospatial schema (map) to enable the analyst to visualize the spatial, temporal, social, or other patterns of criminal activity to better understand patterns of activity and underlying causal factors.

Typical geocoded (e.g., latitude-longitude coded) source information used in crime analysis includes:

- calls for service—date/time group, call number, call category, associated incident report identifier, address, and latitude and longitude of location a police unit was sent;
- reported crimes—date/time group for crime event, case number, crime category, address, and latitude and longitude of the crime location;
- arrests—date/time group of arrest, case number, arrested person information, charge category, address, and latitude and longitude of the arrest location; and
- routes—known routes of travel (to-from crime scene, to-from drug deliveries, route between car-stolen and car-recovered, etc.) derived from arrest, investigation, and interrogation records.

Once the geocoded data has been entered in a database, a GIS tool is used to perform spatial-temporal analysis if the data. One representative example (figure 7.4) illustrates an analysis of crime data. In the first step, the data are displayed in a graduated-size "pointmap" that clusters local data, displaying points with graduated sizes that represent the density of crimes in the area. Next, the analyst can cluster and characterize the top theft locations and can examine in detail the properties of these spatial clusters or hot spots, identifying spatial attributes (e.g., number of buildings, number of families, per capita income, distance to police station, etc.) that make the areas suitable for crime. The analyst can also drill down in the data to zoom into specific events within a cluster to try to determine if there is a common *modus operandi* within a cluster.[26]

Once a crime mapping database is sustained, the analyst can also use these data to identify other areas similar to known crime hot spots, to project that they may be vulnerable to similar criminal activities. The analysis can also reveal spatial-temporal patterns that can be correlated to criminal behavior tempos or profiles. The process can also detect changes in behavioral patterns and distinguish deviations from normal patterns of criminal activity.

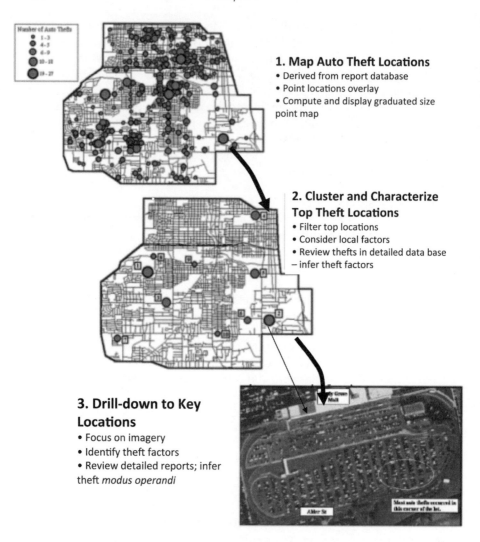

1. Map Auto Theft Locations
• Derived from report database
• Point locations overlay
• Compute and display graduated size point map

2. Cluster and Characterize Top Theft Locations
• Filter top locations
• Consider local factors
• Review thefts in detailed data base
– infer theft factors

3. Drill-down to Key Locations
• Focus on imagery
• Identify theft factors
• Review detailed reports; infer theft *modus operandi*

Figure 7.4 Descriptive crime analysis modeling

A Social Network Analysis (SNA) Example—Intelligence analysts who model organizations apply SNA to quantify the static, topological properties of the structure of the organization, generally to support information operations.[27] The focus of SNA is on the structural properties of relationships, rather than on individual actors.[28] SNA enumerates the actors in an organization and identifies the relationships between them, forming an abstract network graph—an organization model that allows quantitative analysis by applying graph theory where actors are graph *vertices* (or *nodes*), and relationships are *edges* of the graph. *Relationships* or *ties* may refer to a variety of concepts and may be directed (showing a direction of the relationship, e.g., from-to transaction) or not directed (e.g., related by common tribe). Types of relationships may include:

- family, ancestral, tribal or other informal enduring relations;
- organizational roles, interactions, or other interdependencies;
- attitudes or sentiment (positive or negative) between actors;
- transactions by which a material or nonmaterial resource (e.g., capital, communications, or commands) is passed between actors and is a property of a *pair* of actors; or
- events of co-occurrence (e.g., two actors participate in the same event, or they occur at the same time and place).

Once a network model is formed, SNA seeks to characterize the *structures* (regular patterns) in network graphs that represent understood behaviors in real organizations. The structures can be identified by computing structural variables or metrics. The metrics allow analysts to identify actors with different roles, locate structural stabilities or instabilities (potential vulnerabilities), for example.

The metrics measure properties related to the relative flow of information, activity, or influence across actors. The most basic metrics include *degree*, the number of ties an actor has to other actors, and *degree centrality* that includes two components for directed graphs: 1) *indegree*, the number of inbound links to an actor from other actors in the net and 2) *outdegree*, the number of outbound links from an actor to other actors in the net. More sophisticated metrics measure the relative properties of any actor across all actors in a network. Figure 7.5 illustrates a network model represented in the ORA (Organizational Risk Analyzer) tool that enables analysts to perform quantitative social network analysis of large networks. ORA computes over one hundred SNA metrics and is useful for identifying risks or vulnerabilities of an organization's structure.[29]

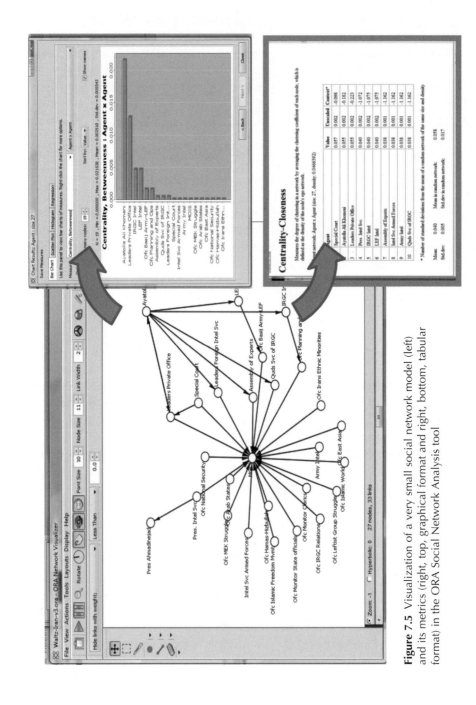

Figure 7.5 Visualization of a very small social network model (left) and its metrics (right, top, graphical format and right, bottom, tabular format) in the ORA Social Network Analysis tool

EXPLORATORY AND PREDICTIVE
SIMULATIONS IN ANALYSIS

Exploratory and predictive models include those models that represent the dynamic behavior of a system to some degree, to anticipate how it will behave under a given set of circumstances. These models are useful to national policy makers and operations planners who desire to explore the potential effects of their planned actions.

Models developed for exploratory and predictive analyses are inherently operated in time as simulations that focus on studying dynamic behavior of the target system, changes in system state, effects, and outcomes. These models require more information than descriptive models because they must represent the dynamic properties of the system:

- transfer functions that represent functional relationships between input and output variables;
- rates of change expressed as first order derivatives (dx/dt), and higher order rates (e.g., acceleration dx^2/dt, jerk dx^3/dt, etc.);
- time constants (τ) — rate measures of the response time a linear component system requires to reach a defined level of its asymptotic value; and
- discrete response choices an actor may make to alternative inputs.

Simulations provide a means of emulating the internal dynamics and external outputs (effects) of a target system (figure 7.6). The system model allows the analyst to experience the behavior to address questions like: *What will happen under specified input conditions (response)? What input conditions are required to cause a certain output (solution)? How sensitive is output z to input x (sensitivity)? Under what conditions will the system become unstable?*

In engineering design, system models are routinely used to represent real systems to predict their behavior and assure they are stable, repeatable, and behave as required under the full envelope of conditions in which they are designed to operate. The engineer controls the system design and conducts tests to compare the real-world system to the model; the model can be refined to an assured level of validity. But in intelligence analysis, the target system model is intended to represent a foreign target that has many unknowns, and the analyst's model is often a *hypothesis* of how the system operates. The simulation is an analytic tool to support several types of analyses:

- Dynamic Description — The simulation provides a tool to explain how a system operates over time and how internal components interact.

- Dynamic Exploration—The simulation is used to evaluate how sensitive alternative options (strategies or courses of action) are to uncertainties in the model and supporting evidence; this analysis supports development of robust plans that are least sensitive to model uncertainties.
- Predictive Support for Hypothesis Testing—Alternative hypotheses of how the target system works may be simulated to produce dynamic results that can be compared to observed actual target behavior; this can guide collection and refine hypotheses (see chapter 9).
- Predictive Support for Planning—Predictive models with a known level of validity may be used to support planning by evaluating the effects of alternative plans. This provides the planner with option awareness and the model is called an "action model."

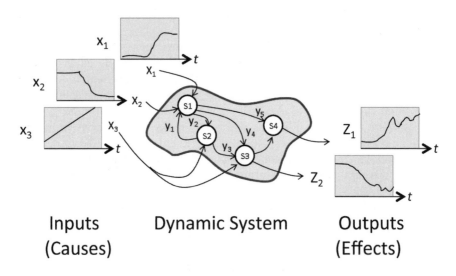

Inputs   Dynamic System   Outputs
(Causes)   (Effects)

Figure 7.6 Simulating the dynamics of a modeled system

We distinguish two fundamental categories of systems that are represented in behavioral simulations to support analysis.

Linear Systems respond deterministically to inputs and the behavior and outputs can be predicted with detail and specificity. The combined system behavior of integrated linear systems is the sum of the component behaviors. For some target systems, such as non-complex continuous manufacturing or production processes, weapon systems, or some military processes, a linear system model may be an appropriate approximation for analysis. In most cases, there exists uncertainty in the system-endogenous variables or the endogenous conditions, and the system, though linear, can only be statistically determined by assigning probability distributions to the uncertain variables, and computing the distributions of the output variables. These system simulations provide a predictable range of behavior patterns, but statistically characterize outcome likelihoods of alternative behaviors.

Nonlinear Systems refer to when we attempt to model systems that include internal independent and adaptive interacting actors (humans or machines), and whose output is not proportional or deterministically derived from a knowledge of its inputs. Real physical and human (social) systems are inherently nonlinear and only when process controls and doctrine or other constraints are applied, can they be approximated as linear systems. Such *complex adaptive systems* are characterized by *complexity*—measured by the scale of its independent actors and the scale and effects of interactions between those actors, and *emergence*—unpredictable behaviors that emerge from the interactions between adapting actors. System behavior is understood in terms of the full interaction of the components, not by the behaviors of the actors themselves.[30]

A wide variety of modeling representations are used to create dynamic simulations for exploratory or predictive analysis. The computational modeling and simulation methods (table 7.10) each adopt a distinct approach to represent the way in which the model moves through time, the approach to dealing with time, space, and functional granularity and representation, and the approach to deal with uncertainty.

Dealing with Uncertainty in Models—The analyst must identify and account for uncertainty in the data on which a model is built and in the model itself; when presenting analytic results based on a model, the analyst must also explain the effect of this uncertainty on results. Two categories of uncertainty must be identified and quantified:

- Uncertainty in System Description (Simulation Inputs)—The analyst must specify and describe the uncertainty in the structure of the system (e.g., uncertain relationships between elements), the variables in the system (e.g., hidden variables, etc.), and the values of parameters that characterize the system (e.g., imprecisely measured variables).
- Uncertainty in System Behavior (Simulation Outputs)—Because the model structure and instantiated parameters have specified uncertainties, the simulation produces computed uncertainty, as uncertainty propagates through the simulation to produce outputs with uncertainty. More complex models produce dynamic uncertainty that arises from the *interaction* of actors (adaptation) and uncertainty due to actor responses, time delays, and phase shifts.

Table 7.10 Dynamic Modeling Representations

Simulation Approach	Description and Example Simulation Tools	Representative Intelligence Applications
Game Theoretic Models	Iterative simulation of game or hypergame computations of competitive decisions to achieve a net payoff, considering each competitor's expectations of how opponents will choose from alternatives. **Tools:** Agent-based models implement game theory in actor decision making	Simulate competitive political, economic or social behaviors to identify equilibrium states, strategies.
General Causal Modeling	Dynamic Bayes nets represent causal chains and propagate input probabilities of causes through the network of conditional probabilities to aggregate posterior probabilities of effects. **Tools:** Norsys Netica™; Bayes Net Toolbox for Matlab™	1. Simulate dynamic systems at a high level of aggregate behavior. 2. Explain causal theories to assess COAs
Discrete Event Simulation	Simulate event-based systems using queuing models of queues-servers, Petri nets, Markov, and other models that define nodes, links, and resources to simulate process interactions, synchronization and scheduling of discrete events. **Tools:** MathWorks MATLAB® SimuLink® and SimEvents®; UC Berkeley Ptolemy; FlexSim Software FlexSim; SIMAN, ProModel, and GPSS/H	1. Detailed simulation of human-technical systems in manufacturing, production, or operations. 2. Model event sequences of weapon systems operations (e.g., integrated air defense systems, command and control systems, etc.)
Discrete Time Simulation	Time-based simulation of continuous or time-discrete processes defined by differential equations; represent continuous processes by state-machine simulation of all processes for each discrete-time increment. **Tools:** Imagine That Inc., Extend™	
System Dynamics Simulation	System dynamics flow models are based on the principle of stock accumulation and depletion, representing the flow of resources to accumulate "stock" variables. System dynamics causal models account for positive and negative feedback across processes and represent nonlinear behavior. **Tools:** ISEE Systems iThink™; Powersim Software PowerSim Studio; Ventana Vensim®	Simulate physical to human-technical systems at a level focusing on the dynamic interaction of system elements.
Agent Based Simulation	Agents represent interacting autonomous rational cognitive actors, their goals, beliefs, and autonomous behavior to study social behavior of individuals, groups, or populations. Goal-seeking adaptation produces realistic emergent behavior not predictable from the underlying models. **Tools:** University of Chicago's Social Science Research RePast; Santa Fe Institute SWARM, University of Michigan SOAR, Sentia Senturion™	Simulate political, social, and economic competitions where many actors interact to produce emergent behaviors

A variety of modeling approaches may be applied to represent and account for uncertainty:

- *Deterministic Model* — A model or simulation in which the results are determined through known relationships among the states and events and in which a given input will always produce the same output. This is suitable only when the model and variables are well-known, and a deterministic approximation is appropriate for the intended propose.

- *Stochastic Model*—A model or simulation in which the results are determined by using one or more random variables to represent uncertainty about a process or in which a given input will produce an output according to some statistical distribution.
- *Multiple Hypothesis Modeling*—Multiple deterministic or stochastic models are simulated with alternative conditions to represent alternative competing hypotheses.
- *Monte Carlo or Sampled Simulation*—Random or other statistical sampling techniques are employed to run multiple simulations across the space of all possible simulations such that the sampled result determines estimates for unknown values.
- *Expected Value Simulation*—Rather than run multiple simulations with sampled values, a single simulation computes the intermediate expected values (the predicted value based on a probability of an occurrence-weighted sum of the possible values) for each uncertain value and produces expected value outputs.

In the next three sections, we illustrate the use of some of these simulation methods to support intelligence analysis for three different challenge problems.

CASE STUDY: SIMULATING A PHYSICAL SYSTEM

In this case study we consider the simulation of physical systems (natural or engineered systems whose operations are dominated by physical laws, and the role of human activity and cognitive decision making is minor and not modeled in detail). Physical system models and simulations are useful to understand the constraints, behavior, and performance (e.g., capacities, rates, stability criteria) of such systems. Physical system models used in intelligence employ physics-based model components that represent, for example, kinematics (e.g., motion of objects), material flows, transportation, production processes, physical weapons effects, sensors, and the phenomena that they detect (e.g., thermal, visible, radar, acoustic, seismic, magnetic, etc.).

Physical system models may focus *only* on the functional performance of the system or may include a 4D (dynamic 3D spatial simulation) simulation of the target system, which includes terrain, buildings, vehicles, etc., to provide a high-fidelity visualization of the system. In the latter case, the functional simulation is coupled with a visual rendering engine, where the game-like visualization is justified to support analysis of physical constraints, comparison with observations, or presentation to decision makers. Examples of intelligence physical-system simulations might include the following:

- Simulation of military facilities and their associated physical activities and the simulated effects of weapons, if used to counter the facilities;[31]
- Simulation associated with narcotics crop growth, narcotics production, and transport flows;
- Simulation of supply chains and manufacturing and industrial processes that involve physical materials and labor.

This specific case study considers a chemical weapons (CW) target system, following the earlier examples of CW analysis subjects introduced in chapter 6:

- *Intelligence Challenge Problem*—Perform a high-level analysis of a new foreign CW production capability, following observation of facilities construction and procurement of precursors. Estimate production capacities and limits of production cycles considering on-site storage of agents. Project the effects of disruption due to alternative COAs (sanctions to precursor procurement, on-site inspections, etc.).
- *Analytic Approach*—Compare site imagery to other known dual-use CW capabilities to estimate range of capacity, develop a high-level process model to simulate production process to support predictive analysis of effects of COAs.
- *Model Purpose*—Model production process and simulate over a range of operating conditions consistent with intelligence sources to provide *predictive analysis* to 1) estimate capacities (and predict effects of precursor sanctions) and 2) estimate production cycles (and predict the potential disruptive effects of on-site inspection timing).
- *Model Schema and Simulation Approach*—For these requirements, a high-level system process model (schema) that provides estimates of production within ± 5 metric tons/ month are appropriate, based on prior experience. The model should include precursor procurement and storage, three-phase processing to produce the agent (reaction, alkylation, distillation), and agent storage. Physical visualization is not required to meet the analytic purpose.
- *Model Validation for Use*—Compare the simulation results to know data sets (process parameters, capacity, and production rates) for prior cases in foreign countries and based on old data sets from U.S. testing.

The analyst and analytic methodologist (modeler) evaluate alternative modeling methods and choose the System Dynamics (SD) methods to provide a graphical representation of the three-phase (reaction, alkylation, and distillation) process and enable rapid simulations of the production dynamics. It is important to note that the SD modeling method is not limited to physical systems, but is well suited to rapid development of aggregate systems models that focus on the dynamics of behavior, flows, and capacities. The causal loop diagram is a high-level conceptual model of the CW process—and can proceed to a validation process that includes a review by CW subject-matter experts for appropriate granularity, completeness, and sufficiency for the analytic purpose.

Conceptual Modeling—The SD modeling process generally includes two elements: a reference description that includes the baseline modes of behavior (called the *reference mode*) and a *causal diagram* that is a conceptual model representing a hypothesis about causation. (We referred to this earlier as the *dynamic hypothesis*.) The reference mode describes the dynamic behavior and the causal diagram captures the feedback structure of the system that produces the behavior. The typical reference mode development steps include:[32]

- Develop a functional theory of how the system operates (the major elements and relationships);
- Define any supporting context and ancillary theories on which the system relies (exogenous factors);
- Define the time frame over which the analysis is being conducted and that the dynamics must represent;
- Identify the major dynamic variables (typically five to nine major variables, although there may be many more) and their relationships;
- Prepare graphs of the dynamics of these variables over time, showing the reference behaviors over the time frame. For example, reference graphs for a manufacturing model might show the typical production run-up and an interruption in production due to lack of resources;
- Postulate the causal behavior of the system by developing causal diagrams that describe the feedback structure of the model.

Causal diagrams distinguish variables (in text) and causal connections (in arrows) that visually show independent variables (e.g., the "cause," X) and dependent variables (e.g., the "effect" Y; so $X \rightarrow Y$; or $Y=F(X)$). The valence (+ or −) of the arrows indicates the direction of change of the dependent variable (Y) by the independent variable (X). The positive sign for the arrows denotes change in the same direction (X goes up, Y goes up); a negative sign denotes a change in the opposite direction (X goes up, Y) goes down. These causal relationships should be monotonically increasing or decreasing; if they are not, the variables require further disaggregation.

Feedback loops are composed of collections of these arrows that form a closed loop, and result in two categories of forward causation or feedback loops:

- Reinforcing Loops have a "plus" sign or an even number of "minus" signs that make a net "plus."
- Balancing Loops have a "minus" sign or an odd number of "minus" signs that make a net "minus."

The model can also introduce delays in the loops (rectangles) and exogenous influences on the variables or causation. A simple example of CW precursor ordering and use in production illustrates two loops (figure 7.7). The precursor loop is shown in this example as a reinforcing loop—the more stock that is built up causes more stock to be ordered. This may occur initially as the success of a CW capability increases confidence in processes, and orders increase to scale up to full production. But this reinforcing loop reaches a point of diminishing returns, and stocks will grow without bound due to positive feedback. In reality, the ordering loop should be a balancing loop (where the polarity of the "precursor stock" to "precursor ordering rate" will be negative), like the production loop that depletes the stock, and the depletion in stock calls for more to be delivered to production.

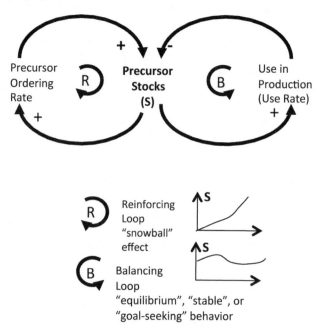

Figure 7.7 Basic causal loop diagram nomenclature

The causal analysis process begins by enumerating the major dependent variables that are being addressed—in this case, precursor chemical stocks and CW agent stocks being produced for warhead or artillery shell fills. Next, the analyst indentifies the key variables that influence the dependent variable (e.g., order arrival rates, process volumes or production rates, production yields due to impurities or effectiveness of distillation, etc.). The next step is the "relate" process where variables are related by causal connections in the causal loop diagram, with exogenous factors that influence the variables. (In this case, shipments of precursor chemicals from other producers inside or outside of the country are key exogenous variables.) Finally, the delays in the process loops are identified.

Computational Modeling—Next, the causal model is translated to a SD computational model using a graphical model-building tool that implements the causal diagram, in system dynamics modeling formalism, adding parameters to further refine the model. System Dynamics tools (e.g., ISEE Systems iThink™, Powersim Software PowerSim Studio, Ventana Vensim®, and XJ Technologies AnyLogic) provide a graphical user interface to translate the causal diagram to system dynamics model nomenclature that distinguishes "flows" of variables and accumulated "stocks" of variables. The variables may represent physical items (e.g., chemical precursor inventory, chemical agents, workers, etc.) or intangible variables (e.g., capital, information, orders, etc.). Stocks are the variables that represent the state of the system and provide the system with inertia and storage; they effectively buffer inflows and outflows from the system. The stock is represented by the basic differential equation for the accumulation of stock over a period of time, integrating the inflow and depletion, added to the initial stock stored at time, t_0.

STOCK: (Integral) Stock (t) = $\int$ Stock (t_0) + [Inflow(S) – Outflow(S)] dS

While the stock is an integral that accumulates, flows are the derivative, measuring the rate of change of a stock over time:

FLOW: (Derivative) Net Stock Change =d(Stock)/dt

The most basic system dynamics process (figure 7.8) defines the abstract flow from a hypothetical infinite supply through "valves" that govern the flow to stocks, and then by depletion to an infinite potential consumption. Converter symbols (circles) specify the flow rates of the valves. (Modeling tools allow significantly more sophisticated functions than these basics, including queues to sequence and hold stocks, processes that delay flow while incoming stock is "processed," and more.) System dynamics texts describe how basic building-block processes (e.g., ordering, inventory control, sequential production, testing, etc.) can be integrated to build more complex models that account for human resources, financial resources, supply chain, inventory control, manufacturing, and distribution models that can be integrated into a full business and industrial system model.

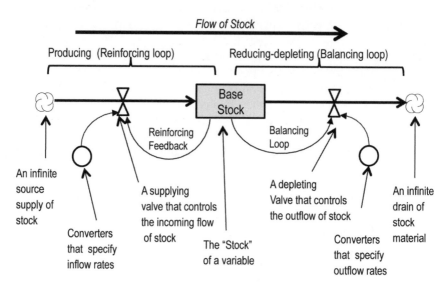

Figure 7.8 Basic elements of a process flow

The CW process Conceptual and Computational Models—The CW process causal model (figure 7.9) shows the basic CW process, proceeding from precursor chemical acquisition (ordering process loop) through reaction-alkylation and distillation stages to storage ready for weapons filling.[33] Notice that this is not a typical functional flow diagram; in this diagram, the "functions" are arrows, and the variables (inputs-outputs) are the text labels. The high-level model here shows the two basic balancing loops that affect the resulting flows from orders and precursor stocks to end-product agents. The weapons filing process is not represented because the intelligence problem is focused on agent production rates and inventories, not weapons filled for deployment.

The translation of the causal model to a SD model (figure 7.10) requires further description of the factors that define flow rates, delays, initial stock values, and other factors (e.g., statistical model that effects number of successful orders fulfilled) and constraints (e.g., storage capacities). This modeling stage instantiates the model with parameters for the estimated baseline capabilities of the target facility. (A more sophisticated

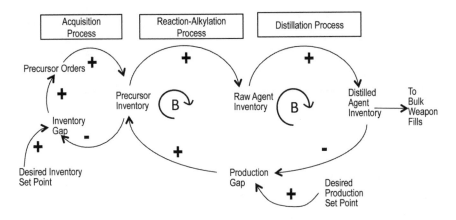

Figure 7.9 Causal model of basic CW production process

model could account for delays in the order fulfillment loop and for the delays in the chemical production loops.)

The modeler has partitioned the simple model to distinguish the ordering-acquisition process, the agent production process (reaction-alkylation-distillation) and the control factors that will be used to assess the effects of sanctions and inspections. The model also accounts for basic factors in the process:

- estimated production yield and conversions from precursors, to raw agents and then distilled agent stocks;
- influence of labor and work duty cycles on production and distillation rates;
- desired set-points for inventory and production levels.

The modeler and analyst simulate the model under a variety of conditions to verify that it performs as the causal model intended. Refinements and additional variables are often introduced at this point to improve the understanding of dynamic behavior before validation and simulation for analysis. Simulations of this model are compared to known production dynamics to validate the behavior of the model for its use to understand production operation and capacities at the scale of the target system.

Once validated to be suitable for the analytic purpose, the model is simulated over a range of conditions to estimate the production capacities and operational dynamics. Then, the simulation can be used to assess, for example, the effects of sanctions to disrupt the inflow of precursors and inspections to disrupt the production process.

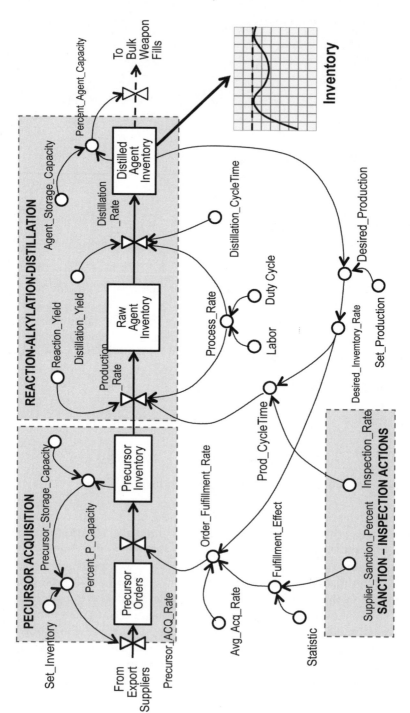

Figure 7.10 System Dynamics Model of basic CW production process

The fundamental patterns of dynamic response in such a system (figure 7.11) are evaluated over a range of conditions to understand the limits of stable, sustained production, and the vulnerabilities of the process to disruptions (sanctions, inspections) that may reduce effectiveness. Notice that such a model may also produce the estimated signatures of observable activities to support collection planning (as described further in chapter 9).

Behavior Mode	Response	Description and Examples in the CW System Model
1. Growth to Equilibrium	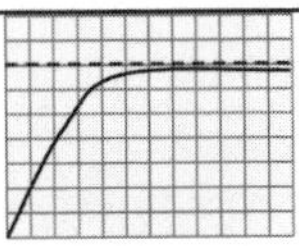	• Variable increases and settles at a stable value (equilibrium) due to balancing control loop •CW example- Production variable rises to full production equilibrium
2. Linear or Exponential Growth	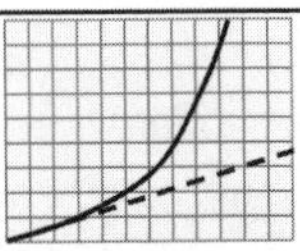	•Linear (dotted line) accumulates proportional to inflow; exponential (solid line) accumulates with inflow rate proportional to accumulated stock •CW example - Production proportional to precursors
3. S-shaped Growth	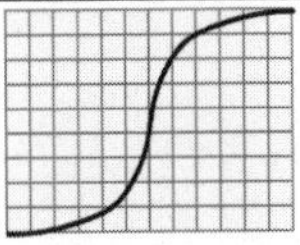	•Exponential growth followed by exponential slowing to value limited by resources (logistics equation behavior) •CW example – Ramp up expecting unlimited precursors; then slow to limited precursor availability
4. Oscillation	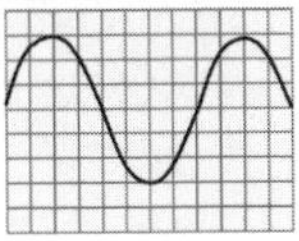	•System is stable but variable moves between two points due to delay in counteracting loops •CW example – Delays between precursor stock delivery and production usage causes production rate fluctuations.

Figure 7.11 Fundamental dynamic behaviors

The System Dynamics formalism, developed by Jay Forrester in 1961 and applied to physical industrial systems like our example, has been widely applied to the analysis of business, cyber-physical, and human systems.[34] Several intelligence-relevant applications implemented in system dynamics models include:

- *Counterterrorism*—Exploratory analysis was conducted on a model of the financial operations and organizational behavior of the "Salafist Group for Preaching and Combat" terrorist organization to study funding relationship to the quantity and type of operations, and expected effects of different counterterrorism policy choices.[35]

- *Cyberwarfare*—A Single Vulnerability Problem (SVP) model of cyber threat activities was developed to provide model-based insights to unobservable hacker behaviors that give rise to observed attack behavior. The model was validated with reference (external) attack behaviors, and applied to explore hacker community activities that produce observed attack behavior.[36]
- *CounterInsurgency (COIN)*—Operations analysts developed an extensive COIN model focused on Afghanistan that includes three fundamental stocks: 1) insurgent-supportive individuals, 2) neutral-minded individuals, and 3) host government-supportive individuals. The model developed the influences (governance, economic development, security, and services) that control the flow of individuals between these three stocks. The model was used to assess aggregate social stability and the factors required to move individuals toward host government support.[37]

Complete introductions to the use of SD are provided in John D. Sterman's comprehensive textbook, *Business Dynamics: Systems Thinking and Modeling for a Complex World* (McGraw-Hill, 2000), as well as Barry Richmond's practical introduction, *An Introduction to Systems Thinking* (see ISEE Systems, 1997).

SIMULATING HUMAN SYSTEMS

In this section we briefly introduce the challenge of modeling human systems composed of people interacting in a cultural context and illustrate the topic with a basic modeling study. Human system models are alternatively called "social" models, "IOS" (individuals, organizations and societies) models, "human social cultural dynamic" models, or simply "human behavior" models. These models support intelligence analysis and operational planning for three categories of human subjects:

- *Leaders* (or elites) are modeled to understand the potential behavior of key individuals based on their beliefs, self-concept, motivations, needs, stress tolerance, relationships, and other factors. The focus of human factor analysis is on individual high-value decision makers, their local network, decision-making calculus and context, and anticipated behavior under specified conditions. The models support influence and information operations.
- *Organizations*, formal groups of people who share a mission and an arrangement to structure roles, relationships, and activities, are modeled to understand group motivations, goals, decision processes, resources, and their network, cultural context, and key actors. Organization models include social network analysis (SNA) models and

agent-based models of organizational dynamic behavior. Models may be used to understand power struggles, organization pathologies, vulnerabilities, and operational styles.

- *Populations or Societies* are the inhabitants constituting an identified group (by nationality, race, etc.) in a specified area that are studied to understand culture, behavior, and sources of influence (e.g., family, media, organization affiliations, economy, security, etc.). These models must consider behavior in the context of national, ethnic, cultural, tribal, familial, political, economic, and other factors. Models may support socio-cultural dynamics analysis, including social movement analysis, political stability warning, or information operations (e.g., target audience identification, analysis, and strategic communication planning).

A number of formal DoD (Department of Defense) terms have been defined to distinguish the kinds of human systems analysis that are performed across the Intelligence Community (figure 7.12).

DoD Human Systems Analysis Terminology

- *Human Factors Analysis* – analytic examination of the behaviors of key national-level decision makers and their associated groups, including social network analysis to assess the characteristics and behaviors of those groups having the greatest influence on these leaders. Understanding the views, roles, and perceptions of these players on a given issue and the stance they will take in the decision is a crucial element in determining effective channels, levers, and messages to support influence operations. (Source - Human Factors Full Spectrum Project Sol. W74V8H-05-T-0320, 01 Sept 2005)
- *Human Terrain Analysis* - A multidisciplinary approach to describe and predict geospatial and temporal patterns of human behavior by analyzing the attributes, actions, reactions, and interactions of groups or individuals in the context of their environment. (DoDD 3600.01 Information Operations (IO), August 14, 2006, Incorporating Change 1, May 23, 2011) [i]
- *Foreign Cultural Analysis.* Analysis of information on the demographics, norms, values, institutions, and artifacts of a population used to assist in anticipating the actions of that population within the operating environment. (DoDD 3600.01)
- *Socio-Cultural Dynamics* - Information about the social, cultural, and behavioral factors characterizing the relationships and activities of the population of a specific region or operational environment.(DoDD 3600.01)
- *Atmospherics* - Information regarding the surrounding or pervading mood, environment, or influence on a given population. (DoDD 3600.01)

---

[i] The National Geospatial Intelligence Agency (NGA) uses the term *Human Geography* to refer to the study of human activities and the spatial differentiation and organization of human activity and its interrelationships with the physical environment. NGA defines five levels of human geography information (from concrete to abstract): *Level 0* - Physical terrain: Natural features; *Level 1* - Material culture: Physical manifestations of culture (Global Foundation Layers); *Level 2* - Human groups: Socio-cultural descriptions of communities; *Level 3* - Cultural Interactions: Social norms and attitudes; *Level 4* - Behavioral level: Estimates of human activity (e.g. socio-cultural dynamics). See Rickert , Craig (NGA/Source/S2) "Human Geography - Human Geography Domain", presented at ISR Forum, Washington DC, 8 February 2011.

Figure 7.12 DoD human systems analysis terminology

A significant study of human system modeling for defense applications was conducted by the National Research Council to assess the state of the art; a cautionary conclusion of the study is worthy of repeat here:[38]

> In our discussions with military personnel and in interactions outside the committee deliberations the committee became aware that many people may have unrealistic expectations of what a model or simulation of human behavior is able to do. No model is ever likely to be able to predict exactly what an individual or group will do, except in a situation so constrained, with alternatives so well understood, that a model is not needed. Human behavior, individually and in groups is governed by so many variables, including many that are not likely to be susceptible to capture in a model, that the best any model will do is to narrow the range of plausible behavioral outcomes of a defined situation. For example, a model may be able to forecast the most likely range of outcomes of a potential course of action. It may be able to direct attention to situational variables that are known to be important but may have been overlooked in a particular engagement. A well-designed model may draw a decision maker's attention to possible unintended consequences ("second-order effects") of a planned course of action. But it will *not* be able to make point predictions, such as "If we take Action A, the adversary will attack at Point B early tomorrow morning with three simultaneous improvised explosive devices (IEDs)." So we speak of models *forecasting* a range of outcomes, rather than making precise *predictions.* Certainly models that can produce such forecasts are a worthwhile objective. They can serve many useful purposes, from supporting training, to serving as tactical decision aids, to examining possible outcomes of alternative strategies or policies.

Indeed, human system modeling provides an insightful tool to explore the dynamics of human interactions, causing analysts to consider the many variables of behavior in a comprehensive and rigorous way, but it is not at all predictive in the strictest sense, recognizing that humans exercise free will and interact with others in complex ways. The case study will consider a typical problem posed to analysts by decision makers who are aware of the benefits—and limitations of analytic methods supported by human system simulation.

CASE STUDY: CIVILIAN POPULATION RESPONSES TO SANCTIONS

We continue the prior case study for the country developing a CW capability, by considering the potential effects on the civilian population if sanctions are applied to deter the government's pursuit of an offensive CW capability.

- *Intelligence Challenge Problem*—Perform a comprehensive analysis of the effects of range of sanctions on the five major population groups. Also consider the effects of social media to empower those groups to mobilize against the regime as a result of economic sanctions. Forecast the kinds of behaviors that may occur over the range of economic sanctions and estimate uncertainties, driving factors, and tipping points.

- *Analytic Approach*—Utilize empirical data (political, economic, stability) for the last five years as a baseline, and use a dynamic model of the population segments to understand the dynamics and estimate economic effects on their cohesion, government support, and potential to mobilize against each other or the government.

- *Model Purpose*—Support the *exploratory analysis* of population dynamics by representing the current conditions (based on empirical data) and the theoretical interactions between population groups under increasing economic stress due to sanctions. Estimate the contribution of communications and social media on economic awareness, formation, and mobilizing behaviors across all population groups.[39]

- *Model Schema and Simulation Approach*—For these requirements, a system schema must generate the complex behaviors arising from interactions among diverse population groups, uneven economic effects across groups, and ready access to social interaction via social media. The model should be isomorphic to the situation in the target country to assess characteristic behaviors, but it is not required to be a virtualization-level model.

- *Model Validation for Use*: For exploratory use, the model's behavioral validity will be judged by comparison to empirical population dynamic data (sentiment toward the government, employment, reported violence). The analyst must compare model data to countries under economic duress and countries that have mobilized using social media. But this will be a challenge because prior examples are sparse, so the analyst may be limited to comparing a baseline case version of the model (with no social media) to increasing levels of social media. With no comparable empirical data, the analysts may be limited to validation by subject-matter expert review. This validation is suitable for the model's exploratory use and will assure that a broad space of model behaviors is examined (e.g., quiescent to rebellious populations). All forecasted dynamics will be reported as exploratory results (not predictive); the analyst will explain that the results represent potential behavioral trajectories and effects, the conditions under which they will occur, and the indicators of their emergence.

Conceptual Model—The analyst and supporting social scientists first consider the relevant social science theories that explain key behaviors being analyzed for the problem: economic duress, group dynamics, political polarization, social communication, and movement. Prior empirical data and theoretical modeling studies are reviewed to formalize a conceptual basis for the factors to be included in the model. The conceptual model for this case includes population groups and their demographic representation, economic categories and the influence of sanctions on each category, the distribution of economic effects across population groups, access to social media and the effects of communication on polarization and mobilization. The conceptual model represents an integration of these theoretical social behavior mechanisms (backed by empirical studies); it is described in narrative with a graphical representation of the key factors and their relationships.

Computational Model—The analyst and supporting social scientists evaluate the alternatives for human system modeling (table 7.11) and choose an agent based model (ABM) over an aggregated top-down model. This is because of the complexity of the interaction among the populations groups and the host government response to economic sanctions and popular unrest. The high degree of interaction between government

Table 7.11 Alternative Human System Modeling Categories Considered

Category	Modeling Method	Example Modeling Methods
Individuals	Apply psychological characteristics to instantiate a cognitive model (or agent) to represent an individual with a defined context (e.g., operational, social, political, etc.)	• Cognitive agents (e.g., ACT-R; Soar), Bayesian causal analysis (e.g., Netica™ tool or Influence nets (e.g. SIAM)
Organizations	Define the structure of the organization as a network, and the cognitive behaviors of individuals in the network; simulate interactions within the structure.	• System dynamics (aggregate) • Dynamic Social Net • Agent based simulation
Populations	Define the demographics (distribution and attributes) of the populations and interaction characteristics and restrains. Identify the appropriate level of analysis: Macro-level (top-down) modeling of aggregate behaviors, or Micro-level (bottom-up) generation of behavior by heterogeneous agents interacting in a synthetic environment.	• System dynamics (Macro-level aggregate behavior simulation) • Agent-based models (behavior-generating simulation of interacting agents) • Hybrid multiple-level simulation

policy-making actors in such situations alone makes aggregate analysis difficult because 1) results of the system cannot be predicted from separate actions of individuals, 2) strategies of any actor depend upon the strategies of others, and 3) the behaviors of interacting actors even change the very environment in which they interact.[40] The ABM offers a bottom-up simulation that can generate a wide range of behaviors of both government actors and the diverse populations.

The ABM is simulated over time to generate macro-scale emergent behaviors resulting from the complex nonlinear interaction of the micro-scale agents and their adaptation to achieve individual or collective (negotiated) goals. The agents also observe the changing environment around them (e.g., increasing economic stress, reduced security, government actions) and may adapt their expectations. The agents include the following properties:

- Perception—Agents perceive the synthetic environment in which they operate, comparing their perceptions with their goals to make judgments about the state of the environment.
- Autonomy—Agents perform goal-directed cognitive behavior, applying a basic set of rules to make decisions and act in the environment; they can learn, respond, and adapt.
- Activity—Actions include interaction among agents (e.g., competition, negotiation, cooperation, etc.), expression of attitudes, and interaction with the environment (e.g., purchasing/selling, changing location, etc.)

The Simulation Workflow (figure 7.13)—The computational model is constructed by the methodologist (a computational social scientist) who translates the abstract conceptual model and the current real-world state into ABM abstractions (the agent properties and synthetic environment). The social scientist then establishes the range of future conditions and events over which the nation's behavior will be observed (e.g., over a range of sanctions, regional political and economic conditions, and military stresses). This range of conditions creates a "simulation matrix" of individual runs to be performed by simulation. A typical simulation matrix results in hundreds of individual simulation runs, each run representing a simulated time period (e.g., 24 months). Two categories of model data are created. First, the methodologist uses an agent builder tool (or suitable software language) to define the classes of agents (e.g., government actors, population groups), the agent cognitive parameters, their goals and constraints and relationships with other agents; agents are replicated based on the demographics and are interconnected. The methods for agent interactions with other agents or with the environment are defined,

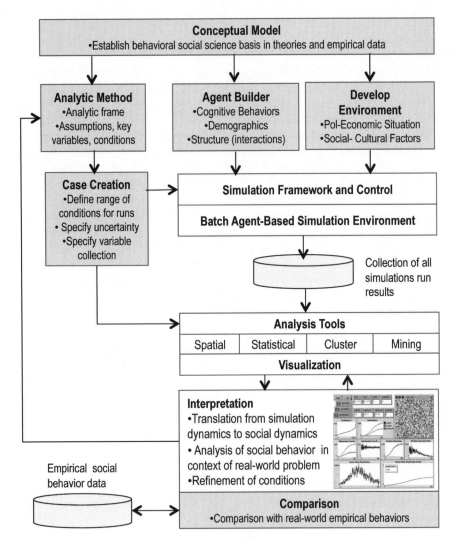

Figure 7.13 Agent based simulation and analysis flow

as well as the ways in which agents respond to these interactions. Second, the methodologist develops the models that represent the environment (e.g., political, economic, geospatial, etc.) and parameters.

The analytic method defines the range of simulation matrix "cases" that describe the envelope of exogenous conditions over which simulations will be run. Exogenous events (e.g., economic shocks) that are planned to stimulate the social systems are also defined. The agent-based simulations are then run in batch mode over the conditions defined by the matrix of excursions. The simulations are indexed and stored for subsequent analysis; the input data sets used to create the runs, and the simulation control parameters are also stored with the results to support analysis.

The analyst visualizes the abstract top-level parametric summaries across all simulations in the batch, as well as drilling down to the detailed outcome metrics for each run against the dimensions of the excursions. The analyst may also choose individual simulations of interest and explore the detailed increment-by-increment social-interaction activities within the run to understand the behavior of populations, social groups, and influential actors. Based on the quick-review assessment, the analyst may perform more detailed studies of the results.

The data across all runs may be analyzed with standard statistical tools to identify trends, volatility, stability, etc.; results may also be statistically compared with empirical social data to support the validity of the simulation abstraction. Cluster analysis and data mining analysis (automated induction) may also be performed to identify behavioral clusters across all simulations to locate similar effects; the analyst may drill down to details to understand the causal relationships that influence emergent clusters.

The analyst must interpret the results, translating the abstract and quantitative simulation behaviors (behavior trajectories, instabilities, oscillations, clusters, etc.) into behavioral explanations in qualitative social dynamic terms (e.g., fractionalization, cohesion, competition, polarization, etc.). The analysts may select results from individual simulations to illustrate and support analytic judgments. Based on results of the simulations, the social analyst may refine and update the actors and environment to improve the fidelity of representation and to expand the envelope of environment and actor excursions.

While ABMs may be built in common object-oriented programming languages (e.g., Java, C++), an increasing number of agent-based development tools, modeling frameworks and model libraries exist to support re-use and minimize development time.[41]

HYBRID MODELING SOCIO-TECHNICAL SYSTEMS

The preceding case studies illustrated modeling system dynamics and agent-based methods to represent specific physical or human system problems, respectively. Socio-technical systems that integrate human, cyber, and physical elements may require a hybrid approach that integrates several modeling methods introduced earlier (table 7.10), with each representing an appropriate element of the overall system. Hybrid modeling frameworks enable the integration of models into a combined multiple-model configuration. The framework controls multi-model simulation such that the models share and exchange variables in synchronism across the common framework, while maintaining internal consistency within each model.[42] The following section illustrates the use of a hybrid model in support of exploratory and predictive analysis for the intelligence preparation and planning processes.

CASE STUDY: MODEL-BASED SUPPORT TO PLANNING: JOINT INTELLIGENCE PREPARATION OF THE OPERATIONAL ENVIRONMENT (JIPOE)[43]

While the last section illustrated how model-based methods support collection to discriminate difficult target systems, this section illustrates how model-based methods can also support the intelligence preparation and planning process, using integrated models that include both human and physical infrastructure systems. DoD Joint Publication 2-01.3, "Joint Intelligence Preparation of the Operational Environment" (JIPOE) describes the analytical process used by joint intelligence organizations to produce intelligence assessments, estimates, and other intelligence products in support of the joint force commander's decision-making process.[44] It is a continuous process that includes defining the operational environment, describing the effects of the operational environment, evaluating the adversary, and determining and describing adversary potential courses of action (COAs).

In current practice, joint intelligence analysts (J2) apply the JIPOE process with representations of static models, in explicit but static forms (e.g., map graphics, tables, network diagrams, etc.) and perform tacit, mental simulations to project the estimated outcomes of alternative COAs. Model-based computational simulations offer a number of potential benefits to analysts:

- a common means to explicitly represent the attributes, structure, and dynamics of the operating environment and adversaries operating in the environment;
- an explicit representation of the dynamics of the environment—one that can be measured and objectively validated (unlike tacit mental simulations and experience);
- the potential for exploration of a wider range of COA excursions and diverse operating environments—and the ability for analytic teams to share the experience in a visual environment that allows them to understand the dynamic behavior of the environment.

While the doctrine defines a rigorous analytic process, it does not specify the use of computational simulations—and the typical implementation of the method applies the analyst's tacit mental and conceptual models, not explicit computational models.

The four-step JIPOE process (figure 7.14) is focused on understanding the operational environment and its influences (constraints, restraints, opportunities, etc.) and impacts on operations and effects, before anticipating the COAs that may be chosen by an adversary.

The four sequential steps are:

1. Define the characteristics of the operational environment that are relevant to the mission (commander's intent). This typically includes the relevant elements of the political, military, economic, social, information, and infrastructure (PMESII) systems of society.
2. Describe the characteristics of the environment that impact the mission, and develop an understanding of the influences.
3. Evaluate the attributes, structure (e.g., network structure) and dynamics (potential objectives, behavior, decision making, capabilities) of the adversary. (In this step, the analyst is creating a conceptual model of the adversary.)
4. Develop a range of conceptual alternative adversary COAs that will achieve the estimated adversary objectives or threaten the objectives of the commander's intent.

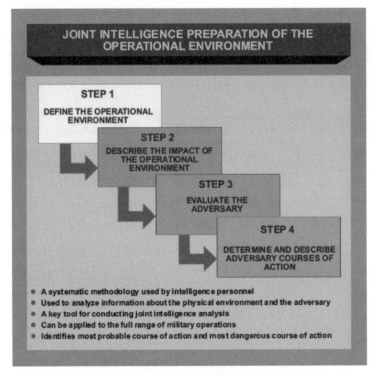

Figure 7.14 Four-step JIPOE process[45]

(It is important to note that this *intelligence* process performed by the J2 precedes the Joint Operations Planning Process (JOPP) performed by the J5 that *plans* joint operations to counter adversary COAs. The development of models in the JIPOE process provides a simulation that may then be used by JOPP planners to wargame and evaluate candidate plans, in accordance with the JOPP process.[46])

The four steps of the process can be translated into computational modeling activities (table 7.12) that are performed when the J2 employs computational models to explicitly represent the environment and the adversary in that environment.

Table 7.12 JIPOE Modeling Activities

JIPOE step	Representative Computational Modeling Activities (with JP 2-10.3 references)
Step 1—Define the Operational Environment	1. Review the Commanders Intent for the JIPOE effort (JP2-10.3; II-4). 2. Review and identify key effects relevant to the Commanders Intent, and the systems within the environment that must be represented. 3. Perform cursory review of the models developed previously and maintained in a Model Library by the J2 (JP2-10.3; II-5); identify the appropriate models and data required to instantiate component models and meta model for the environment. 4. Compose a baseline model, calibrate and validate behavior compared to prior months as appropriate for the environment and current situation. 5. Prepare Step 1 summary data.
Step 2—Describe the Effects of the Operational Environment	1. Review current situation in the operational environment (JP2-10.3; II-11e Information Domain; II-12 Systems Perspective). For human social cultural behavior issues, evaluate policy leaders, political parties, key population groups, spoilers (e.g., terrorist groups) and their relations, positions, and relative political-social power. For the operational context, assess economics, corruption, security and terrorist trends, and media influences. 2. Accept and update information from current intel systems to establish model initial conditions and parameters. 3. Consider two year outlook and impact of Op environment on Adversary and US COA's: Using baseline simulation, project effects if no Red actions taken and explain dynamics of the environment (JP2-10.3; II-13 Systems Perspective). 4. Prepare Step 2 summary data.
Step 3—Evaluate the Adversary	1. Review the modeled information about the adversaries and their relationships with other groups (JP2-10.3; II-14-16); identify uncertainties and sensitivities. 2. Identify sources of power and relative effects of alternative positions (JP2-10.3; II-17). 3. Identify relevant centers of gravity (JP2-10.3; II-18) across the PMESII systems. 4. Prepare Step 3 summary data.
Step 4—Determine Adversary Courses of Action (COAs)	1. Perform analytic simulations to identify potential adversary Objectives and Endstates (JP2-10.3; II-19-20). 2. Perform a range of exploratory simulations to evaluate potential effects of adversary activities (e.g. recruitment, terrorist campaign, political action, media campaign, etc.) to achieve their desired objectives and endstates (JP2-10.3; II-21). 3. Develop and evaluate the effectiveness of alternative adversary COA's (e.g. media campaigns, adverse influence-economic actions, terrorism, maritime piracy, maritime disruption campaign). 4. Prepare Step 4 summary data.

To illustrate a model-based JIPOE process, the process has been evaluated adopting a phase 0 situation (shaping operations) for a fictitious southwest Asian country, "Ficta," that is threatened by terrorist activities while its political leaders are wavering in cooperation with U.S. and regional partners. In this scenario, the U.S. commander's intent is to support the Ficta government, reduce corruption and instability, and move the government toward participation in counterterrorism initiatives while building democratic institutions.

Situation—The JIPOE analysis was to consider a three-year period, 2007–2010, during which the economy experienced marginal growth (1 percent), and the government had weak institutions and ineffective rule of law with high and growing corruption. The country's trade was stable, with a potential for decline, and maritime security faced rising piracy, as emerging insurgency-terrorist groups gained strength from external support and some internal recruiting.

The high-level meta-model of this situation (figure 7.15) shows the top-level influences (interdependencies) between models of the major actors and the context of the nation's environment within which they operate. The simulation integrates two agent-based models of the major power

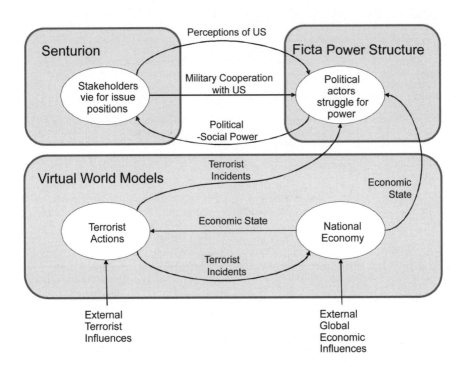

Figure 7.15 High-level Ficta composed model structure

actors, representing their competition for positions (relative to cooperation or resistance to U.S. economic and counterterrorism support) and competition for political power over the weakened state. These models operate in an economic- and terrorist-threat environment represented by the contextual model.

The component models include two agent-based models (table 7.13) of approximately 40 major actors of influence (leaders, organizations, population segments) that vie for positions on the two major issues and for political power in Ficta policy making. These actors include government leaders and ministries, political parties, terrorist organizations, and key segments of the population.

Table 7.13 Agent-Based Models Representing Political and Social Behaviors

Model	Sentia Senturion™ Political Landscape Model[1]	Soar Technology Power Structure Simulation[2]
Model Function	Pol Landscape Model: simulates how the policy positions of competing interests evolve over time by cooperating (bargaining) and competing, to track the dynamics of shifting opinion.	Power Structure Model: simulates competition for relative political-social power in a network of interacting agents that transfer power to within competing networks.
Focus of Model	Policy Positions	Political-Social Power
Complementary integration of the two HSCB models	• Senturion focuses on aggregate positions of many actors and their interactions relative to their interests on multiple, concurrent issues. • Power Structure Simulation focuses on the competition of networked individual actors, based on their relative goals and abilities to gain political-social power. • Competition for power changes a stakeholder's influence in the political landscape. Relative positions of key leadership actors in the political landscape affect their support among other actors.	
Simulation Paradigm	Agent-based simulation	Agent-based simulation
Key Social Theories	Game theory, decision theory, spatial bargaining, and micro-economics	Social capital and political power competition; agents gain and apply social (political) capital to achieve relative power goals
Behavior Modeled	Aggregate behavior of actors relative to a space of policy interests	Individual behavior of actors who perceive the environment, make decisions and compete for relative power

1. For an overview of the Senturion model, see: Abdollahian, Mark, Michael Baranick, Brian Efird, and Jacek Kugler, "Senturion: A Predictive Political Simulation Model", (Washington DC: Center for Technology and National Security Policy, National Defense University, July 2006).

2. For an overview of the PSTK model, see: Taylor, Glenn, Robert Bechtel, Ed Waltz, and Jeffrey White, "PSTK: A Toolkit for Modeling Dynamic Power Structures," *Proc.2008 Conference on Behavior Representation in Modeling and Simulation (BRIMS)*, April 14–17, 2008, Providence, RI, (2008).

The agent-based models of decision-making actors operate within an environment of models of the nation's economic, governance, and security environments, as well as of major media influences on the civilian population groups (table 7.14).

The intelligence analyst can apply hypothesized actions (e.g., hypothesized red COAs) to create simulated effects in JIPOE step 4 to game the potential effects that can be achieved by the adversary terrorist groups. This allows the analysts to explore the effects of alternative red COAs, within a range of economic and security environments, under alternative Ficta and U.S. actions.

Table 7.14 Virtual Environment Models That Provide Context for Agent-Based Models

Model	Model Type; Modeling Tool	Description
Event Generator	Bayesian Network; Netica	Models major and minor violent and nonviolent events per week, based on grievances, violence, and mobilizing structures.
Economy	System Dynamics; Vensim	Models economy and related infrastructure activities. Key outputs include GDP growth, unemployment rates, and poverty rates.
Media Influence	Agent Based; custom modeling tool	Models the influence of media sources, via channels, on the attitudes of target audiences (relative to specified themes associated with positions in the Senturion model).
Rule of Law	System Dynamics; Vensim	Models the legal system, including police, prisons, and judiciary.
Military	System Dynamics; iThink	Models military force readiness positioning and effects.
Corruption	System Dynamics; iThink	Models the non-legitimate flow of finances in the underground economy, and collateral effects.
Computational Interface Models	System Dynamics; Vensim	Provide model services (e.g., simple calculations, transfers, unit conversion for other models).

The framework also allows J5 and J8 joint planning cells to perform JOPP wargames on the same models to evaluate alternative U.S. COAs over the range of adversary COAs and operational contexts provided by the J2.

For these case studies, the typical JIPOE step 3 and 4 analyses were characterized by:

- Six-month to 3-year simulation outlooks (a typical simulation run on the COMPOEX server takes 2–4 minutes).
- The Ficta country is partitioned into distinct (typically 4–10) geospatial regions, distinguished by their population segment, cultural, and economic makeup. Separate and independent virtual-world models represent each region.
- Time increments of the time-based simulation were one-week intervals (all models exchange state variables at this rate.
- Over 5,000 PMESII model variables across all models are represented on the backplane; all may be viewed in time series visualizations to assess the effects of alternative COAs.

The JIPOE process was demonstrated and evaluated by independent reviewers to assess the value of model-based JIPOE analysis and the contributions to the JIPOE process—with an emphasis on the contribution to rigorous analysis of human, social, cultural behavior aspects in irregular warfare.

METHODOLOGY AND TECHNOLOGY CHALLENGES

The broader application of target system models that aim to represent the real world face challenges in methodologies to make them useful to intelligence analysts, as well as the computational technologies that implement them. The following paragraphs identify the major challenges and areas of R&D in modeling and simulation science that hold promise to enhance their usefulness to analysts in complex problem solving.

Model-Building Methodologies and Analytic Methods—model-based methods are required to appropriately apply computation science to analytic problems; progress in this area is being made in the operational research community.

- *Model-based Analytic Methodology*—The analytic community still requires a methodology to translate an analytic purpose into a quantitative description of model requirements appropriate for the problem, defining the level of model abstraction and multiple levels of resolution, model granularities, data accuracies, etc.
- *Model Instantiation*—Methods and supporting technologies are required to automatically extract content from structured and unstructured raw data sources (e.g., published data tables and raw text, respectively) for automated instantiation of model structures (e.g., social networks) as well as model parameters.

- *Participatory Modeling*—Enhanced analytic methods, visualization, and model interaction mechanisms will make model-based analytic methods more natural and useful to analysts. Furthermore, these methods will increase confidence in the analysts who have greater intellectual ownership in the model content.
- *Uncertainty Analysis*—Methods to explicitly represent model and data uncertainty and then present uncertainties in results will improve analyst confidence in model-based analyses. Current uncertainty representations (discrete probabilities, probability distributions, fuzzy variables, etc.) and computational methods (e.g., Bayesian propagation, Monte Carlo simulation, etc.) must be improved to provide useable results by analysts.

Data Modeling—In addition to broad research are data mining and massive data analysis; active research in two areas of data analysis hold promise for increasing the value of information that can be extracted from data observed about target systems.

- *Causal Inference*—Inferring the causal impact of independent variables $X=(x_1, x_2, \ldots x_N)$ on a dependent variable, Y remains the most difficult challenge when using observational data (non-experimental data)—as is the general case in intelligence problems. The inference process is plagued by confounding variables (hidden extraneous variables in the statistical model that correlate with both the dependent and the independent variables that bias or distort causal estimates if not controlled or measured. Unless the analyst develops "probes" to stimulate a target to increase observation data to increase potential for unbiased estimates, the analyst is limited to scant observation data. Research in quasi-experimental research-design methods hold promise to minimize bias in inferred causal relationships from passively observed data alone.[47]
- *Model Learning*—machine learning, a field of artificial intelligence focused on developing algorithms to learn from observational data, is broader in application that causal inference alone. One area of promise is the induction of process models from time-series data alone. For example, a model learning capability useful to intelligence is where the function and causality of process may be known or hypothesized (e.g., manufacturing, electrical production), but the learning algorithm must estimate the model parameters (performance) or structure (number of parallel activities, sequencing, etc.).[48]

Theoretical Modeling—improvements in key areas will make theoretical modeling more accessible to intelligence analysts and will increase confidence in their use and results.

- *Theory Capture and Modeling*—Representation of concepts and theories by analysts has benefited from modeling tools that allow more natural representation and model experimentation; graphic user interfaces to system dynamics, discrete event simulation, and Bayesian modeling tools will make these capabilities even more accessible.
- *Microsystem Modeling*—Agent-based generative modeling methods will continue to benefit from increased computational capabilities to build, test, and explore these models. Modeling human behavior, social systems and their interactions with information and physical systems will benefit from advances that improve scale, sophistication of agents and interactions, and abilities to quickly compare simulation results to real life.[49]
- *Behavior Explanation*—Complex models and simulations require natural interfaces that explain the behavior of the simulation and allow a user to drill down to detail, enabling causal paths, driver variables, sensitivities, tipping points, and phase shifts to be observed and understood.

Integrated Empirical Theoretical Modeling—A combined methodology for applying empirical and theoretical models in an integrated way is yet to be fully developed. The National Science Foundation Directorate for Social Behavioral and Economic Sciences' Empirical Implications of Theoretical Models (EITM) Project has conducted workshops for a decade to study the joint contributions of formal models and empirical research methods the fields of political science and economy.[50]

Hybrid Multi-modeling—Memory and processing capacities and computational infrastructure enable ever more complex models to be implemented, with several computer science challenges:

- *Model Integration Frameworks*—Computational infrastructures and associated analytic techniques are required to compose interoperable validated model components from a model library, to enable rapid assembly and validation of hybrid models.[51]
- *Multi-resolution Models*—Model frameworks must also accommodate the integration of models of a common situation at different levels of abstraction or implementation granularity to allow analysts to define model parameters at different levels appropriate for the problem.[52]
- *Model Docking*—Testing methods are desired to determine if two dissimilar computational models are equivalent or aligned and if one model can subsume another. Models shown to be equivalent provide a validation for each model, a means to distinguish the strengths and weaknesses of each model, and a means to jointly validate the set of models beyond the level of validation of each model's independent validation.[53]

- *Model Scale*—Management of models of increasing scale is required as analysts are required to understand large-scale dynamic systems; as modeling frameworks enable computational integration of hundreds of models, the analytic framework to manage such large-scale models must also be scaled.

Model-based Analysis—As computational power increases, it is enabling new methodologies that require large numbers of simulations (thousands to hundreds of thousands) to support analysis.

- *Exploratory Analysis*—More sophisticated methods are required to conduct and analyze computational experiments to explore the behaviors of target system models characterized by insufficient knowledge and unresolved uncertainties. In such cases, modelers may make guesses at model structures, parameters, and functions. Such alternative exploratory models are dynamic alternative hypotheses that can be simulated to reveal how the system would behave over alternative guesses. Exploratory modeling is the use of series of such computational experiments to explore the implications of varying assumptions and hypotheses.[54]
- *Model Behavior Search*—Models are applied to the study of complex situations and their underlying systems because closed-form (analytic) solutions to their behavior cannot be derived. Simulations are useful to represent systems behavior, but even when validated, it does not mean that solutions to locate certain behaviors with the massive space of behaviors can be located. For example, if a course of action is sought that will minimize resources and risk, while maximizing output variables (e.g., the most information gained from a collection), the analyst must "solve" a typical optimization problem. This requires a "search" across the space of behaviors to locate local or global maxima (optimum solutions). Because an exhaustive search of the entire space, of all possible policies over all sets of conditions) is infeasible, more effective forms of computational search are required. Research in search methods includes goal-directed control methods, such as genetic algorithms that sample the space (e.g., run point simulations), and reason about the behavior surface to locate maxima.
- *Robustness and Resiliency Analysis*—Simulation-based analysis of resilience and robustness of policies (or courses of action) to modify system behavior require rigorous analytic methods in order to address highly adaptive situations and target systems that exhibit deep uncertainty beyond traditional statistical uncertainty.[55] Such methods seek robust policies that trade off some degree of optimal

performance for less sensitivity to assumptions for which there is greater uncertainty. These methods will require multiple time-scale simulations representing processes and option sets at multiple scales.[56]

Model Visualization—As models grow in complexity, so do the internal and output variables to be presented to users. Geospatial, temporal, behavioral, and operational views of system interdependencies, causal linkages, and effects are required. Visualization of the behavior and outputs of such simulations require representation of high-dimensional data in manners that provide comprehensive explanation.

Model Validation—The procedures and standards for validating purely physical models are generally well defined and accepted; the processes for validating complex social-system and hybrid socio-technical system models are not. Referring to the challenges of validating such models, the National Research Council has acknowledged that "There are many open questions about the analytical basis for such complex models, and validation is still more of an art than a science."[57] Challenge areas include:

- *Validation of hybrid models* of diverse social and technical systems; methodologies to validate model components and a fully-integrated model and provide a measure of confidence in validity.
- *Validation of models for non-stationary target systems* are continually undergoing adaptation (e.g., terrorist organization dynamics); development of on-the-fly validation and daily updating of validity measures.
- *Validation of low base rate models* (rare or sparse events and catastrophic high impact events such as nuclear or biological events with very limited empirical data.)[58]

NOTES

1. Hodges, James S., "Six (or so) Things You Can Do with a Bad Model," N-3381-RC, RAND March 1991.

2. For a text that focuses specifically on target modeling and analysis in intelligence that is complementary to the topics of this chapter, see Clark, Robert M. *Intelligence Analysis: A Target-Centric Approach*, revised edition (Washington, DC: CQ Press, 2007).

3. This was a comment by Albert Einstein to Herman E. Mark, quoted in Holton, Gerald James, *The Advancement of Science, and Its Burdens*, (New York: Cambridge University Press, 1986) 13.

4. For an excellent account of the historical basis for the empiricist-theoretical divide within science, see Henry E. Brady, "Factors Contributing to the Split

Between Formal Theory and Empirical Modeling" Appendix B in *EITM Empirical Implications of Theoretical Models Report,* (Washington, DC: National Science Foundation, Political Science Program, Directorate For Social Behavioral and Economic Sciences, 2002) 28–31. For a statistician's perspective, see Breiman, Leo, "Statistical Modeling: The Two Cultures," *Statistical Science,* Vol. 16, No. 3, (2001) 199–231.

5. For an introduction to Data Models, See Nisbet Robert, John Elder, and Gary Miner, *Handbook of Statistical Analysis and Data Mining Applications,* (New York: Academic Press, 2009). Theoretical modeling texts are provided in subsequent sections of this chapter.

6. Typical goodness-of-fit functions include the root means squared error (square root of the sum of squared deviations between empirical and model-predicted data divided by the number of data points fitted) and the more general coefficient of determination (R2) that measures the proportion of variance in the empirical data set that is accounted for by the statistical model; when R2=1, the model has perfectly accounted for all of the variance of the model's errors.

7. For an early overview of these efforts, see Davies, John L. and Ted Robert Gurr, *Preventative Measures: Building Risk Assessment and Crisis Early Warning,* (New York: Rowman and Littlefield, 1998), Section II "Dynamic Indicators and early Warning Models."

8. Jacobs, A. M., and J. Grainger, "Models of visual word recognition—sampling the state of the art" *Journal of Experimental Psychology: Human Perception and Performance,* 29 (1994), 1311–34.

9. This criterion is based on the heuristic principle of *Occam's razor,* which is often stated as a preference to choose the simplest hypothetical explanation of an effect, over more complex ones.

10. O'Brien, Sean P., "Crisis Early Warning and Decision Support: Contemporary Approaches and Thoughts on Future Research," *International Studies Review* 12, (2010) 87–104 and Kettler, Brian, "Mixed Methods Stability Forecasting and Mitigation for the DARPA ICEWS Program," *Proceedings of the Third International Conference on Computational Cultural Dynamics (ICCCD),* 2009.

11. Nye, Joseph S. Jr., "Peering into the Future" *Foreign Affairs,* Vol. 73, No. 4, (July/August 1994). 82.

12. Gannon, John, "The Outlook for China: A CIA Perspective," Address at the College of the Holy Cross, Worcester, MA, November 20, 1996.

13. Taleb, Nassim Nicholas and Mark Blyth, "The Black Swan of Cairo: How Suppressing Volatility Makes the World Less Predictable and More Dangerous" *Foreign Affairs,* Vol. 90, No. 3, (May/June 2011) 36. Taleb is the author of *The Black Swan: The Impact of the Highly Improbable* (New York: Random House, 2007).

14. Lustick, Ian S. and Dan Miodownik, "Abstractions, Ensembles, and Virtualizations: Simplicity and Complexity in Agent-Based Modeling," *Comparative Politics* (January 2009) 223–44.

15. These definitions are adapted from the *DoD Modeling and Simulation Glossary,* Department of Defense Publication 5000.59–M, January 1998.

16. Sterman, John D., *Business Dynamics: Systems Thinking and Modeling for a Complex World* (New York: McGraw Hill, 2000) 86; the entire chapter 3 of this text is an excellent detailed introduction to the modeling process.

17. Box, G. E. P., "Robustness in the strategy of scientific model building," in R. L. Launer and G. N. Wilkinson (eds.), *Robustness in Statistics,* (New York: Academic Press, 1979).

18. Definition from DoD Directive 5000.59, "DoD Modeling and Simulation (M&S) Management," January 4, 1994.

19. Law, Averill M. "How to Build Valid and Credible Simulation models," Mason, S. J., et al. (eds.), *Proceedings of the 2008 Winter Simulation Conference,* (2008). The seven steps here also summarize and integrate Law's ten techniques to achieve validity and credibility. Also see Law, A. M., *Simulation Modeling and Analysis* 4th edition (New York: McGraw-Hill, 2007). An excellent resource on Validation is the DoD guide, "A Practitioner's Perspective on Simulation Validation" RPG Recommended Practices Guide Reference Document, August 15, 2001, accessed June 20, 2012 at http://vva.msco.mil/Ref_Docs/Val_Lawref/Val-LawRef-pr.pdf.

20. DoD Modeling and Simulation (M&S) Verification, Validation, and Accreditation (VV&A), DoD Instruction 5000.61, December 9, 2009.

21. Bigelow, James, and Paul K. Davis. *Implications for Model Validation of Multiresolution Modeling,* (Santa Monica, CA: RAND, 2003) 16.

22. Zacharias, MacMillan, Van Hemel (eds.), *Behavioral Modeling and Simulation: From Individuals to Societies,* (Washington, DC: National Research Council, National Academies Press, February 28, 2008), 8.

23. Axelrod, Robert, *The Complexity of Cooperation,* (Princeton: Princeton University Press, 1997) 6.

24. For an excellent set of defense and intelligence applications of GIS, see the ESRI series *GIS Technology in the Defense and Intelligence Communities,* Vols. 1–4, (Redlands, CA: ESRI Press 2007–2008).

25. Liu, H. and D. E. Brown, "A New Point Process Transaction Density Model for Space-Time Event Prediction. Systems," *IEEE Transactions on Man and Cybernetics,* Part C, Vol. 34, No. 3, (2004) 310–24; Smith, M. A. "Choice Modeling of Bombing Attack Site Selection," Master's Thesis, Dept. of Systems and Information Engineering, University of Virginia (May 2005) and Brown, Donald E. and Stephen Hagen, "Data Association Methods with Applications to Law Enforcement," *Decision Support Systems,* 34 (2002) 369–78.

26. Velasco, Mary and Rachel Boba , *Manual of Crime Analysis Map Production,* DOJ Office of Community Oriented Policing Services, November 2000. For a more general introduction, see Harries, Keith, "Mapping Crime: Principle and Practice," NCJ 178919 (Washington, DC: National Institute of Justice, U.S. Department of Justice, December 1999) accessed online June 20, 2012 at https://www.ncjrs.gov/pdffiles1/nij/178919.pdf.

27. For an introduction to organization analysis and modeling in support of Information Operations, see the author's chapters: "Know The Enemy: Acquisition, Representation and Management of Knowledge About Adversary Organizations" (chapter 1) and "Means and Ways: Practical Approaches to Impact Adversary Decision-Making Processes" (chapter 4) in Alex Kott (ed.) *Information Warfare and Organizational Decision-Making* (Boston: Artech, 2006).

28. A standard reference text on the subject of SNA is Wasserman, Stanley and Katherine Faust, *Social Network Analysis: Methods and Applications,* (Cambridge: Cambridge University Press, 1994).

29. Carley, Kathleen M., Dave Columbus, Matt DeReno, Jeff Reminga and Il-Chul Moon, *ORA User's Guide 2008,* CMU-ISR-08-125, (Pittsburgh, PA: Carnegie Mellon University, July 2008). A number of other tools are used for social network analysis, including: Social Science Automation's Critical Node Analysis Tool (CNAT) and UCINET.

30. Casti, John L. *Complexification: Explaining a Paradoxical World Through the Science of Surprise,* (New York: Perennial, 1995). Casti identified five properties of such systems: 1) They are *unstable,* subject to large effects being produced by small inputs or changes; 2) They are *chaotic* (they are not random, although they may appear to be), in that relatively simple deterministic process rules produce apparently random behavior; 3)They are *irreducible* and defy decomposition into their independent components and relationships, 4) They are *paradoxical* in the sense that there may be multiple independent solutions or explanations for behavior, and 5)Their behavior is *emergent*—it arises from the interaction of all of the independent actors in the system. The emergent behavior patterns form out of interactions and self-organization, not strategic plans.

31. Integrated Munitions Effects Assessment/Underground Targeting and Analysis System (IMEA/UTAS) Brochure, UNCLASSIFIED unlimited dissemination, Defense Threat Reduction Agency, Brochure v-imeadtra-03, 2003.

32. I am indebted to Dr. Corey Lofdahl for introducing me to these steps when he coached me on my first system dynamics model as we modeled elements of a foreign city years ago. A more complete illustration of these steps can be found in his book, Lofdahl, C. L., *Environmental Impacts of Globalization and Trade: A Systems Study,* (Cambridge, MA: MIT Press, 2002). Also see Randers, J. "Guidelines for Model Conceptualization" in J. Randers (ed.), *Elements of the System Dynamics Method,* (Cambridge, MA: Productivity Press, 1980), 117–39.

33. The very basic CW model used here is for illustration purposes only to place the method in a typical intelligence context. Actual models are significantly more detailed to account for the large number of constraints and methods of performing the target system functions. The model is based on chemical agent production information provided in, U.S. Congress, Office of Technology Assessment, *Technologies Underlying Weapons of Mass Destruction,* OTA-BP-ISC-115 (Washington, DC: U.S. Government Printing Office, December 1993), the examples are based on chapter 2, Technical Aspects of Chemical Weapon Proliferation.

34. Forrester, J. W. *Industrial Dynamics,* (Cambridge, MA: MIT Press, 1961).

35. Grynkewich, Alex (USAF) and Chris Reifel (USAF), "Modeling Jihad: A System Dynamics Model of the Salafist Group for Preaching and Combat Financial Subsystem," Naval Postgraduate School, *Strategic Insights,* Volume V, Issue 8 (November 2006).

36. *Source:* Preliminary System Dynamics Maps of the Insider & Outsider Cyber-threat Problems Version 1.0. CERT Group Modeling Workshop February 16–20, 2004 at SEI/CERT, Pittsburgh, PA , accessed April 5, 2012 at www.cert.org/research/sdmis/cyber-threat-maps.ppt.

37. Pierson , Brett (CAPT U.S. Army), Warfighting Analysis Division J8/WAD, "A System Dynamics model of the FM 3-24 COIN Manual," Accessed 06 April 2012 at http://www.mors.org/UserFiles/file/meetings/07ic/Pierson.pdf.

38. Zacharias, MacMillan, Van Hemel (eds.), *Behavioral Modeling and Simulation: From Individuals to Societies,* National Research Council, (Washington, DC:

National Academies Press, February 28, 2008) 19. This extensive study is an essential reference for modelers and analysts involved in developing or applying human system models. See also the earlier NRC study: Breiger, Ronald, Kathleen Carley, and Philippa Pattison, *Dynamic Social Network Modeling and Analysis: Workshop Summary and Papers*, National Research Council, Committee on Human Factors, Board on Behavioral, Cognitive, and Sensory Sciences, Division of Behavioral and Social Sciences and Education, (Washington, DC: The National Academies Press, 2003).

39. For an example of an ABM model that considers the effects of social media mechanisms and social behavior, see Makowsky, Michael D. and Jared Rubin, "An Agent-Based Model of Centralized Institutions, Social Network Technology, and Revolution" Towson University, Working Paper No. 2011-05, October, 2011. Accessed online April 6, 2012, at http://www.towson.edu/econ/workingpapers/2011-05.pdf.

40. Jervis, Robert, *System Effects: Complexity in Political and Social Life*, (Princeton, NJ: Princeton University Press, 1997); see also Jervis "Complex Systems: The Role of Interactions," in David S. Alberts and Thomas J. Czerwinski (eds.), *Complexity, Global Politics and National Security*. (Washington, DC: National Defense University, June 1997) 45–72.

41. See the Open Agent Based Modeling Consortium at http://www.openabm. org. ABM Modeling Platforms include NetLogo, MASON, SWARM, REcursivePorous Agent Simulation Toolkit (Repast), Repast S (Symphony), and AnyLogic ™.

42. For examples of hybrid modeling methods and results, see: Kott, Alex, Jeff Hansberger, Pete Corpac, and Ed Waltz, "Whole-Government Planning and Wargaming of Complex International Operations: Experimental Evaluation of Methods and Tools" in *International C2 Journal (IC2J), Special Issue on Interagency Experimentation*, (December 2009). See also Waltz, Ed, "Modeling the Dynamics of Counterinsurgency (COIN)" and, "COMPOEX Validation"; two papers in *Proceedings of the of NATO System Analysis & Studies Panel Specialists Meeting SAS-071/ RSM-003 Conference on Analytical Tools for Irregular Warfare,* Ottobrunn, Germany, March 24–26, 2009 and Waltz, Ed, "Situation Analysis and Collaborative Planning for Complex Operations" in *Proceedings of the 13th International Command and Control Research Symposium*, Office of Assistant Secretary of Defense, Bellevue, WA, June 17–19, 2008.

43. This section is adopted from the author's presentation, "Anticipatory Intelligence Analysis: Integrating Multiple Models for Joint Intelligence Preparation" at the *IEEE Conference on Security and Informatics: Workshop on Predictive Analytics for Intelligence and Security Applications*, May 2010; the paper was approved by the ODNI for public release May 21, 2010.

44. Joint Chiefs of Staff, Joint Publications (JP) 2-01.3, *Joint Intelligence Preparation of the Operational Environment*, (June 16, 2009).

45. Ibid.

46. Naval War College, Joint Operations Planning Process (JOPP) Workbook, JMO Department, Naval War College, (January 21, 2008).

47. Nichols, Austin, "Causal Inference with Observational Data," *The Stata Journal*, Vol. 7, No. 4, (2007) 507–41.

48. Langley, Pat, Dileep George, Stephen Bay and Kazumai Saito, "Robust Induction of Process Models from Time Series Data" *Proceedings of the Twentieth Conference on Machine Learning*, Washington, DC, 2003.

49. Cioffi-Revilla, Claudio, "Invariance and Universality in Social Agent-Based Simulations," *Proceedings of the National Academy of Sciences*, 99 (Suppl. 3) (May 14, 2002) 7314–16. Although a decade old, the challenges in this paper remain fundamental to progress in this promising field.

50. *EITM Empirical Implications of Theoretical Models Report*, National Science Foundation Political Science Program, Directorate for Social Behavioral and Economic Sciences, (Washington, DC: National Science Foundation, 2002). For the 2011 workshop materials, see http://harrisschool.uchicago.edu/Blogs/EITM/.

51. Waltz, Ed, "Computational Modeling Technology for Unconventional Situations," chapter 4 in Kott, Alex and Gary Citrenbaum (eds.), *Estimating Impact: A Handbook of Computational Methods and Models for Anticipating Economic, Social, Political and Security Effects in International Interventions* (New York: Springer, 2009).

52. Davis, Paul K. and James Bigelow, "Experiments in Multiresolution Modeling (MRM)" RAND MR-1004-DARPA, DTIC ADA355041 (Santa Monica: CA: RAND, 1998) and Davis, Paul K. and James H. Bigelow, "Introduction to Multiresolution Modeling (MMR) with an Example Involving Precision Fires," *Proc. SPIE 3369*, 14 (1998).

53. Axtel et al. identify three categories of model equivalence: 1) numerical equivalence is when two models produce quantitative measures that are identical, 2) distributional equivalence is when two models produce distributions of results that are statistically indistinguishable, and 3) relational equivalence is when two models produce the same internal, qualitative relationships among their results. See Axtell, Axelrod, Epstein, and Cohen, "Aligning Simulation Models: A Case Study and Results" *Computational and Mathematical Organization Theory*, 1 (2) (1996) 123–41.

54. Bankes, Steven "Exploratory Modeling for Policy Analysis" *Operations Research*, Vol. 41, Issue 3 (May–June 1993), 435–49.

55. Bankes, Steven, "Tools and Techniques for Developing Policies for Complex and Uncertain Systems," *PNAS*, Vol. 99, Suppl 3, (May 14, 2002) 7263–66.

56. Bankes Steven, "Robustness, Adaptivity, and Resiliency Analysis," *Complex Adaptive Systems — Resilience, Robustness, and Evolvability: Papers from the 2010 AAAI Fall Symposium* (FS-10-03).

57. *Defense Modeling, Simulation, and Analysis: Meeting the Challenge*, Committee on Modeling and Simulation for Defense Transformation, (National Research Council, 2006) 22; furthermore, the Committee noted, "*How might one assess validity, even for limited purposes of exploration?* The committee is skeptical about the value of bureaucratic processes to assess validity, since they are expensive, time-consuming, and frequently reinforce conventional wisdom and standard databases even when the reality is massive uncertainty. Nonetheless, validity is an important matter" (page 31).

58. JASON Study Group, "Rare Events," JSR-09-108, (Washington, DC: The MITRE Corporation, October 2009).

8

✛

Analytic Wargaming
in Intelligence

A thought-provoking passage of the 9-11 Commission report noted that within the Intelligence Community, "It is therefore crucial to find a way of routinizing, even bureaucratizing, the exercise of imagination."[1] While it may not be possible to make routine the process of thinking imaginatively, capabilities to think critically and enhance shared analytic exploration will greatly encourage imaginative thinking. Nobel laureate (2005) Thomas Schelling once described the benefit of the kind of exploration described here, conducted by analytic games: "Games have one quality that separates them qualitatively from straightforward analysis and permits them to generate insights that could not be acquired through analysis, reflection, and discussion. During ordinary analysis *one thing a person cannot do is to draw up a list of the things that would never occur to him or to think of all the ways a statement he has carefully composed could be misinterpreted under pressure*"(emphasis added).[2] In this chapter, we show just how games, and models and simulations, can help analysts transcend "ordinary analysis"—and therefore gain the power of imagination and insight that is inspired by competition.

Military planners have long used *wargames* to prepare for conflict; business and government today apply the term *serious games* to refer to game-play applied to market competition and policy development. In this chapter we adopt the term *analytic games* to introduce and distinguish the application of the games process to support the intelligence process—collection, analysis, and operations. The intelligence environment is a competition for information and the game-play process has been used by intelligence organizations to explore potential futures, test analytic capabilities, develop collection and analysis strategies, and assess potential intelligence operations (e.g., covert operations). The focus of this chapter is on analytic gaming applied to collection and analysis challenges.

In all of these applications, game participants (*players*) are placed in an artificial situation (that may be based on a current reality, of course) that causes them to think ahead, explore the uncertainty in their knowledge of the situation, make judgments about the situation, project the effects of their actions, and make decisions that impact the outcome of the game. Players are forced to consider: *How did we get here? What do I know and what do I need to know? What are my alternatives? What are the potential effects of actions that I take?* And in the process of the game, the players see the emerging effects of their actions and are confronted with: *How could it have played out differently?* Game players benefit from the immersive experience in the situation and the knowledge gained by exploring alternative strategies. Game organizers (who design, run, and analyze results) benefit from the knowledge about the behaviors exhibited in the game and the kinds of decision trajectories that the players take. Unique to this methodology is that the decisions of the players guide the flow of the game—and the ultimate outcome.

Agreeing with Schelling, game advocates assert that games provide unique human experience and analytic insights that can be gained by no other form of operations analysis—and that games develop situations that are intractable to conventional analysis.

PRINCIPLES OF GAMING
AND CATEGORIES OF GAMES

Gaming methods are used for several purposes, and the purpose(s) for any game must be clearly defined to guide scenario development, game design, and data collection-analysis to achieve the intended purpose(s). The major purposes to support intelligence include:

- *Exploration and Learning*—Exploration of the behaviors, dynamics, and effects of alternative actions under a range of circumstances. Examples: 1) An open exploration of the range of outcomes of a foreign government's response to a regime of inspections, sanctions, embargoes, and overt intelligence collections; 2) An exploration of the possible policy paths that a regime may consider to respond to circumstances or military actions.

- *Assessment*—Evaluation of alternative methods (policies, strategies, tactics, techniques, procedures) in a range of situations. Example: Assess the potential impact of alternative intrusive collection and supporting analysis strategies, the expected target responses, the potential for adverse effects (blowback).
- *Training*—Immersive training for analysts in a given situation to gain an understanding of alternative futures, the constraints, and consequences. Example: Place multi-disciplinary teams of collection managers, analyst, methodologists, and area specialists in a foreign situation game so they will gain experience as a team confronting a hard target.

The Marine Corps recognize that *wargaming* is an exploratory and assessment methodology that applies to a broad range of situations outside of "war" proper and offers the operational definition of wargaming as:

> The artificial replication of a situation of competition or conflict not involving actual military forces, and is characterized by human decision-making, which impacts the course of events throughout. It revolves around the interaction of two or more opposing forces guided by predetermined objectives, rules, data, and procedures designed to depict an actual or assumed real world situation. Wargaming is particularly suitable for generating, refining, and assessing concepts, plans, issues, and technologies; assessing alternatives; identifying capabilities and deficiencies; replicating conditions difficult to reproduce in peacetime; and reducing surprises.[3]

We adopt the term *analytic game* to refer to gaming methods that replicate a situation for intelligence collection managers and analysts to consider uncertainties, alternative explanations, internal processes, and outcomes of intelligence and policy activities. Unlike wargames, conflict and opposing forces are not necessarily required—but the realities of obfuscation may be represented by denial and deception. We apply the term *analytic* to refer broadly to the analytic intelligence discipline. Wargame developer and researcher Peter Perla, makes the careful distinction that wargames are not *analytic* in the technical sense—meaning that games are unlike other forms of repeatable operations analyses: closed-form or stochastic solutions, Monte Carlo analyses, stochastic simulation-based analyses. Games are uniquely human events or live performances and are not replicable, as Perla emphasizes:

> The players will never be identical, even if they are the same persons. Once you have played the game, you have learned and experienced something that changes your "state of nature," if you will. As a result, wargames are not

universally applicable tools to solve all problems. Wargames are exercises in human behavior, human interaction, and human decision making. The interplay of those human decisions and actions and the myriad ways they may change the game universe makes it impossible for two games to be the same. Wargames are best used to explore the role and potential effects of human behavior and human decisions. Other tools, such as analysis, are better tuned to deal with the more technical aspects of reality.[4]

For wargaming, Perla prefers the terms *artists* and *architects* (as opposed to *analyst*) to refer to game developers who create *unreal* game scenarios that are intellectually and emotionally engaging (the artist) and creatively challenge the judgment and decision making of players (the architect). All of these characteristics apply to analytic games.

The terms *simulation, games,* and *exercises* are too often used interchangeably in the literature and have caused some confusion. The general distinction between categories of operations analyses, analytic games, and exercises is helpful to distinguish the categories of games that we refer to in this chapter (highlighted in table 8.1).

The *game* categories are generally distinguished by:

- Human participants interact in a synthetic environment (with game facilitators or computers).
- The participants are confronted with an unfolding situation that causes analysis of the situation and consideration of alternative choices and "move" decisions at points in time ("turns").
- Participants are also confronted with time pressures that drive their specific decisions, rather than allowing them to agonize over uncertainty or deal in generalizations.
- The game is inherently competitive, involving intense social dynamics of team versus team.
- The trajectory of events (or game "path") is determined by the choices of the participants (and within limits determined by game controllers).
- Game controllers may inject conditions or situations to keep the game on course toward meeting the game's objectives.
- Participants experience a sense of consequentiality; actions have effects and may limit future options.

Simulations, as we have defined them in this text, are computational tools that operate models over time. Even in this chapter, we cite some authors who use the term *simulation* to refer to a human competitive game, not a computational tool.

Table 8.1 Categories of Analyses, Games, and Exercises

Category	Description
Operations Analyses	*Closed Form Mathematical Solutions*—deterministic (e.g., Lanchester equations), or stochastic computational models (even formal game-theoretic models) of operational situations. *Simulations* that measure objective functions (performance, effectiveness, utility) across scenarios and strategies. Emphasis on accuracy, validity and realism of results to real-world situations (past, current, hypothesized futures).
Individual Experience Games immerse an individual or multiple players in a computer game environment.	*Individual Game*—A single player performs a role in a computer-generated environment with other synthetic players; the environment dynamically responds to the player's actions.
	Multiple-Player Game—Insert multiple players, playing different roles, in a common simulated dynamic environment. The environment dynamically responds to the players' combined actions.
Discussions-Based Games familiarize participants with challenging situations, and the issues involved in taking alternative actions.	*Seminar or Workshop Game*—Facilitator confronts multiple-discipline teams with situations to generate discussions about issues, approaches; multiple, or sequential situations are generally introduced for discussion. A sequence of situations may be presented to provide the feel of a progressive game; but the sequence need not respond to prior discussions or "moves" by the participants. .
	Tabletop Game—Facilitator guides multiple (parallel or competing) teams in separate "tabletop" discussions to cause teams to consider issues, develop alternatives, and choose solutions (make a "move") at the end of each turn. The sequence of rounds may last one to several days.
	Large or Complex Tabletop Game—A simulation of operations that involves two or more teams operating in separate areas, usually in a competitive environment, using rules, scenario data, gameboards and procedures designed to depict an actual or realistic future situation. The game is played out over many turns across multiple days.
Operations-Based Exercises validate plans and policies; clarify roles and responsibilities, in an actual operational environment.	*Drill*—A coordinated, supervised activity usually employed to test a single, specific operation or function within a single entity.
	Functional Exercise—A functional exercise examines and/or validates the coordination, command, and control between various multi-agency coordination centers (e.g., emergency operation center, joint field office, etc.). A functional exercise does not involve any "boots on the ground" (i.e., first responders or emergency officials responding to an incident in real time).

ANALYTIC GAMES IN INTELLIGENCE

The United States maintains a National Strategic Simulation Center at the National Defense University that focuses on the seminar-category games to provide military policy makers, civil servants and war fighters a place to work together to explore options and examine assumptions about political-military issues. The games generally focus on strategic-level interaction under a series of specified constraints that allow players to crucially examine their assumptions, options, and the potential effects of actions.[5] The center hosts *analytic games* that focus on analyzing situations and options, and *educational games* that provide an intense introduction to a situation. While this center includes intelligence as one participant in strategic games, it is not dedicated to the unique problems of intelligence collection, analysis, and operations. Arguments for a dedicated game and simulation center for intelligence have been detailed by Hanig and Henshaw, asserting benefits similar to those cited throughout this text.[6]

> Simulations [games] are not predictive, but they can allow analysts to explore key analytic questions and conclusions in far greater depth than is possible from behind a desk or in meetings with other analysts. A properly organized geopolitical simulation forces analysts into dynamic, social, stressful situations that simulate real-world conditions to expose the participants' thinking, mindsets, biases, and assumptions to colleagues and observers positioned to identify analytic weaknesses.

The purposes for such games cited by Hanig and Henshaw include: 1) to provide participants opportunities to share information, ideas, theories, and best practices in structured, realistic environments, 2) to help analysts remain both timely and strategically relevant by simulating as many events as possible before emerging crises unfold, 3) training, and 4) experimentation with new analytic tradecraft. In addition, analysts are exposed to alternative, unexplored futures.

To illustrate the applications of gaming already applied, consider five categories of games that can uniquely benefit intelligence.

1. *Strategic Policy Analysis*—The most common use of game-based analyses is to evaluate geopolitical situations to develop plausible, likely, or worst- or best-case outcomes. In these games, intelligence analysts often team with policy makers to proceed through the game, and the benefit to the analyst is in understanding key policy questions and essential intelligence needs to address those questions. In 2010 a series of Iran situation games were conducted by nongovernmental organizations to assess the outcomes of alternative policies adopted by the United Nations, the European Union, Israel, and Iran. A summary by White and White of these games noted:

> Games can be highly effective at emulating the dynamic and competitive nature of real-world situations. They also replicate the uncertainty (misunderstanding, miscommunication, misperception, and misrepresentation) that

characterizes actual situations. In addition, the compelling and immersive nature of war games often leads to revelatory moments for the participants. All in all, the process of testing complex strategies and decisions in a competitive human gaming environment may be the best we can do short of the real world.[7]

Each game examined the objectives and strategy options of Iran, as well the outcomes of alternative strategies of the United States, Israel, and allies. In each case, a critical assessment was the interpretation, by Iran, of opposition moves to prevent it from developing nuclear weapons and the effect of actions on cohesion between U.S., Israel, and allies' relationships. Geopolitical games highlight the issues that policy makers confront, and the information that intelligence must provide.

2. *Operational Threat Analyses* — Assessments of potential threats require the anticipation of adversary course of action (COAs); games can provide a process for exploring these COAs and their consequences. DoD Joint Publication 2-01.3, "Joint Intelligence Preparation of the Operational Environment" (JIPOE), is the analytical process used by joint intelligence organizations to produce intelligence assessments, estimates, and other intelligence products in support of the joint force commander's decision-making process.[8] JIPOE requires definition of the operational environment, the effects of the operational environment, and the adversary, before wargaming potential adversary courses of action (COAs). A later section illustrates how games supported by computer simulation aid these operational analyses.

3. *Hard Target Assessment* — Games can also be used to focus analysts on the issues associated with understanding a difficult target. The target may be an organization, a facility, or a system (e.g., economic, infrastructure, media, etc.) that must be understood, explained, and described to support operations. The game is based on an uncertain description of the target and the game moves require actions that will reveal more information about the target without violating constraints (e.g., political blowback, collection discovery, etc.). The analysis requires deep assessments of target uncertainties, hypothesized alternative explanations, and creative collection targeting. Chapter 9 further develops this category of games.

4. *Collection Contribution Assessment* — Games provide training experience to a user for complicated collection operations, where collectors are competing with targets who seek to hide. A game can provide training experience in asset management, coverage, target denial and deception, and overall utility. For example, McCaffrey has illustrated the use of a computer-based naval game to assess the relative impact of SIGINT

information on operational outcomes.[9] The game allowed a single player to compete against a software competitor; players were provide historical levels of SIGINT (baseline) as well as varied levels of SIGINT. Using a historical naval situation, the results of many game plays could be compared to actual data (to support validation confidence building) and could assess alternative outcomes (e.g., due to contributions of SIGINT).

5. *Indication and Warning to Prevent Surprise*—A Defense Science Board studied approaches to prevent "capability surprise"—the unexpected threat occurring from a scientific breakthrough in the laboratory, rapid fielding of a known technology, or new operational use of an existing capability or technology. The study identified five steps that, when integrated, constitute a robust approach to managing surprise.[10] Notice that steps 2 and 3 explicitly consider analytic modeling, simulation, and game play:

1. A scanning and sifting process that narrows the many possibilities to the most worrisome few;
2. A "red" capability projection function that takes a "deeper dive" on the worrisome few through analysis, simulation, experimentation, and/or prototyping;
3. A net assessment process in which the deeper understanding of "red," gained through capability projection, is played against blue capabilities in order to assess the degree to which the nation can address the threat or adapt capabilities already in hand;
4. An options analysis team to provide an unbiased evaluation—or "rack and stack"—of the alternatives should blue capabilities prove inadequate; and
5. An ability to produce a decision package that can be acted upon by senior leadership.

Each of these categories of analyses can be performed at different levels of game play—ranging from small individual games to major games involving a large number of players. Table 8.2 illustrates this range of analytic game activities, identifying the objective, duration and typical number of participants, and activities. Perla surveyed the uses of games across defense communities, including intelligence. Citing a Defense Intelligence Agency military officer, he noted that "Wargaming in the intelligence community can be an important tool in trying to think beyond the conventional wisdom. It is a quintessential tool for exploring alternate or competing hypotheses and applying alternative analytical techniques."[11]

Table 8.2 A Range of Representative Analytic Intelligence Games

Category	Objective	Example Game Description
Individual Game	Immerse a single analyst in a situation to familiarize the analyst with analytic issues	• Duration: Many one-hour simulation explorations, by different analysts, with different capability "treatments" • Analysts play a simulation across different treatments to determine the relative performance. • Example: SIGINT Game (See p. 201)
Analysis Seminar	Orient a multi-disciplinary analysis team on a situation and the collection, analysis challenges	• Duration: One-day (5–15 participants) • Orient participants or provide an overview of authorities, plans, policies, procedures, concepts, and ideas. • Guide discussion on collection and analytic issues. • Guide discussion on policymaker needs.
Situation Analysis Workshop	Facilitate group(s) of participants to discuss, assess a situation, and develop a situation assessment product	• Duration: 1–2 Days (5–25 participants) • Place participants in a situation to allow open-ended discussions about the options they would consider; focus is on open and interactive discussion with no competitive interaction. • Collect results of discussions in a situation report.
Typical Tabletop Game	Facilitate a role-playing game that reveals issues of policy and intelligence to develop a policy or intelligence capability assessment	• Duration: 2–3 Days (10–25 participants) • Facilitator leads role-playing participants to role-play in a multiple-phase reality-based, but hypothetical, situation; in each turn, the facilitator describes an evolving situation before participants discuss issues and responses. • Participants must address issues of policy, collection, analysis, uncertainty, decision-making, and consequences. • Post-game analysis identifies intelligence and policy issues, critical intelligence impact on policy; Report on analysis is produced within 30 days. • Example: Iran Nuclear Games (See p. 208)
Large or Complex Tabletop Game	Facilitate a role-playing game that reveals issues of policy and intelligence to develop a policy or intelligence capability assessment	• Duration: 3–5 Days (25–50 participants) • Create a situation that confronts two or more interacting (competing) cells in an operational situation. • Game controllers lead role-playing competitors in a multiple-phase situation; in each turn, participants must develop actions (or "moves") to confront the situation. White cell adjudicates the results of each round and sets the situation for the next round. • Post-game analysis identifies analytic lessons learned from perspective of each competing team; report on analysis is produced within 30 days.

THE GAME PROCESS

While we have emphasized the wide range of game categories, the general process of developing and conducting a game is similar for all, and can be illustrated (figure 8.2) as a series of seven key steps (nominal duration of each step for a major game is provided):

1. Define Objective—The first step is to clearly define the purpose (e.g., analytic exploration, concept assessment, or training) and specific

objective of the game, as well as the game stakeholders (sponsor, information contributors, recipient of the analytic results, etc.). The objective should clearly describe the questions to be answered, and the expected insights to be gained.

2. Game Design (3–6 months)—The game is an exploration, a controlled environment within which human creativity, competition, and conflict can be evaluated. The design process creates the environment within which humans will be immersed to achieve the game objective. The process includes:

   - Based on the objective, identify the situations in which players must exist to confront problems, create an option space, make decisions, and take actions ("moves"), then observe effects and learn from the consequences of interacting with a simulation or a second (or more) human competitor.
   - Design a scenario to represent the situation, define the levels of play (e.g., strategic, operational, or tactical—each with associated time-scale), and the rules of interaction between levels for multi-level games (synchronous or asynchronous). Develop the scenario storylines and the branches and sequels that result from likely player decisions. Define the rate of play and number of "turns" or "rounds" (time increments for players to take action and observe results) in the game.
   - Identify the number of "sides" (e.g., competing teams; a two-sided game has two competing teams), the roles of all game participants, game controllers, white cell adjudicators, and observers or analysts.
   - Define the "gameboard" representation (e.g., map, event timeline, relative state of competitors, etc.) of the state-of-play (situation) throughout the game.

3. Game Development (1–3 months)—The game is tested and evaluated in this step, using a prototype with sufficient fidelity to assess the potential option space that the players may take, to determine if the game objectives can be met. The analysis must consider: *Will the players be confronted with the desired decisions? Are the interactions at a sufficient rate? Is the scenario rich enough to make the game environment realistic? Are there potential traps, dead-ends, or early completions that threaten to result in an incomplete game? Do game controllers have sufficient control to prevent play that does not achieve the experimental objectives?* A game review is held so the sponsor may assess the design to determine if it meets the objectives.

4. Game Preparation—The game developer arranges logistics (facility, equipment, networks, etc.) for the event and then nominates, invites, and confirms participants. Read-ahead and training materials are prepared, and a detailed game-day schedule is approved.

5. Conduct the Game (2–4 days)—All participants are provided training on the game objective and situation, their roles, and constraints on game play (e.g., policies, commander's intent, rules of engagement (ROE), and resources). Training is also provided for the game board, the means of initiating actions, and any special provisions in the game (e.g., mock interviews, mock policy-board reviews, videotaping, etc.). The game is initiated with all players in their appropriate roles, being guided by controllers who feed scenario situations to them, record their actions, and "adjudicate" (judge the likely results of the joint actions of all parties and determine the outcome) and then provide situation updates that begin each new "turn." Controllers and facilitators guide the pace of the game and can limit the trajectories of play to ensure that the game objectives are met. Observers monitor the activities of the human participants, and data are collected on the activities on networked computers. The importance of the game facilitators cannot be understated; a good game is the result of thorough preparation, careful selection and preparation of participants, and active facilitation and control throughout the game. Facilitators recognize the challenge of effectively involving all participants. Teams often separate into dominant members, supporting contributors, and marginal participants. Facilitation requires strong leaders to keep all participants involved and contributing.

6. Game Outbrief (1–4 hours)—A Quicklook Review is a quick summary for the participants and stakeholders immediately at the conclusion of the game, not an in-depth analysis. Participants brief their own impressions and lessons learned while the experience is fresh on their minds, and game controllers share their top-level observations.

7. Game Analysis (1–3 months)—An After Action Report (AAR) is disseminated after sponsor review, reporting the lessons learned against the initial stated objectives for the game.

The flow of these steps, the participants in each step, and the major activities are summarized in figure 8.1.

While these steps are intended to provide a rapid overview of the game process, a more comprehensive understanding of the game design process can be found in texts on the subject of military wargaming[12] [13] [14] and analytic games for business.[15]

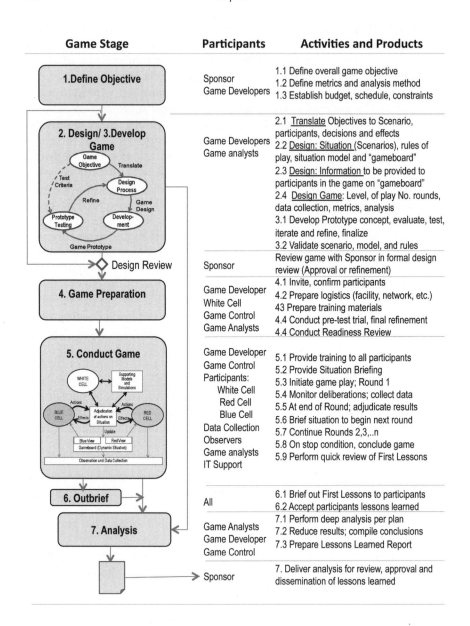

Game Stage	Participants	Activities and Products
1.Define Objective	Sponsor Game Developers	1.1 Define overall game objective 1.2 Define metrics and analysis method 1.3 Establish budget, schedule, constraints
2. Design/ 3.Develop Game	Game Developers Game analysts	2.1 <u>Translate</u> Objectives to Scenario, participants, decisions and effects 2.2 <u>Design: Situation</u> (Scenarios), rules of play, situation model and "gameboard" 2.3 <u>Design: Information</u> to be provided to participants in the game on "gameboard" 2.4 <u>Design Game</u>: Level, of play No. rounds, data collection, metrics, analysis 3.1 Develop Prototype concept, evaluate, test, iterate and refine, finalize 3.2 Validate scenario, model, and rules
◇ Design Review	Sponsor	Review game with Sponsor in formal design review (Approval or refinement)
4. Game Preparation	Game Developer White Cell Game Control Game Analysts	4.1 Invite, confirm participants 4.2 Prepare logistics (facility, network, etc.) 43 Prepare training materials 4.4 Conduct pre-test trial, final refinement 4.4 Conduct Readiness Review
5. Conduct Game	Game Developer Game Control Participants: White Cell Red Cell Blue Cell Data Collection Observers Game analysts IT Support	5.1 Provide training to all participants 5.2 Provide Situation Briefing 5.3 Initiate game play; Round 1 5.4 Monitor deliberations; collect data 5.5 At end of Round; adjudicate results 5.6 Brief situation to begin next round 5.7 Continue Rounds 2,3,..n 5.8 On stop condition, conclude game 5.9 Perform quick review of First Lessons
6. Outbrief	All	6.1 Brief out First Lessons to participants 6.2 Accept participants lessons learned
7. Analysis	Game Analysts Game Developer Game Control	7.1 Perform deep analysis per plan 7.2 Reduce results; compile conclusions 7.3 Prepare Lessons Learned Report
	Sponsor	7. Deliver analysis for review, approval and dissemination of lessons learned

Figure 8.1 A general game development process flow

INCORPORATING COMPUTATIONAL MODELS
AND SIMULATIONS IN ANALYTIC GAMES

We earlier distinguished the *game* (a competitive and distinctly human intellectual activity) from a *simulation* (a computational tool that operates a model over time to produce dynamic behavior). While games may be played with paper-based products (boards, charts, maps, rules, and human adjudication of the results of each round of sequential play), computers may be useful in games in several ways:

- Recording and Collaboration—Computers are used to collaborate across team members and record the actions of team deliberations and decisions; these logs benefit the game monitors in understanding the deliberations and actions of individual players and teams. The records are also used in preparation of the game assessment report.
- Analytic Tools—Computer-based tools such as geographic information systems, spreadsheets of force allocations, simulations of satellite collection performance, or weapon simulations may aid teams in making decisions with greater depth and breadth of considerations.
- Outcome Simulation—Computational models may also be used by the white team to adjudicate the outcomes of competing team actions at the completion of each round. The adjudication has traditionally been performed by "mental simulations" of the white team subject-matter experts. Computational simulations may supplement the adjudication process, estimating the effects of individual teams' actions (e.g., the effect of a collection plan) or the combined effects of competing teams' actions (e.g., the effect of team A's collection plan and team B's deception plan) in a complex and changing environment (e.g., under weather conditions).

In the second two areas, computer simulations hold increasing promise to provide competing teams and white cells the potential for a richer game experience. Within the gaming community there remains, however, a debate over the degree to which models and simulations should be used in games. The arguments advanced for and against simulations center on the constraints that simulations may place on game players—limiting their level of play and available actions and limiting the scope of play to the scope of a situation that was pre-programmed into the simulation. Consider these two views:

- Con—Computer-based simulation will never reach the breadth and depth of real-life situations represented in games. The pre-programmed constraints in a simulation may severely limit a player's creativity, keeping the player "inside the box" that is confined by the simulation—and limiting the effectiveness of the overall game.
- Pro—The constraints imposed by computer-based simulation pre-clude much of the out-of-bounds, infeasible, and downright cheating play that bedevils many games and limits their ability to focus on game learning objectives. A good simulation allows rich out-of-the-box thinking and creativity, while limiting fanciful and wasteful activities that detract from the game objective.

The next section provides a case study for a basic intelligence game with human adjudication, and a game that illustrates a JIPOE analysis with a supporting computer simulation.

CASE STUDY: CONDUCTING ANALYTIC GAMES TO SUPPORT INTELLIGENCE

We now illustrate the use of games in intelligence by describing, in some detail, two of the types of intelligence-focused analytic games described earlier in table 8.2. In both cases, the modest uses of computational simulation support are included in the two fictitious, but representative games. The two games are:

- CRYSTALLINE is a *seminar game* that exposes interagency teams to a difficult problem with a single objective: to focus the analytic energies of the best-qualified personnel in a short period of time on a key problem. The specific challenge to the game participants is to develop alternative hypotheses to explain the internal operations of foreign leadership and their options, as well as approaches to collection targeting and analysis. The seminar game provides in-depth exposure to the problem with a minimal time commitment to participants.
- VERTIGO is a more expensive *major game*, performed only semi-annually, that challenges teams of analysts, in a competitive environment, to assess a regional geopolitical situation—the objectives of this game are twofold: 1) an analytic objective to expose regional analysts to the complex interplay between the two rivals and their neighbors, and 2) a training objective to expose a broader community of analysts to a key challenge area.

CRYSTALLINE

The CRYSTALLINE game addresses a difficult, closed foreign country whose belligerent leadership has threatened neighbors and U.S. interests abroad. The leadership's threatening rhetoric and activities (support to terrorist operations, military operations on their borders and beyond their territorial waters) has risen sharply over recent weeks, and increased understanding of the internal dynamics of the unstable government is required. The game gathers a wide range of knowledgeable personnel from across the Intelligence Community and other agencies.

The layout of the CRYSTALLINE seminar (figure 8.2), representative of a typical two-day event, shows the carefully scheduled sessions across two days that include three "rounds"—that address increasingly narrowly focused aspects of the problem. Round 1 asks the teams to develop hypotheses to describe the possible course of action that the target system may take and their leader's decision calculus. Round 2 asks the teams to

GAME DAY 1			GAME DAY 2		
Objective: Base Case			Objective: Refinement Cases		
Overview, Game Objectives Roles, assignments			ROUND 2 Brief teams on Problem 2		
Intelligence Briefing Situation Background; Issues			Team A Analysis-Plan	Team B Analysis-Plan	Team C Analysis-Plan
A Group Intro	B Group Intro	C Group Intro	A Outbrief	B Outbrief	C Outbrief
Lunch Break			Lunch Break		
ROUND 1 Brief teams on Problem 1			ROUND 3 Brief teams on Problem 3		
Team A Analysis-Plan	Team B Analysis-Plan	Team C Analysis-Plan	Team A Analysis-Plan	Team B Analysis-Plan	Team C Analysis-Plan
A Outbrief	B Outbrief	C Outbrief	A Outbrief	B Outbrief	C Outbrief
End of Day Summary brief; Teams excused			End of Game Summary brief; Teams excused		
After Hours Assess Round 1 data; adapt Rounds 2 and 3			After Hours Collect Rounds 2-3 data		

Figure 8.2 CRYSTALLINE two-day game schedule

develop options for collection and assess the risks and likelihood of success of each alternative. Round 3 then focuses on the effects of alternative events or operational actions that may significantly change the situation or change the target's COAs over the next eighteen months.

Three teams (A,B,C) of eight members each are selected to assure that each team has a complementary diversity of analysts, subject-matter experts, and collection experts. The first day begins with an overview and clear statement of the question to be addressed by the game and the analytic objective to be achieved by the game. Roles of participants and game facilitators are explained, and the schedule of activities and administrative information are provided. Next, an intelligence briefing is provided to the participants, describing the context and current situation and the gaps or uncertainties in current intelligence. Participants then convene in teams in separate rooms to get to know each other and establish an operating approach; a facilitator is provided to guide each team.

After lunch, the teams are briefed on the round 1 questions and then the teams reconvene in their separate rooms to begin a facilitated discussion, focused on completing a solution to the round 1 question. The teams complete a general template to summarize conclusions of play, and the facilitator monitors and logs their analytic activities, assumptions, and lines of reasoning. At the completion of the round, the teams meet in a general session to brief the entire group on their results. Game facilitators ask questions about their conclusion, solutions, and analytic approaches applied. Rounds 2 and 3 are identical, each receiving a pre-brief addressing an update on the situation (news on recent changes, new intelligence updates, etc.) and an instruction to the new question to be addressed in the round.

There are numerous opportunities to apply models to support such a seminar game; the following examples show the range of possibilities:

- Situation models—Model tools can be used to represent and then present the situation to game participants; for example, geographic information system (GIS) representing the spatial situation and key locations, network model representing a political organization, spreadsheet representing the resources available to an adversary.
- Situation exploratory and effects models—In a step further, the model tools may be made available to game participants during the game-play periods (with a facilitator to use the tool). This allows the participants to ask questions and explore the situation models (e.g., review GIS map layers, explore effects of influence on a political network in the network model, and explore effects of actions in an economic model).

- Situation development models—The game may, in fact, be used to develop a model of the participants' understanding of a situation and expected effects and outcomes. Buede et al. have described an APOLLO workshop method to elicit expert knowledge and build a Bayesian network model representation of expert knowledge.[16] Such a model can be used to support facilitated elicitation and model building during the game. (Indeed the objective or the question to be addressed by the game may be the development of models that represent the collective knowledge of the participants.) The APOLLO approach, similar to an analytic game, is conducted in a two-day, facilitated workshop. A discussion facilitator guides the elicitation of model structure and parameter estimates, while a second facilitator implements the model in the tool, and the graphical representation of the model is projected on a screen for all participants to view the emerging representation. Alternative models can be developed and the model captures assumptions, underlying logic, and supporting evidence that is used.

Seminar games, among the most popular and cost-effective game form, provide an opportunity to expose a diverse team to a critical problem and immerse them into an intensive analytic exercise within a few days.

VERTIGO

The VERTIGO game addresses a longstanding regional rivalry between nations and the complex interactions with their regional neighbors and global powers. Competition for regional power, leadership stability in each state, threatening rhetoric and provocative military maneuvers, and potential disruption of global trade are perennial issues that are addressed in semiannual games. Each year has a different emphasis, as the competitive scenario changes and different disruptions are considered. The leadership's threatening rhetoric and activities (support to terrorist operations, military operations on their borders and beyond their territorial waters) has risen sharply over recent weeks and increased understanding of the internal dynamics of the unstable government is required. The game gathers a wide range of knowledgeable personnel from across the Intelligence Community and other government agencies.

VERTIGO is a week-long strategic or high-operational-level game structured to explore strategies to collect on, analyze, and influence the behavior of the rival nations in the complex geopolitical situation. In this case the game objective is to explore the potential options of political leaders in the rival nations. VERTIGO is a 2-sided intelligence-focused game that pits a "Nation A" BLUE cell (a team comprised of policy makers, operations officers, collection managers and analysts) against a competing "Nation B" RED cell in the context of a well-defined situation.

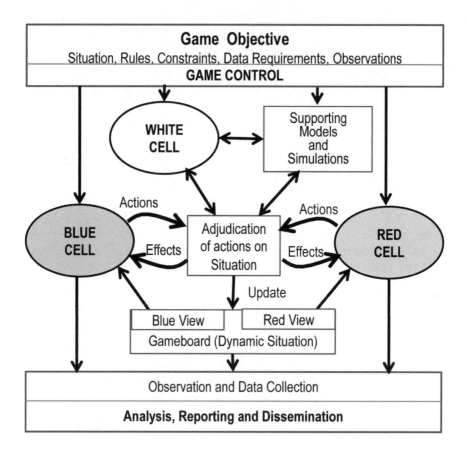

Figure 8.3 Elements of the two-sided VERTIGO game

The elements of the game structure (figure 8.3) include the following:

- A "game book" establishes the objective of the game, prepared by a development team to document the game schedule of events, the scenario, game procedures, rules, and constraints of play. The game book is made available to all participants as a pre-read document, and guides all play throughout the game event.

- A game control team of five individuals implements and enforces the game rules to ensure that the game will accomplish its analytic objectives; the game control team monitors and facilitates the game to keep participants focused and on schedule with the pace of the rounds in the game.
- The BLUE cell is comprised of ten individuals representing the Nation A government; participants are assigned roles in the government, military, and political factions to represent the different interests and perspectives of each. These assignments carefully apply the knowledge and experience of the selected players. The cell must represent the internal rivalries within the government, as well as competition with opponent Nation B, in accordance with the scenario presented at the beginning of each round and the constraints of the game book.
- The RED cell is comprised of a similar set of ten participants representing Nation B in competition with A. The number of players is a function of the analytic importance of the game: If the game is focused on studying RED considerations of strategy, a larger number of RED players may be assigned.
- The gameboard provides a display of the dynamic situation (updated each turn) that can be viewed by each cell. The views by each cell may be limited to the aspects of the situation that are observable to them (for example, RED government players have full visibility into RED information, but has only limited visibility into what BLUE nation's activities are at any time). The gameboard is implemented as a series of pages that summarize each nation's position (decisions, political and policy positions, actions, military force allocations, leadership popularity, economic situation, etc.) and provide the players with a snapshot of the situation during any round of the game.
- The WHITE cell adjudicates the actions of RED and BLUE at the end of each round—judging the outcome of their actions and defining the resulting effects of their *combined actions* and the situation that sets the stage for the subsequent round. The cell may employ supporting models and simulations to assess the potential effects of combined RED and BLUE actions in each turn of the game. In addition, the cell may introduce GREEN events, actions, or situations that represent conditions in the environment other than RED or BLUE actors (e.g., civilian social, economic, infrastructure, weather, etc.). It must also be prepared to respond to unexpected or unrepresented situations to keep the game on course to achieve game objectives.

**SimBAT: Simulation-Based Analysis and Training
for Intelligence Analysts**

Timothy Smith, an Analytic Methodologist at the Office of Strategic Analysis, Office of Naval Intelligence (ONI) has pioneered the application of games to develop analytic skills for teams of naval intelligence analysts. The games he leads build collaborative teams and competence in situation assessment. The games also expose juniors to the dynamism, complexity, and fascination of warfare and intelligence; senior analysts are exposed to the challenges of team leadership and higher-order military analysis and planning. The focus of Smith's games is to conjoin creative to critical thinking, embrace hypothetical reasoning, and to encourage reasoning about the possible future trajectories of dynamic situations. Specific analytic methodology objectives are in 3 areas;

- Area 1-Cognition: Develop advanced reasoning skills that are: 1) *strategic* in scope – large-scale and long-range, 2) *critical* in depth for comprehensive situation analysis, and 3) *creative* in perspective to apply problem-solving discipline with originality and innovation.
- Area 2 - Management & Staff work: Exposure to intelligence requirements assessment, asset allocation, situation awareness, and operations planning.
- Area 3- Leadership & Command: Immersion in decision-making under constraints of uncertainty, time pressure and stakes in a team environment.)

The games are conducted as 3-5 day analytic workshops to promote mastery of high profile, high stakes analysis and production. The workshops leverage commercial wargames (board games and computer simulation games) of historical, contemporary and future scenarios to expose analysts to a range of situations. Minor adaptation is required to use these tools to achieve the learning objectives. The games adopt a Naval War College three-cell structure. Red and Blue cells are comprised of trainees role-playing competitive command and control personnel of respective combatant forces performing situation awareness and command decision-making activities based on ISR collection/analysis; a separate White cell of event managers represents echelons above the Red/Blue cells and adjudicate the ISR & combat outcomes. Aspects of the "fog and friction" of war are added by injecting external surprise events and conditions into the game. SimBAT methodology has also been applied to analytic production using computer simulation, a potential growth area in national intelligence production. [i]

[i] Source: Smith, Timothy,"SimBAT" presentation at IDGA Intelligence Analysis and Processing Conf, Washington DC, 8 Dec.2010. See also Smith, Timothy, "Simulation-Based Training for Intelligence Analysts: Promoting Analytic Standards, Structured Techniques, and Community Collaboration," Finalist paper in the Director of National Intelligence Galileo Essay Contest, 2008.

Figure 8.4 SimBAT: Simulation-based analysis and training for intelligence analysts

Similar to the seminar game, the first day begins with a joint session of RED and BLUE teams; an overview is provided of the game objectives, rules of play, and roles of the game control facilitators and white team. The roles of participants and the schedule constraints are explained. An overall regional situation briefing is given to the joint session before the competing teams are separated to receive detailed briefings on the situation in each country. (The competing teams then remain separated for the entire game, until rejoining at the end of the week to receive a final out brief of the game and to share experiences.) This process may take most of the first day before the first round begins; game control facilitators guide each team to begin developing the positions and actions they will take at the end of the first round. Participants review the round 1 conditions on the gameboard and deliberate within their subgroups (presidency, political party offices, ministries, military, etc.) to develop positions; then, the national decision-making authorities establish a national plan of action. The facilitators assure that the teams report their positions and actions on schedule (e.g., actions including public rhetoric, economic, public security stance relative to protests, covert, and military actions, etc.).

At the completion of each round, the WHITE cell evaluates the actions (or "moves") chosen by the competing teams and determines the outcome of their combined actions. The choice of round outcome by the WHITE cell is based on several factors: 1) providing a realistic and reasonable outcome based on the RED and BLUE actions, 2) keeping both teams in competitive play to achieve analytic objectives, and 3) maintaining the pace and trajectory of the game. The WHITE cell can also inject surprise into the game by introducing new, external factors into each new round; these can include, for example, actions by other countries, economic shocks, threatened interventions, or catastrophes (e.g., nuclear detonation, natural disaster, etc.). By this method, the WHITE cell can confront the competitors with ever-increasing challenges, guiding the trajectory of the game toward its analytic and learning goals, maintaining game tensions, and avoiding early termination. WHITE cells have employed simulations in several ways to support their adjudication process:

- Component simulations—WHITE cell uses simulations of individual components of the competition to evaluate expected outcomes, such as weapons effectiveness, media influence, economic effects, political competition, or social behavior.
- Integrated simulations—WHITE cell uses simulations that account for the wide range of available RED and BLUE actions can be used to assess the complex interactions of both sides to support the WHITE cell's judgment.
- Pre-simulated results—The WHITE cell may also use pre-computed simulation results to guide the human judgment in the adjudication process, where time between rounds precludes the exercise of the simulation to support decisions.

The WHITE cell formats the outcome of the first round in the game board and the second round is initiated as the teams are reassembled and briefed on the new situation they confront to begin round 2. In the

VERTIGO game, the rounds are each a logical progression of the competitive game play by both sides, guided by the WHITE cell to keep the game trajectory to achieve the analytic objectives of the game. Note that in some games, the rounds may simply be a set of cases to be considered by the participants and not a progression at all.

Subsequent rounds throughout the week follow the same pattern, and the game controllers observe and record the deliberations of the participants. Their perceptions of the situation, their considerations, and decision making are recorded for subsequent analysis.

On the final day, the participants reconvene for a quick-look review of the game and lessons learned. The WHITE cell and game controllers provide an overview of the outcomes and top-level assessment of the achievement of analytic objectives. Each team then briefs their first-look lessons learned and insights developed from the perspective of the country they represented. Participants complete a questionnaire that allows them to assess the specific analytic and learning values of the game and to comment on their view of strengths, weaknesses, and issues in the game. In the weeks following the game, the game control team conducts an analysis of the game results by reviewing the observer notes, gameboard trends, WHITE cell notes and outbriefs by both teams. A draft of the final report is developed for the game sponsor, and upon approval, the report is disseminated.

ANALYTIC GAMES TO ENHANCE WORK-GROUP EFFECTIVENESS

An Intelligence Science Board study conducted research to identify the conditions that foster the effectiveness of analytic teams, focusing on two key approaches to organizing teams:[17]

- *Coacting Groups*—Individual analysts work in parallel and each analyst is held accountable for his or her personal output; individual contributions are then aggregated into a unit-wide product. Analysts interact and consult extensively with one another, but the exchanges are for the purpose of helping individual members competently fulfill their individual responsibilities.
- *Work Teams*—A team of analysts is collectively responsible for a significant piece of analytic work—work that, since it is being performed by a team, can be larger in size and potential significance than usually is possible for a task performed by any single individual. Members of work teams bring their own special expertise to the work, of course, and over time evolve specialized team roles—but it is the team as a whole that produces and is accountable for the analytic product.[18]

The research evaluated a wide range of Intelligence Community teams; the work teams achieved a higher level of effectiveness, based on three criteria: a team diagnostic survey, an on-site observer survey, and a multiattribute ranking measure. The researchers showed that the work teams clearly outperformed the coacting groups because they more effectively met five criteria of effectiveness:

1. The organization of analysts made up a *real* team (bound together, stable, and members are clearly interdependent to perform a task).
2. The team has a compelling *direction/purpose* (a purpose that is challenging, clear, and consequential).
3. The team has a *structure* that facilitates interdependent team work (task design, team composition, norms about behavior).
4. The team has a supportive *organizational* context (recognition for team performance, appropriate training, information, and resources to complete the task)
5. The team has access to competent team *coaching* (facilitation of the task with appropriate expertise that is focused on task processes).

Analytic gaming events, when properly developed, can be very effective because they form and facilitate intensive analytic work-team activities, focused on a compelling problem that demands the interdependent work of real teams. The game designers must invite analysts to provide a team structure that fosters interdependence and is supported by appropriate pre-game training and preparation. And the game must be conducted with appropriate facilitation to guide teams in the game toward a result that has evident analytic results.

NOTES

1. *The 9-11 Commission Report*, (Washington, DC: Government Printing Office, 2004), 344.

2. Schelling, Thomas C., "The Role of War Games and Exercises," in Ashton B. Carter, John D. Steinbruner, and Charles A. Zraket (eds.), *Managing Nuclear Operations*, (Washington, DC: Brookings Institution, 1987) 436.

3. Marine Corps Warfighting Laboratory (MCWL), Wargaming Division, Quantico, VA.,

4. Perla, Peter and Ed McGrady, "Wargamming and Analysis," Presentation for MORS Special Meeting, Center for Naval Analysis Report DOOI6966.A1I, October 2007, 12; See also Perla, Peter P., "So a Wargamer and a Black Swan Walk into a Bar . . . ," *MORS Phalanx*, Vol. 41, No. 4 (December 2008).

5. McCown, Margaret M. "Strategic Gaming for the National Security Community," *Joint Forces Quarterly*, Issue 39 (2009) 34–39.

6. Hanig, Rachel K. and Mark E. Henshaw, "To Improve Analytical Insight: Needed—A National Security Simulation Center," *Studies in Intelligence*, Vol. 52, No. 2. (Washington, DC: Center for the Study of Intelligence) 11–18.

7. White, Jeffrey and Loring White, "Serious Play: War Games Explore Options on Iran," PolicyWatch 1626, (Washington, DC: The Washington Institute for Near East Policy, February 4, 2010); for a report on one of the games, see Pollack, Kenneth M., "Osiraq Redux: A Crisis Simulation of an Israeli Strike on the Iranian Nuclear Program, Middle East, Memo No. 15, Saban Center for Middle East Policy (Washington, DC: the Brookings Institution, February 2010).

8. Joint Chiefs of Staff, Joint Publications (JP) 2-01.3, *Joint Intelligence Preparation of the Operational Environment*.

9. McCaffrey, Charles W., "An Analysis of the Influence of Signals Intelligence through Wargaming," DTIC 20010221, (December 2000).

10. Office of the Under Secretary of Defense for Acquisition, Technology, and Logistics, "Report of the Defense Science Board 2008 Summer Study on Capability Surprise" Volume I: Main Report, (September 2009), xii–xiii.

11. Perla, Peter P, and Michael C. Markowitz, "Conversations with Wargamers," Center for Naval Analysis Report D0019260.A2, (January 2009) 35 ff.

12. Dunnigan, James F., *Wargames Handbook: How to Play and Design Commercial and Professional Wargames*, 3rd edition, (Bloomington, IN: IUniverse, 2000).

13. Perla, Peter P., *The Art of Wargaming*, (Annapolis: Naval Institute Press, 1990).

14. Herman, Mark, Mark Frost, and Robert Kurz, *Wargaming for Leaders: Strategic Decision Making from the Battlefield to the Boardroom*, (New York: McGraw Hill, 2008).

15. Gilad, Benjamin, *Business War Games: How Large, Small, and New Companies Can Vastly Improve Their Strategies and Outmaneuver the Competition*, (Pompton Plains, NJ: Career Press, 2008).

16. Sticha, Paul, Dennis Buede, and Richard L. Rees. "APOLLO: An Analytical Tool for Predicting a Subject's Decision Making"; See also Sticha, Paul J., Dennis M. Buede, and Richard L. Rees, *The Role of Personality and Situational Variables in Predicting Decisionmaker Behavior*, 7, January 4, 2006, Technical Report, Contract, 2002-N181400-000, reported in *Proceedings of the 3rd MORS Symposium Working Group 7*, (January 2006).

17. Hackman, J. Richard and Michael O'Connor, *What Makes for a Great Analytic Team? Individual versus Team Approaches to Intelligence Analysis*, Intelligence Science Board Task Force Report (Washington. DC: Office of the Director of the Central Intelligence Agency, February 2005).

18. Ibid., definitions on pages 3–4.

9

Model-Based Support to Collection and Operations

A 2008 Joint Intelligence and Defense Science Board report recommended the development of a rigorous model-based collection support approach (called *model-driven fusion*) for the most difficult targets:

> In the model-driven fusion approach, a complicated intelligence problem is broken down into its constituent pieces, with the goal that understanding or confirming existence of these parts can be integrated together to address the original question. . . . These models will identify what is needed to discern the appropriate details of the target; what is required to characterize it; and how that could/should be accomplished with the sensors at hand—model-driven tasking of sensors to support model-driven processing and exploitation.[1]

In this approach, the models represent alternative hypothetical explanations of the structure and/or behavior of the target, and sensor measurements are compared to alternative hypotheses. Successive hypothesis tests yield the hypothesis with the least variance from sensor measurements. Iterative testing eliminates falsified candidates and refines likely models; in this model, the *fusion* process compares collected evidence to that expected by the models, and refines the likely model as evidence accumulates, *driving* the collection tasking.

The joint Science Board recommended:

- development of improved models of hard target problems coupled to multidimensional signature models that produce expected signatures for alternative models of the target;
- development of processing tools for multisource data that take advantage of models of intelligence targets to support ISR (intelligence, surveillance, and reconnaissance) the collection process.

This chapter develops the model-based fusion approach applying computational models and illustrates its application in a representative case study. As explained in earlier chapters, the intelligence process is inherently model based, where analysts' mental models form the basis for guiding collection and analysis. In many cases this is sufficient and appropriate. But difficult and enduring targets that pose significant challenges to collection and analysis require a more rigorous approach in which model hypotheses must represent the complex structure and the dynamics of the target. For example, the observed activities of a manufacturing facility (such as freight movements, energy consumption, personnel activities) over a thirty-day period of time may be too difficult for a mental model to distinguish among four different hypotheses of the products being manufactured. The difficulty may be compounded by active denial and deception measures being employed to defeat collection by hiding some activities, while inserting false activities (such as empty freight deliveries). In this case, rigorous explicit models of the four hypotheses may be required to represent the internal processes that produce the externally observable activities, to allow rigorous comparison.

Because intelligence data is often sparse and relationships among the entities and actors may be difficult to observe, there is a premium on formulating and testing hypotheses that can explain the observed data. The rationale for applying model-based methods in this context may be summarized as follows:

- Model-based intelligence collection and analysis enables quantifiable expressions of hypotheses.
- By creating a family of models (that spans the space of feasible hypotheses), one can perform statistical tests to determine how well each model fits or is refuted by the data.
- Hypotheses can be tested on the basis of statistical validity (actual data compared to model-predicted values with a statistical test criteria) and, under some conditions, the verification of causal relationships required by the hypothesis. (The cause is verified as *necessary* because without it, the effect will not occur, and as *sufficient* because with it, the effect will result regardless of the presence or absence of other factors.)
- There are methods that can select the information that has the most potential value added—that is, the information that most effectively reduces the variance in the data relative to the model.

It must be recognized that the model-based methods introduced in this chapter are not easily accomplished. First, it is difficult to build models that have the power to discriminate among competing hypotheses; it is the challenge of the analyst to understand which structural and dynamic properties of a system enable discrimination. Second, even if such properties are identified, it may not be feasible to observe and collect the data on those properties. Third, there may be hidden (unobserved) factors that may produce observed effects not accounted for in the models—this is what keeps analysts and modelers awake at night.[2]

Two model-based approaches to collection, analysis, and operations support are introduced in the following sections, distinguishing approaches to physical systems and then human systems targets, followed by an example that integrates models of both human behavior and physical infrastructure.

MODEL-BASED APPROACHES TO ISR COLLECTION SUPPORT FOR PHYSICAL TARGET SYSTEMS

The model-based approach to support collection is based on the concept that a hypothesized model of the behavior of a target system can produce *synthetic* signatures, indicators, or other phenomena that can be compared to the observations of a real target system to refute the validity of the hypothesis or provide a degree of confirmation. The hypotheses may distinguish the *state* of a system (e.g., in production, in testing, in maintenance) or the *function* of a system (e.g., plastic production, explosives production, etc.) The model-based concept includes several necessary conditions:

- The target system produces observable phenomena that are uniquely traceable to its core structure or internal behaviors.
- There is sufficient knowledge of the problem context to conjecture hypothetical target systems and then to represent them in a conceptual and computational model.
- There is a means to observe the target with sufficient revisit or persistence to provide multiple perspectives and measurement of dynamics to enable progressive refinement of promising hypotheses and elimination of falsified ones.
- The observable phenomena are *diagnostic*; that is, they provide the ability to differentiate between alternative hypotheses. The degree to which a set of observables is able to differentiate is called *diagnosticity*.[3]

The elements of the model-based analytic approach (figure 9.1) can be illustrated by following eight stages of the process being performed to discriminate the function and characterize the state of a foreign facility with limited access.

1. *Define Target Hypotheses*—The process begins as the analyst identifies the target as a system, describing the objective of analysis (e.g., "To determine if a facility is conducting illicit activities banned by treaty"). The set of hypotheses (just consider two, for example: H_1—legal activities as advertised or H_2—illicit drug production) are defined by the best conjecture of potential explanations. The hypotheses are first represented in conceptual models as the analyst decomposes the facility into its component parts: the buildings, people, their communications, equipment, manufacturing processes, energy consumption, and the transport of materials in and products out. The model of each hypothesis is developed using these component building blocks to represent the attributes of each. The model also synthesizes the unique observables for collection.

2. *Develop and Simulate Modeled Behaviors for Each Hypothesis*—Next, the model is simulated over time and refined to represent the hypothesized dynamic behaviors of activities and the observable effects of those behaviors for each hypothesis. This may require the analyst to represent ISR collection systems to determine what can be examined about internal system activities by external observables. This process is an *exploratory analysis* phase, acquainting the analysts with the dynamics of the target, and may include a review of historical data to interpret prior behaviors.

3. *Collection Management*—Based on an understanding of the important dynamics of the target, a collection plan is developed that tasks sensors and sources, coordinating the timing and characteristics (coverage, time of day, dwell, resolution, etc.) required to capture the observables that will help to establishes the target state or characteristics and distinguish between hypotheses.

4. *Conduct Intelligence, Surveillance, and Reconnaissance (ISR)*—Following the plan, ISR systems observe the target with coordinated collection by sensors and other assets to meet the required sampling or persistence requirements. The observations of target structure (physical structure, process structure, transportation structure, organizational structure, etc.) and time sequences of observations represent behaviors of the components of the target system.

5. *Compare Simulated Results to Observed Phenomena*—The results of collections over time are compared to simulations of a range of conditions—across all hypotheses to determine which hypotheses may explain observed behavior and to learn from unexpected results.

6. *Refine Hypotheses and Models Based on Comparison*—Based on the comparisons, refinements are made to the hypotheses and models. Over time, the desire is to converge on the most likely hypothesis and eliminate (falsify) those models that fail to describe the target behavior.

7. *Conduct Diagnostic Analysis*—As the models are refined, the observables are evaluated to determine their diagnostic contribution.
This may result in a refinement of the collection plan or the request
for collection that is supported by an active probe of the target to
stimulate a response that improves diagnosticity (e.g., if the target
is H_1, it will respond differently than if it is H_2). This analysis is supported by the models that can be stimulated to explore which kinds
of probe actions may cause responses that are highly diagnostic.
The procedure is a search, running many simulations (hundreds or
thousands), with each simulation measuring the effect of the probe
on the models representing each hypothesis and scoring the ability
to observe and distinguish between hypotheses.
8. *Develop Probing Operations*—Simulated probes (sets or sequences of
actions) are translated to operational actions that are coordinated
with ISR collection.

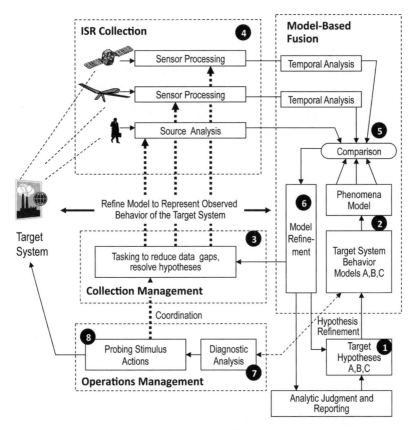

Figure 9.1 Model-based support to collection and analysis

MODEL-BASED APPROACHES TO SUPPORT ACTIVITY-BASED INTELLIGENCE (ABI) FOR HUMAN TARGET SYSTEMS

Activity-based intelligence (ABI) is an evolving strategy for developing intelligence using the combined capabilities of persistent surveillance, tailored collection management, multi-INT analytic tradecraft, and flexible and discoverable data management.[4] The Office of Undersecretary of Defense, Intelligence (OUSD [I]) has led the conceptual development of ABI sources and methods that focus on the detection, identification, and tracking of *activities* (rather than on the *entities* as in traditional target-based intelligence). The focus of surveillance is to capture, characterize, and geolocate activities (e.g., planning, bomb making, assembly, etc.) or transactions (e.g., exchanges of people, weapons, finances, materiel), capturing these activities and transactions as they occur, allowing analysts to develop and unravel insurgent networks.[5] ABI responds to the need to locate human target systems (e.g., terrorists, insurgency groups) that hide among civil populations.[6]

Emerging ABI concepts hold promise for exploiting the increased data collection capabilities of advanced full-motion video (FMV), wide-area motion imagery, and SIGINT/GMTI sensor systems. ABI leverages the persistent surveillance of large areas to distinguish the most difficult target systems by understanding the context within which they operate—the "patterns of life" that characterize normalcy and allow discrimination of subtle deviations.

Pattern of life analysis refers to the detailed analytic process that develops (learns) the patterns of normal behavior of a persistently observed target to identify the target, characterize its activities, and detect changes from normalcy. Flynn et al. described the operational art of such methods to locate elusive high value individual (HVI) targets. Analysts developed target intimacy "to the degree that they could easily recognize something unusual and in some cases even detect a visual signature of how the target walked, traveled in groups, or engaged other people. The ability to recognize a target's gait, dress, companions, parking patterns, and so forth became high-confidence targeting indicators because of the hours of pattern of life observation."[7]

Flynn described the three essential elements of persistent surveillance and analysis in pattern of life analysis:[8]

- The *Unblinking Eye* provides an opportunity to learn about the network in action and how it operates. It is long dwell, persistent surveillance directed against known and suspected terrorist sites or individuals. The purpose of this long dwell airborne stakeout is to apply multisensor observation 24/7 to achieve a greater understanding of how the enemy's network operates by building a pattern of life analysis. This is an important concept and has proven itself time and again with hundreds of examples of successful raids.

- *Nodal analysis* is spatially connecting relationships between places and people by tracking their patterns of life. While the enemy moves from point to point, airborne ISR tracks and notes every location and person visited. Connections between those sites and persons to the target are built, and nodes in the enemy's low-contrast network emerge. Nodal analysis has the effect of taking a shadowy foe and revealing his physical infrastructure for things such as funding, meetings, headquarters, media outlets, and weapons supply points. As a result, the network becomes more visible and vulnerable, thus negating the enemy's asymmetric advantage of denying a target. Nodal analysis uses the initial start point to generate additional start points that develop even more lines of operation into the enemy's network. The payoff of this analysis is huge but requires patience to allow the network's picture to develop over a long term and accept the accompanying risk of potentially losing the prey.
- *Vehicle follow* is tracking vehicle movements from the air. These are important in illustrating the network and generating fix-finish operations. . . . Vehicle follows were surprisingly central to understanding how a network functions. They are also among the most difficult airborne ISR operations to conduct and often require massing of assets to ensure adequate tracking.

Such analysis is largely a patient, manual process, where the pattern of life representations are maintained as mental models formed by the ABI analyst assigned to a target area of interest.[9] The role of conceptual and computational modeling in ABI includes the following areas:

- Representation of *general* patterns of normal behavior and the patterns of threat behavior. These representations can include marked map graphics to capture spatial patterns and tables or timelines that represent sequences of activities or daily routines.
- Representation of *specific* patterns observed at each specific target site, target route, or target activity.
- Representation of quantitative models of the empirical data observed over time—captured in spreadsheets or a database to allow quantitative comparison and trend analysis.
- Representation of the dynamic behavior in computational simulations to explore the possible meaning of certain behaviors or project the effects of alternative actions to disrupt a target (e.g., simulation of the effects of roadblocks to disrupt vehicle movements).

In each of these cases, the explicitly captured models can support handoff from analyst to analyst, representation to support targeting and planning, and training for pattern of life analysts.

CASE STUDY: MODEL-BASED COLLECTION SUPPORT

We can illustrate the model-based ISR concept described in the Joint Intelligence-Defense Science Board report by two published examples of model-based methods that focus on representing a foreign organization and its associated facilities and activities. The first example is a conceptual modeling approach that focuses on understanding structure and process, and the second is a computational approach that focuses on the organization's process dynamics.

Bodnar has described a conceptual modeling approach, Multidimensional Analysis (MDA), that combines top-down reasoning (moving from a conceptual hypothesis "down" to component parts) and bottom-up reasoning (moving from pieces of evidence "upward" to the components they support and the hypotheses they support) about a model that represents a foreign target system, using maps, timelines, and organization charts.[10] He presents a series of analytic axioms that lead to an MDA model that integrates the aspects of organization, process complexity, and development time. The process Bodnar has illustrated in the MDA model uses a notional biological weapons (BW) program as the target systems being studied (figure 9.2). In this example, the model integrates three fundamental aspects of the system:

- **Organization structure** of organizational elements from a national command authority down to required organizational elements: research, supporting (dual use) public health and production organizations and the deploying armed services.
- **Process flow** describes the stages of activity proceeding from research to development, testing, production, and deployment.
- **Timeline of major activities** or milestones that are required to be achieved to lead to a deployed biological weapon capability. The analyst can also label the expected indicators of each milestone accomplishment.

The MDA process begins with the conceptual model, hypothesized from the top (the required capabilities to develop BW, then moving downward to the component parts). Working from the bottom up, the analyst instantiates (populates) the model with supporting evidence as it is acquired—individual and organization names, facilities, places, identified activities, etc. The model establishes the top-down analytic context—a model of how a hypothesized BW program would operate in the context of the foreign country under study. The bottom-up analysis studies the role and activities of entities or activities revealed in reporting; the analysts then seek to identify their potential role of each element of evidence in the overall MDA model.

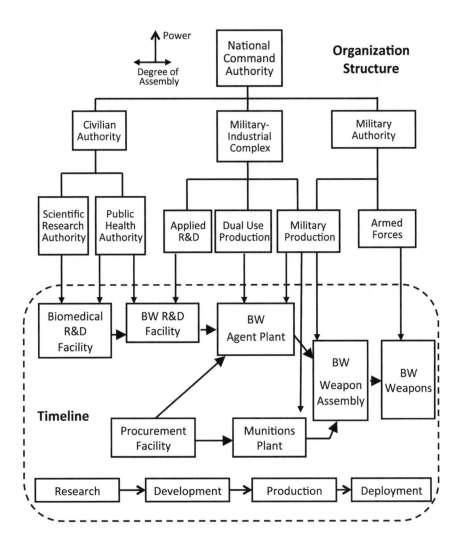

Figure 9.2 Multidimensional model of a basic biological weapons program[11]

Notice that the MDA model can be used in two ways:

1. **Model Refinement**—Working from the model downward, and the evidence upward, the analyst revises and refines the model to more accurately represent the actual program being studied. The goal is to build a conceptual representation of the target system. In such cases, the analyst may know what the target system is (for example, an equipment production facility) but needs to better understand its operation (the production rate and processes used).

2. **Hypothesis Testing**—When the analyst does not know what the target system is, two (or more) alternative hypotheses may be modeled, and the analyst tests the evidence against the alternative models. The bottom-up evidence is tested against each alternative hypothesis represented by its model. Because the goal of this use of the model is to distinguish between alternative hypotheses about the structure or behavior of a target system, the development of such models must carefully represent the attributes that discriminate between hypotheses or they will be of little value. For example, if the analyst is trying to distinguish between military and commercial equipment manufacturing, the model must capture the specific differences in behavior between these two processes.

The MDA model can be updated, annotated, and refined to present an accumulating body of knowledge about an intelligence target system. The model and supporting information can be maintained in a variety of computer tools to allow rapid update as the model is refined and new information is added. For example, the linked data can be stored in a relational data base such that the user can see the data from the three different views—who is performing an activity, where are they in the development process, and what is the timeline of their (observed or projected) activities.

While the MDA employs a conceptual model, the dynamics of the target systems processes are not explicitly represented, other than by the timeline. For the most difficult targets, the analyst may require a model that represents the dynamics of the target organization to experiment with alternative behaviors of the organization over a range of conditions. This may be necessary for several reasons:

- to understand internal activities (or combination of activities) or the explanations of observed external activities (e.g., what the internal production processes related to deliveries of raw materials are, and what the internal storage capacities being used to sustain production are)

- to understand the potential behaviors of the target system under different conditions (e.g., natural disasters, imposed sanctions, perceived threats, etc.);
- to explore potential strengths (e.g., the robustness to sanctions), vulnerabilities (sensitivity to deliveries, resources, or personnel), or unique operating constraints (e.g., critical timing).

Dynamic computational models, or simulations, can provide insight into these aspects of a target system. Such an approach is illustrated by an MIT team that represented a foreign organization using systems dynamics models.[12] The effort integrated multiple modeling approaches to develop active probes to determine the activities at a target biotechnology organization; the model was applied to a hypothesis testing problem to determine if probes of the organization could discriminate between H_0 (benign commercial activities) and H_1 (nefarious activities). The multiple model simulation includes four integrated model elements to represent the organization:

1. a social network model that represents the structure of high-level leadership;
2. a decision model that represents management-level decisions;
3. a discrete event simulation model that represents the development and production processes that proceed from development to production for two different activities, V1 and V2; and
4. a systems dynamics model that represents critical external resources that supply the development and production processes.

The models exchange data to form an integrated simulation (figure 9.3) that represents the behavior of the organization to a sufficient degree to allow the analyst to explore the effects of external actions on the system. The figure illustrates one example of many causal chains that may be considered by an analyst: the effects of a reduction in a critical resource (skilled personnel, material, energy, etc.). The hypothesized effects of a probing action are illustrated in arrows representing the flow of a chain of effects through the organization: (1) resources to the organization are reduced (e.g., due to a sanction on materials), (2) the resources that are allocated between V1 and V2 must be rationed, causing delays in development and production schedules, (3) management must make decisions on priorities between V1 and V2 allocations, and (4) reallocates resources according to priorities that sustain the (military) V2 development over the commercial V1 development, (5) sustaining the critical activity (V2) to restore schedule, while (6) stopping the observable commercial (V1) activity.

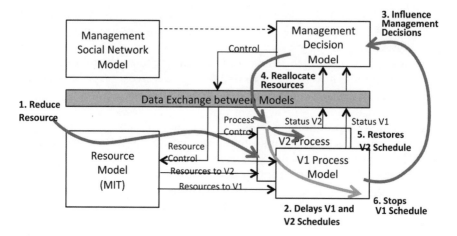

Figure 9.3 Multimodel simulation structure for an organization and its development activities [Adapted from Anderson, et al.]

Each of the model components simulates the dynamics of the internal process and the effects are coupled to dependent models in the causal chain. MIT illustrated the analysis of effects in a very simple, but complete model implemented as a systems dynamics model (figure 9.4).[13] The model was used to illustrate the effect of a reduction in the ability of the human resource process to provide skilled personnel for development. The subsections of this simple model are shown in dotted lines:

- Human Resource model produces experienced personnel to support the development "pathway" model. The system dynamics model has two "stocks" to deliver to the pathway model to increase productivity: Workforce (the volume of development personnel) and Experience (the degree of experience in the personnel provided). The two stocks account for both the quantity and quality of the workforce given changes in the workforce flows ("hiring" and "attrition").
- Pathways model productivity (and subsequent output) is a function of Workforce, Experience (as well as other factors, like Material, Energy, etc.)
- Management Decisions model represents management decisions, such as the desired level of workforce and the time with which to adjust workforce.
- The probe input section of the model contains inputs to simulate a probe to reduce workforce ("workforce reduction" caused by, for example, a sanction on foreign workers).

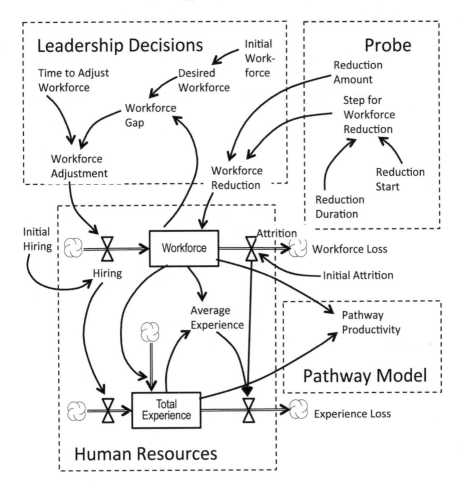

Figure 9.4 Human resources model component [Adapted from Anderson, et al. p. 19]

The model illustrates the analyst's explicit thinking about how the organization may work, and how management may respond to actions that impact human resources. This model, like the static MDA models, requires the analyst to explicitly represent the structure of the target system hypothesis, but further requires the explicit representation of dynamic characteristics (e.g., hiring, training, production rates). Of course, the real-world system is more complex than the model and the analyst must always recognize that the model is intended to represent the first-order dynamics, but that real world may exhibit emergent behaviors not captured in the model.

MIT illustrates (figure 9.5) how the model is used to explore the dynamics of the system response to workforce reductions, using simulation results that compare a base case (the system in equilibrium where hiring and training are sustaining a normal level of productivity) and the response of the organization to a probe that reduces the supply of human resources. The figure represents the base case (solid line) and the response to a probe (dashed line). The graphs show how a probe increases the loss of workforce (bottom left), creating a decline in workforce and experience (middle). The leadership responds by increasing hiring (top left), though while the workforce recovers there are delays in the development pathway progress (far right).

In the same research program, Malinchik and Wedgewood developed an efficient search method that could discover robust strategies of probing actions that would produce observables to discriminate among alternative hypotheses about the activities or capabilities of the target systems.[14] A genetic algorithm guided a "search" for discriminating probe sequences by running many iterations of the multimodel simulations, examining the "landscapes" of simulation results and refining probing actions to seek regions of maximum response by the target system. The approach generated probe sets (or sequences), injected them into the multimodel simulations for hypotheses H_0 and H_1, and computed a

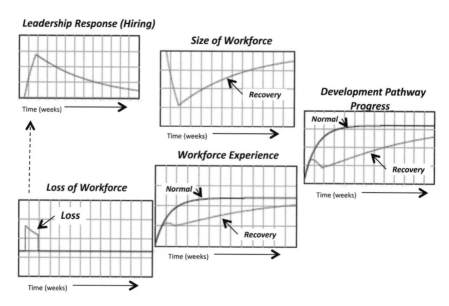

Figure 9.5 Example model response to a loss of workforce [Adapted from Anderson et al. p. 18]

diagnosticity value that measured the degree to which the probe set distinguished between H_0 and H_1. This process continued until the number of iterations (generations) reached a predetermined threshold of diagnosticity (a maxima, representing a probe set that provides acceptable discrimination between hypotheses). This approach provided an automated means to enable the analyst to search for effective probe sets to stimulate the target model to test the hypotheses, (i.e., reveal internal activities by outward observables).

HYPOTHESIS TESTING ANALYTIC METHOD

The analytic methodology that integrates causal inference, simulation, diagnosticity evaluation and hypothesis testing into the operational process introduced earlier in figure 9.1 is illustrated in figure 9.6.

Target Development and Evaluation

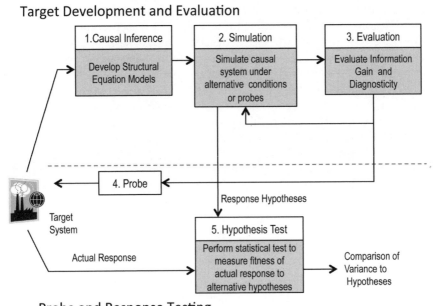

Figure 9.6 Integrated Hypothesis Testing Method

The method proceeds in the following five major steps, numbered in the figure.

Step 1, Causal Inference—The target system (often a cooperative target system used for analytic purposes) is observed and key variables are used to induce a causal model of the system, describing the independent (cause) variables, mediating variables, and observable (effect) variables. Structural equation models (SEM) represent these causal structures in directed acyclic graphs, and an associated system of equations describe the variances and covariances among the variables. The process attempts to specify every causal factor that is correlated with an observable variable of interest, Z, in alternative SEM models (alternative causal hypotheses). The model guides the collection of data for subsequent hypothesis testing to compare how well the covariance matrix is fit by alternative models.[15]

Step 2, Behavior Simulation—The causal analysis allows a simulation of the effect on the observable, Z, of alternative normal activities of the target, or of responses to probing stimuli. The first-phase model may also be a contributor to a theoretical or hypothesized model, based on information other than the empirical measurements.

Step 3, Diagnosticity Evaluation—The practical implementation of a methodology to evaluate collected evidence against alternative hypotheses generally measures the difference (or similarity) between probability distributions of measurements of the evidence for each of the hypotheses. The difference metric (previously described as *diagnosticity*) can be easily visualized as the separation of the sets of predicted measurements for two hypotheses, H1 and H2. Consider for example, the four cases in which the circles (figure 9.7) represent the statistical distributions of measurements (random variables being measured) used to distinguish H_1 and H_2. In the case where the diagnostic value is D=0, the observables are consistent with both hypotheses (H_1 and H_2) and therefore provide no ability to distinguish between the two hypotheses. As D increases, the measurements provide an increasing number of observables that can distinguish between the two hypotheses. For D=1, the measurements are mutually exclusive and provide distinct separation between the two hypotheses. For D>0 there are overlaps in the measurements and the uncertainty provides the potential for a decision error. The overlap is called *mutual information* and is a measure of mutual dependence of the random variables for H_1 and H_2.[16]

Selecting the appropriate measurements and probes to stimulate responses from target systems are critical to developing highly diagnostic capabilities. In addition to a measure of diagnositicity, the analyst requires a measure of the relative contribution of each additional measurement, or of a probe to determine their value. What is required in this case is a measure of the information gain attributable to the additional measurement or probe. Here, an information theoretic approach is useful to quantify the relative gain from a new measurement or probe-induced change in state (that produces a change in measurement). Applying information theory, we let $M=(x_1, x_2 \ldots x_i \ldots)$ be the set of all possible measurements

Hypothesis Measurement Distributions	Diagnostic Value
 H_1 and H_2 Overlapped	No diagnostic value; H_1 and H_2 Indistinguishable)
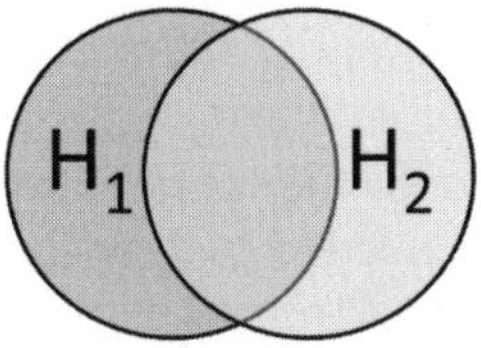 H_1 H_2	Low diagnostic value
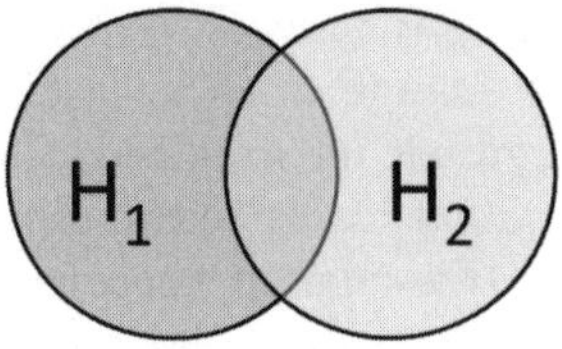 H_1 H_2	High diagnostic value but some uncertainty in region of overlap
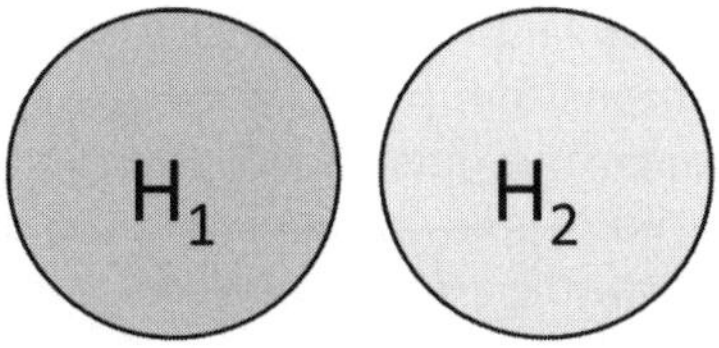 H_1 H_2	Assured ability to distinguish between Hypotheses H1 and H2

Figure 9.7 Representative separation between measurement distributions and diagnostic value

from the system X which may take on any one of n states, and define the information content of any particular measurement, m_i, about the state of X as a function of m_i. The primary information-related metric (for each measurement) is called *entropy* (*H*) and is a function of the probability of occurrence of the measurement. Entropy (*H*) is then defined as:

$$H = \sum_{i=1.,n} p_i \log p_i$$

Where:
H = Entropy (measured in bits when log2 is used)
Pi = Probability that the random variable is in state i
n = Number of possible states of the system X

H is the measure of average uncertainty in the random variable and is represented as the average number of bits needed to describe the random variable. It is a measure of the "disorder" or "uncertainty" about the state of the system.

Entropy is not, *per se*, the measure of information, but the *decreases* in entropy due to additional measurements can be used to measure gains in information. As additional measurements (or measurements resulting from stimulating probes) are added, the change in *H* quantifies the decrease in uncertainty and increase in diagnostic information. The entropy change or information gain is then the measure of reduction in uncertainty about the state of X, determined by the change in entropy, *H*, due to an added measurement, or a diagnostic probe-induced measurement:

$$I_i = H_{Before\ Probe} - H_{After\ Probe}$$

Step 4, Probing Stimuli—The causal events that produce the desired dynamic response occur. If the conditions that produce the response are natural (e.g., weather event, calendar event, operational event, etc.), the collection awaits the conditions that aid in discrimination. If the method requires a controlled active stimulation, the probe is issued to measure the target response.

Step 5, Hypothesis Testing—Finally, the observed results of changing conditions, or active probing stimuli, are compared against the expected measurements predicted by the alternative hypotheses. The statistical variance between model-predicted values and actual measurements are used to determine which model best fits the observed behavior of the target.

THE FUTURE ROLE OF
MODELS AND SIMULATIONS IN JOINT
INTELLIGENCE OPERATIONS

Joint Intelligence Operations Centers (JIOCs) have been organized to integrate assessment, planning, and execution functions to the highest degree possible. These centers integrate the operations (J3 operations and J5 plans) and intelligence (J2) processes by co-locating operators in the intelligence center and placing intelligence personnel into other boards, centers, cells, working groups, and teams.[17] The intelligence, planning, and operations personnel can share a common operating picture and products and can more effectively converse about intelligence collection and operations planning needs.

In the future, the dynamic simulations illustrated in the prior sections can play a critical role in the integration process by allowing analysts and planners to share a common (dynamic) operating model (COM) that enables (figure 9.8):

- J2 analysts to run simulations to explore the dynamics of the targets to guide collection and perform JIPOE analyses.
- J5 planners to run simulations on the common operating model to assess plan effects and outcomes. The model enables rapid evaluation of candidate courses of action (COAs) in the plan and the assessment of alternatives.

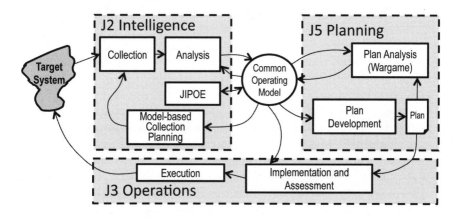

Figure 9.8 The common operating model as an integrating element in a JIOC

The CONOP for using this process allocates model building and update to the J2—just as intelligence report authoring and update is performed today. In fact, the COM is the next step in the current movement from static intelligence reports to dynamically updated web pages. J2 JIPOE analysts and J5 planners are the primary consumers of the COM to perform exploratory analysis and plan assessment.

Unlike current static intelligence reports or common operating pictures, the COM simulations will represent the underlying dynamics (causality) of the current situation, allowing analysts to simulate the effects of red COAs in support of JIPOE, and planners to wargame candidate blue COAs. Of course, the COM concept may not be suitable for all mission applications, but it can provide significant aid to the most complex missions, or the most difficult target systems. The DoD is conducting research to develop simulation capabilities suitable to implement the COM CONOP in several key areas:

- Complex Battlefield Situations—The Defense Advanced Projects Agency (DARPA) has developed complex battlefield scenario simulations suitable to support in-theater analysis planning support to commanders, enabling them to run extensive simulations of alternative COAs and outcomes. Tools developed for the Deep Green program allow the ground forces commander to generate and analyze maneuver and fires options quickly, including simulating the many possible futures that may result from a combination of friendly, enemy, and other courses of action. As the ground engagement moves on, Deep Green tools use information from the current operation to assess which futures are becoming more likely in order to focus the development of more branches and sequels; and make decisions cognizant of the second- and third-order effects of those decisions. At the core of Deep Green is a simulation (a common operating model) that is updated with current intelligence, and runs fast simulations of potential futures to support S-3 (operations) and S-2 (intelligence) officers.[18]
- Underground and Deeply Buried Facilities—The Defense Threat Reduction Agency (DTRA) maintains an Integrated Munitions Effects Assessment/ Underground Targeting and Analysis System (IMEA/ UTAS) suite of models to represent hardened and deeply buried targets to support analysis, planning (targeting), and post-attack assessment. The model suite includes 3D spatial models, event fault tree models, and process models (systems dynamics simulations) to represent the hypothesized properties of an underground target systems, and assess munitions effects.[19]

- Human Social Cultural Behavior Systems—The Office of Secretary of Defense Human, Social, Cultural, and Behavior Modeling (HSCB) Program has developed a modeling and simulation framework to support command-level intelligence analysis, planning, and operations decision processes. The models will provide a COM capability for social, cultural and behavioral domains.[20]

NOTES

1. Office of the Undersecretary of Defense for Acquisition, Technology and Logistics, *Report of the Joint Defense Science Board and Intelligence Science Board Task Force on Integrating Sensor-Collected Intelligence*, (November 2008) 49 ff.

2. Such factors are called "confounding" because they are extraneous variables that may influence both the cause and effect variables in a model; results of tests that do not consider the presence of such factors cannot correctly evaluate causal relationships.

3. We use the term *diagnosticity* to refer to the extent to which any item of evidence helps the analyst determine the relative likelihood of alternative hypotheses, following the definition of Heuer, Richards, *Psychology of Intelligence Analysis*, 41.

4. Arbetter, Robert and Mark Phillips, "Advancements in Intelligence Analysis: Activity Based Intelligence and Human Domain Analytics," Presented at Intelligence Analysis & Processing Summit, Washington, DC, December 6, 2011.

5. Timm, Adam, "Persistent Surveillance Support to Targeting," NGA Briefing to Precision Strike Association Technology Symposium, October 28, 2009.

6. See chapter 3 "Intelligence in Counterinsurgency," in FM 3-24, Counterinsurgency, (Washington, DC: Headquarters Department of the Army, December 15, 2006).

7. Flynn, Michael T ., Rich Juergens, and Thomas L . Cantrell, "Employing ISR SOF Best Practices," *Joint Forces* Quarterly, issue 50, (3rd quarter 2008) 59. At the time of writing, MG Michael T. Flynn was the Deputy Chief of Staff, Intelligence (CJ2) for the International Security Assistance Force (ISAF) in Afghanistan.

8. Ibid., 58; the three bullet paragraphs are quoted in their entirety.

9. For a description of pattern of life analysis process in a joint targeting cell to determine the identity and "targetability" of an individual or group and the roles in developing a collateral damage estimate (CDE), see pages14–15 of Garrett, James F. Col. (USA), *Necessity and Proportionality in the Operation Enduring Freedom VII Campaign*, United States Army, Strategy Research paper, (Carlisle Barracks, PA: U.S. Army War College, 2008). See pages 19–21 for a description of the use of pattern of life information derived from full motion video (FMV) in monitoring, selecting, and targeting a Taliban compound in Afghanistan during Operation Mountain Thrust in July 2006.

10. Bodnar, John W., *Warning Analysis for the Information Age: Rethinking the Intelligence Process*, Washington, DC: Joint Military Intelligence College: December 2003, chapter 9, "Modeling the Target."

11. Ibid.

12. Anderson, Ed; Nazli Choucri, Daniel Goldsmith, Stuart E. Madnick, Michael Siegel, and Dan Sturtevant, *System Dynamics Modeling for Proactive Intelligence*, Final Technical Report, AFRL-RI-RS-TR-2010-32, ADA514594, (January 2010), 15–21.

13. For a description of systems dynamics modeling methods and the graphical nomenclatures, see Sterman, J., *Business Dynamics: System Thinking and Modeling for a Complex World*, (New York: McGraw-Hill, 2000).

14. Malinchik, Sergey and Janet Wedgewood, "Dynamic Gaming Platform," Final Technical Report AFRL-RI-RS-TR-2009-100, ADA498356, Lockheed Martin Corporation, (April 2009).

15. Pearl, J. *Causality: Models, Reasoning, and Inference*, 2nd edition (New York: Cambridge University Press, 2009). See also Spirtes, P., C. Glymour, and R. Scheines, *Causation, Prediction, and Search*. 2nd edition (Cambridge, MA: MIT Press, 2000) and McClendon, McKee J., *Multiple Regression and Causal Analysis*, (Utasca, IL: Peacock Publishers,1994).

16. The ability to discriminate between two distributions is fundamental to statistical classification theory, and the performance measures for any decision rule to distinguish between H_1 and H_2 are the detection probability and false alarm probability (PD and PFA, respectively). Texts on statistical classification, detection theory (in radar and communications) and decision theory develop the methods to select decision rules, using the receiver operating characteristic (ROC) curve to establish the PD and PFA for any given set of statistical distributions for H_1 and H_2. For a basic introduction, see the author's derivation in chapter 4 "Sensors, Sources and Communication Links" in E. Waltz, and J. Llinas, *Multisensor Data Fusion*, (Boston: Artech, 1990), 80–88.

17. Chairman of the Joint Chiefs of Staff Message, "Joint Intelligence Operations Center (JIOC) Execute Order (EXORD) (U)," April 3, 2006. For example, see, Maritime Headquarters with Maritime Operations Center Concept of Operations (CONOPS), U.S. Fleet Forces Command, March 13, 2007, 41–42.

18. Deep Green BAA 07-56 Defense Advanced Research Projects Agency (DARPA) Information Processing Technology Office (IPTO), (October 16, 2007).

19. Integrated Munitions Effects Assessment/ Underground Targeting and Analysis System (IMEA/UTAS) Brochure, UNCLASSIFIED unlimited dissemination, Defense Threat Reduction Agency, brochure no. v-imeadtra-03, 2003.

20. Human, Social, Cultural, and Behavior Modeling (HSCB) Program, BAA 09-Q-4590, Combating Terrorism Technical Support Office, R2531 HSCB Scalable Modeling System Prototype (May 14, 2009) 6–10.

10

✛

Implementing the Discipline of Explicit Quantitative Modeling and Analytic Gaming

The modeling, analytic gaming, and simulation capabilities described in this text are not widely deployed throughout the Intelligence Community, but the increasing capabilities of technology and availability of empirical data are expanding opportunities for the disciplines to contribute to analysis. The appropriate and effective application of these explicit analytic methods will require a greater awareness of their capabilities and use, as well as training, organizational development and deployment of tools to reach their full potential.

Prior texts published by the National Intelligence University, *Critical Thinking* and *Sensemaking* by David Moore, have fully developed the basis for critical and rigorous analytic methods and have included recommended training to instill the discipline across the workforce.[1] This text complements those texts on methods with a focus on the use of models, simulations, and analytic games to enable critical and rigorous methods. It includes a recommended curriculum (appendix B) to train analysts in the methods of quantitative analysis and applied modeling, analytic gaming, and simulation for intelligence problems. We also provide considerations and approaches to support the broader implementation of models, analytic gaming, and simulation methods by analytic teams.

Because this text goes beyond introducing quantitative methods by encouraging the use of computational tools, we must first address the issues confronting the implementation of these methods that affect policy, organization, and technology implementation. The first section of this chapter identifies the challenges to implementing computational modeling capabilities and recommended approaches, before describing a recommended

241

training curriculum for analysts in the second section. The intelligence analyst is not alone in applying these capabilities and the third section identifies the numerous DoD and IC modeling and simulation organizations that are available to provide policy, standards, model repositories, and other support to intelligence modeling needs.

IMPLEMENTING MODELING CAPABILITIES

We have noted throughout this book that modeling capabilities are indeed being implemented throughout the Intelligence Community, and pioneers are applying these models, games, and simulations in creative ways to collection planning, analysis, and operations.

The analytic methods introduced in chapters 4–9 go beyond requiring the mental discipline of a methodology because they introduce the adoption of modeling and simulation technology and tools to externalize analytic thinking and represent targets of analysis. Likewise, the methods of analytic wargaming also require the application of resources that go beyond the training of another analytic methodology.

Questions about implementation that ultimately arise include:

- Where will the data to instantiate the models be acquired, and who will manage the configuration of the models?
- Who will implement the actual models and operate the modeling tools? Who will instantiate the models with data?
- Must the analysts be trained in the mathematics and computer operations of the modeling tools? Will the analysts be trained in the hands-on use of the models?
- Where is the budget for acquisition, licenses, and maintenance of the models? Will the models reside on stand-alone computers for special projects or reside on networks as organization-wide assets?

These questions require answers to issues of the appropriate roles for model-based analysis (an organizational issue) and responsibilities for resources (a policy issue). Before we answer these questions, it is helpful to recount how the IC addressed these questions over a decade ago. Consider the progress that has been made in the area of implementing spatial modeling (geographic information systems [GIS]) since the early 1990s when the Community made the transition from paper maps to digital cartographic products. In the mid-to-late 1980s the adoption of TERCOM (Terrain Contour Matching) and Digital Scene Matching Area Correlation (DSMAC) navigation methods for the Tomahawk Land Attack Missiles (TLAM) required the development of digital terrain and land-feature models.[2] The IC successfully employed these large-scale spatial modeling GIS systems by a CONOP that distinguishes model developers (today, this generally includes a support group of ArcGIS™ experts with detailed GIS methodology knowledge) who maintain foundation layers for GIS users (geospatial and all-source analysts) who have more general knowledge of GIS and focus on analytic applications. We distinguish GIS spatial modelers-methodologists who develop and maintain shape files, terrain data, and feature data sets from the complementary GEOINT and all-source intelligence analysts who are focused in a particular problem domain and use the GIS data as a tool to produce intelligence products.

This same distinction certainly applies for the spatial and nonspatial descriptive and causal models described in this text. While an individual analyst may take on the ownership of a modeling project to act as modeler and analyst, the more likely operational concept distinguishes the roles of modelers (also referred to as analytic methodologists) and analysts (table 10.1). Analytic methodologists develop and apply analytic methods to add rigor and precision to intelligence analysis and collection, providing

Table 10.1 Roles of Methodologists and Analysts

Analytic Methodologists With Modeling Expertise	Intelligence Analysts With Substantive Expertise
• Expertise in modeling methods: synthesis of computational models (data models or causal models) and use of quantitative methods to represent real-world systems. • Performs data analysis, data and causal model building, model hypothesis testing and exploration, and model validation studies. • Maintains competency in modeling tools and techniques. • Maintains repositories of data, models and results of analyses.	• Expertise in analytic methods and subject matter expertise in designated subject areas (e.g., language, culture, target systems, countries, geo politics, etc.). • Performs analysis of intelligence data, building mental, conceptual, and computational models, as appropriate, of designated subject areas. • Maintains competency in subject areas of analysis. • Maintains repositories of intelligence information and reports.
• Translates analysts' hypotheses and ⟵ contextual data to computational models. • Test models and runs exploratory ⟶ excursions for analyst. • Conduct studies of model validation ⟵ and defines data need to enhance model validity and utility of models for analytic purposes.	• Develops intelligence requirements, analyzes evidence, frames problems, and develops hypotheses. • Evaluates model-based representations of hypotheses. • Recommends hypothesis refinements and needs for additional data.

statistical, operations research, econometric, mathematical, or geospatial modeling support to intelligence analysis.[3] The benefits of teaming analytic methodologists, including quantitative modelers, with analysts with substantive expertise has been described by Johnston, who concluded,

> In order to overcome heuristic biases, intelligence agencies need to focus personnel, resources, and training on developing intelligence methodologists. These methodologists will act as in-house consultants for analytic teams, generate new methods specific to intelligence analysis, modify and improve existing methods of analysis, and increase the professionalization of the discipline of intelligence.[4]

The largest looming issues facing any effort to introduce a new modeling, analytic gaming, or simulation capability into an organization is the assignment of responsibilities to those who will build, maintain, and accredit for use the models within the simulation. Any organization initiative must consider the benefits of data and model reuse (e.g., cost-savings, cross-validation, learning curve, etc.) to allow the resources to be amortized across multiple users where appropriate. Reuse and collaborative model development can be accomplished with a data and model library (DML) that maintains baseline component models and integrated models and results. The DML maintains raw data sets (e.g., demographic data on a particular urban population) as well as basic models (e.g., a general urban population model) and model instantiations (e.g., a population behavior model instantiated for a particular province). The model repositories of the DML can be implemented as an electronic model code repository, "ModelForge," in a centralized location for approved model developers to control and manage open-source model development.[5] The efforts required to maintain a modeling support unit include the following key functions:

1. *Model requirements definition and analysis*—Perform and document the requirements for conceptual and computational models; document these requirements, the analyses that developed them, and traceable links to underlying theories and empirical data.
2. *Model concept planning and development*—Based on model requirements, develop conceptual model descriptions (narrative, graphical, network, spreadsheet, etc.) and define the appropriate computational modeling paradigms (e.g., discrete-time, system, dynamics, agent-based, Bayesian, Markov, Petri net, etc.) to implement the model requirements.
3. *Component model design and development*—Design, implement and develop (test, refine, debug) model components using commercial and custom model-building tools.

4. *Integrated model design and development*—Design, and integrate (or "dock") model components into composite models that represent entire interacting systems.
5. *Model verification test and evaluation*—Define testing and evaluation criteria to assess the structure and behavior of computational models (component models and integrated models) for purposes of verification that the models meet requirements. Prepare model test and evaluation plans; conduct verification testing and document results.
6. *DML repository and ModelForge maintenance*—Maintain the data set and model code repository for authorized users. Provide appropriate services to allow model sharing, reuse, collaborative development, configuration management, and access authorization.
7. *Configuration management*—Maintain configuration control over models within the DML implemented in ModelForge.
8. *Component/system certification*—Provide certification criteria and services to allow users to distinguish models that have achieved a level of certification by certifying authorities (e.g., Afghan opium production model version 3.2.2 certified for use by CENTCOM).
9. *Training services*—Develop and provide modeling training courses to introduce the principles, methods, and procedures to enable analysts to apply modeling, analytic gaming, and simulation capabilities.

TEACHING MODELING, GAMING, AND SIMULATION

There exist graduate-level structured analysis courses across the agencies of the Intelligence Community, and there exist more narrowly focused courses on quantitative analysis in specific domains (e.g., financial analysis, geospatial analysis), but there is no formal training in applied modeling, gaming, and simulation to intelligence analysis.

Appendix B provides a recommended twelve-section course to provide the background necessary to acquaint intelligence analysts with the theory, principles, literature, and application of the capabilities of modeling, simulation, and analytic gaming to a wide range of intelligence problems. The course is suitable for graduate-level training with sufficient exercises to provide practical knowledge that will enable an analyst to apply the methods to range of problems.

PARTNERING WITH THE DOD MODELING, GAMING, AND SIMULATION COMMUNITY

The DoD and Intelligence Community maintain extensive and diverse modeling, wargaming, and simulation capabilities that may be leveraged by the intelligence analyst seeking to apply these methods. The DoD analytic community includes a wide variety of applications:

- *Operational Analysis*—J8 and other analytic organizations support planning by conducting operational analyses of future threats and situations to evaluate alternative force structures, weapon systems, and operational concepts. Simulation and wargames are applied to explore future scenarios to analyze the effects of alternative operational plans.
- *Planning*—Operational planning units develop courses of action (COAs) and perform a rigorous COA analysis process using wargaming methods and modeling and simulation tools.[6]
- *Training*—Realistic models and simulations are used to present visual, geospatial, temporal, and causal information to students and operational forces in individual or combined training exercises combining live, virtual, and constructive simulations.[7]
- *Experimentation*—As in training, models and simulations of advanced systems and future threat scenarios are used to evaluate the relative benefits of candidate operations and systems.
- *Acquisition*—Financial, programmatic, and logistical modeling are used to support the planning and monitoring of system acquisition programs.
- *Testing and Evaluation*—System performance and force effectiveness modeling is conducted to support system and operational concept testing.

The DoD modeling and simulation community has a senior-level steering group that fosters coordination and collaboration across these applications to provide the benefits of:

- establishing common standards for data and model representations to facilitate interoperability between models;
- establishing model use, validation and accreditation procedures;
- maintaining registries (and in some cases repositories) of models, simulation tools, analysis, simulation results, scenarios, best practices, and reference data sets to enable sharing and reuse. and
- providing mechanisms for collaboration among model developers and analysts.

The DoD Modeling and Simulation Coordination Office (M&S CO) performs the key corporate-level coordination functions necessary to encourage cooperation, synergism, and cost-effectiveness among the model and simulation activities of the DoD components; the Executive

Secretariat for DoD M&S Management, in fostering the interoperability, reuse, and affordability of crosscutting model and simulation, provides improved capabilities for DoD operations.

The DoD modeling, wargaming, and simulation community (table 10.2) also has professional organizations that share analytic methods, results, and best practices; similar modeling and simulation communities within the IC can be found on Intelink. The Military Operations Research Society (MORS) is a society for DoD, industry, and academia professionals, holding an annual symposium in June of each year (with both unclassified and classified sessions) as well as four to five workshops each year. MORS publishes symposia proceedings as well as a newsletter

Table 10.2 Defense Modeling, Simulation, and Wargaming Organizations

US DOD M&S Organizations

- DoD Modeling and Simulation Coordination Office (M&S CO) http://www.msco.mil/
- Information Analysis Center (MSIAC) Modeling & Simulation http://www.dod-msiac.org/
- DoD Modeling and Simulation Resource Repository (MSRR) http://www.dod-msiac.org/
- DoD Standards Vetting Tool (DSVT) http://140.32.24.71/
- DoD VV&A Documentation Tool (DVDT) http://dvdt.nmso.navy.mil

US Military Services M&S Organizations

- Army Modeling & Simulation Directorate http://www.ms.army.mil/
- Army Program Executive Office for Simulation, Training and Instrumentation (PEO STRI) http://www.peostri.army.mil/
- Navy Modeling & Simulation Office (NMSO) https://nmso.navy.mil/
- Air Force Agency for Modeling & Simulation (AFAMS) (Public) http://www.afams.af.mil/
- Air Force Environment Scenario Generator (ESG) https://esg.afccc.af.mil/index.php; and https://ine.aer.com/esgsite/; and ESG Operational Test & Evaluation https://ine.aer.com/
- Marine Corps M&S Management Office (MCMSMO) https://www.mccdc.usmc.mil/MCMSMO/index.htm

NATO M&S Organization

- NATO Modelling and Simulation Group (NMSG) http://www.rta.nato.int/panel.asp?panel=MSG
- Technical Cooperation Program (TTCP)—Joint Australia, Canada, New Zealand, the United Kingdom, and the United States. http://www.dtic.mil/ttcp/

Centers of Wargaming Analysis

- Army Us Army War College (Carlisle Barracks)
- Navy–Center for Naval Analysis (CNA) http://www.cna.org/
- Air Force Wargaming Institute (Maxwell AFB)
- Marine Corps Warfighting Laboratory—Wargaming Division http://www.marines.mil/unit/mcwl/Pages/Wargaming.aspx

(PHALANX), a journal, and professional books.[8] Within DoD, the Joint Collaboration Analysis Conference (JCAC) is a Joint Staff led semiannual forum of J8 and other analysts that is focused on combatant commander analysis needs and capabilities.

The U.S. actively participates in the NATO Research and Technology Organization (RTO) that has responsibility for research and application of operations analysis methodologies and tool technologies, and includes a dedicated Modelling and Simulation Group (NMSG).

These organizations maintain significant experience, methods, and models that may be leveraged by the intelligence analyst who seeks to apply the methods to difficult analytic problems. In addition, many of these users (e.g., operations analysts and planners) would welcome simulation-savvy analysts who provide quantitative modeling products of threats and situations that are suitable for their analytic needs.

Intelligence analysts and units that successfully partner with these organizations have adopted the following practices:

- Attend government and professional conferences that report on current and emerging analytic methods as well as modeling and simulation technologies.
- Participate in relevant wargames to understand the relative benefits of these activities to their domain of analysis.
- Contact R&D investigators (e.g., at IARPA, DARPA and Science and Technology directorates at intelligence agencies) to establish the current state of the art for modeling and simulation technologies applied to different intelligence domains.

This community has steadily expanded the application of quantitative analysis, developing new applied methodologies, increasing confidence in the validity of modeling and simulation results, and supporting analysts with existing standards, tools, and data.

NOTES

1. Moore, David T., *Critical Thinking and Intelligence Analysis*, Occasional Paper Number 14 (Washington, DC: National Defense Intelligence College, March 2007); and Moore, David T. *Sensemaking: A Structure for an Intelligence Revolution* (Washington, DC: National Defense Intelligence College, March 2011).

2. For an extensive history of the transition from paper-based maps to digital cartography and geographic information systems in intelligence, see Cloud, John, "American Cartographic Transformations during the Cold War," *Cartography and Geographic Information Science* 29, no. 3 (2002), 261–82.

3. This description is based on the CIA definition of analytic methodologist. See https://www.cia.gov/careers/opportunities/analytical/analytic-methodologist .html.

4. Johnston, Rob, "Reducing Analytic Error: Integrating Methodologists into Teams of Substantive Experts," *Studies in Intelligence* 47, no. 1 (Washington, DC: Center for the Study of Intelligence), 57–65.

5. The "ModelForge" concept follows the successful sourceforge.net open source software implementation model, allowing model sharing, development, enhancement, and collaboration among the modeling community.

6. Modeling, wargaming, and simulation are specifically applied by operational planners to a rigorous *COA Analysis*, the process of closely examining potential COAs to reveal details that will allow the commander and staff to tentatively identify COAs that are valid and then compare these COAs. COA analysis identifies advantages and disadvantages of each proposed friendly COA. The commander and staff analyze each tentative COA separately according to the commander's guidance. Wargaming is a primary means to conduct this analysis. *Wargaming* is a conscious attempt to visualize the flow of the operation, given joint force strengths and dispositions, adversary capabilities and possible COAs, the operational area, and other aspects of the operational environment. The COA analysis process, using wargaming as well as modeling and simulation analysis tools is described in Joint Publication 5-0 *Joint Operational Planning*, August 11, 2011, pages iv, 27–36.

7. The DoD distinguishes three categories of training simulations: 1) *Live Simulations* are those simulation involving real people operating real systems, 2) *Virtual Simulations* inject human-in-the-loop in a central role by exercising motor control skills (e.g., flying an airplane), decision skills (e.g., committing fire control resources to action), or communication skills (e.g., as members of a C4I team), and 3) *Constructive Simulations* are models and simulations that involve simulated people operating simulated systems. Real people stimulate (make inputs) to such simulations, but are not involved in determining the outcomes. See DoD 5000.59-P, "Modeling and Simulation Master Plan," October 1995.

8. The Military Operations Research Society, www.mors.org.

Appendix A
Glossary

This glossary provides a reference to analysis-related modeling terms that are used throughout the text and in common practice by the modeling, analytic gaming, and simulation community. Some definitions are annotated with sources if adopted from: Joint Publication 1-02, "DOD Dictionary of Military and Associated Terms" (JP 1-02); DoD 5000.59-M DoD Modeling and Simulation (M&S) Glossary (DoD M&S); or Joint Forces Command (JFCOM).

Abductive Reasoning—The informal or pragmatic mode of reasoning that synthesizes alternative explanations and then assesses their feasibility to identify the "best explanation"; abduction is the imaginative or creative process that extends a belief *beyond the original premises.*

Analytic Game—An exploratory and assessment methodology that employs human players participating to achieve objectives, often competitively, in a synthetic situation that requires human decision making under constraints of the game with consequences of their actions determined by the dynamics of play.

Assessment—An evaluation or estimation of the nature, characteristics or properties of an intelligence subject.

Cognitive Task Analysis—The process of analyzing the knowledge, thought processes, and goal structures that underlie observable performance of cognitive tasks, such as intelligence analysis.

Convergent Forms of Reasoning—Thinking processes that marshal information to converge on a solution or belief.

Counterfactual (Hypothetical) Reasoning—The thinking processes that conceives conditional claims about alternate possibilities (*hypotheticals*) and their consequences.

Critical Thinking—The conscious style of thinking that improves the quality of thinking by applying skillful disciplines of reasoning that conform to critical intellectual standards.

Descriptive Model—A model used to depict the behavior or properties of an existing system or type of system. Contrast with: Prescriptive Model.

Deterministic Model—A model in which the results are determined through known relationships among the states and events and in which a given input will always produce the same output. Contrast with: Stochastic Model.

Diagnosticity—The significance or diagnostic value to support, refute, or distinguish between hypotheses; evidence that uniquely supports a single hypothesis is more diagnostic than evidence that supports multiple hypotheses.

Dimensions—Independent and measurable aspects of a domain; generally the number of degrees of freedom available for movement within a domain, represented as a vector space.

Discovery of Causal Relationships—Methods of inferring structural information on causal relationships from behavioral data about a system. This information may be used to develop causal models (by induction) that generalize descriptions of internal causal processes in the system that give rise to the observed behavior.

Deductive Reasoning—The inferential process that moves from general beliefs to particular beliefs (or from cause to effect); a conclusion is inferred by applying the rules of a logical system to manipulate statements of belief to form new logically consistent statements of belief.

DIME—A decomposition of actions that may be taken by a nation in competition, conflict, and combat: Diplomatic, Information, Military, Economic (JFCOM).

Divergent Forms of Reasoning—Thinking processes that are stimulated to explore a wide range of perspectives, lines of thinking, and alternatives to search for novel or creative solutions not immediately apparent.

Domain—A category of reality to be abstracted, represented, and modeled within the modeling environment.

Effect—1. The physical or behavioral state of a system that results from an action, a set of actions, or another effect. 2. The result, outcome, or consequence of an action. 3. A change to a condition, behavior, or degree of freedom. (JP 1-02) 4. The physical or behavioral state of a PMESII system that results from a military or non-military action or set of (DIME) actions (JFCOM).

Empirical Data Models—Mathematically derived functions that relate dependent output variables to independent variables; the mathematical derivation of the model function is based on the analysis of empirical data sets, and these models are also referred to as *empirical models*.

External Cognition—The means by which people augment their normal cognitive processes with external aids, such as external writings, visualizations, and work spaces. External cognition combines internal cognition with perception and manipulation of external representations of information.

Extraction—The process of detecting, classifying, parsing, and organizing entities, relationships and attributes from unstructured data (e.g., free text) and translating that data to a structured format (e.g., a relational database, or RDF "Resource Description Framework" triple sets of subject-predicate-object) suitable for use in computational models and simulations.

Generic Model—An Instantiated Model created using a set of generic objects, entities, behaviors, etc., and their interactions, based on general substantive knowledge.

Hypothesis A proposition or tentative explanation that is asserted with supporting reasoning; tests may be deduced from the hypothesis to determine if belief in the hypothesis is justified.

Inductive Reasoning—The inferential process that moves from particular beliefs to general principles or hypotheses; a more general or more abstract belief is developed by observing a limited set of observations or instances.

Instantiated Model—The result of employing a Modeling Tool to create a specific instance of particular objects, entities, behaviors, etc., and their interaction, based on substantive knowledge.

Intellective Model—A model that contains analogous entities, constructs, and complexities of the modeled systems rather than mimicking each specific behavior. Used to explore complex system behavior. Opposite: Demonstrative Model.

Judgment—The result of a logical inference from available information or the result of explicit tests of hypotheses.

Metareasoning—The process of reasoning about the reasoning process itself; introspection about self.

Model—1. A physical, mathematical, or otherwise logical representation of a system, entity, phenomenon, or process. (DoD M&S) 2. An instantiation of a PMESII system using the formal data structures of a Modeling Tool. Given appropriate initial or boundary conditions, the Model may be evolved, optimized, or otherwise solved by a Modeling Tool.

Model Accuracy—The degree to which a parameter or variable, or a set of parameters or variables, within a model or simulation conforms exactly to reality or to some chosen standard or reference. (DoD M&S)

Model, Computational—Conceptual models and simulations implemented on computers that allow manipulation of the structure and dynamics to perform analysis, exploration, gaming, and planning.

Model, Conceptual—An analyst's *explicit knowledge*, or codified and shareable representations of mental models that are used to describe, explain, and explore concepts.

Model Fidelity—The degree to which a model or simulation reproduces the state and behavior of a real-world object or the perception of a real-world object, feature, condition, or chosen standard in a measurable or perceivable manner; a measure of the realism of a model or simulation; faithfulness. Fidelity should generally be described with respect to the measures, standards, or perceptions used in assessing or stating it. (DoD M&S)

Model Granularity (or Resolution)—The degree of detail and precision used in the representation of real-world aspects in a model or simulation.

Model, Mental—The cognitive structures of associated concepts held consciously or subconsciously, forming an analyst's perception of reality; they are the mechanisms whereby humans are able to generate descriptions of system purpose and form, explanations of system functioning and observed system states, and predictions of future system states.

Model Validation—The process of determining the degree to which a model and its associated data are an accurate representation of the real world from the perspective of the intended uses of the model. (DoD M&S)

Modeling Paradigm—A general class of modeling technology or approach, such as agent-based simulation, dynamic network, or Bayesian Network.

Modeling Tool—Capabilities to aid users in the construction of static models and dynamic simulations that represent particular instances of real-world behavior. A software application that captures a modeling formalism, structure, and dynamic representations and then provides the ability to develop, edit, store, visualize, and operate the model or simulation.

Multi-Resolution Model (MRM)—A composite model that incorporates multiple related models that operate at different levels of functional and causal granularity. A system of interacting models that are organized to account for different levels of descriptive granularity. In a multi-resolution model, all component system models are not required to be modeled at a common granularity (e.g., spatial or functional resolution).

PMESII—The decomposition of a society into six fundamental elements for purposes of description and modeling: Political, Military, Economic, Social, Information, and Infrastructure. (JFCOM)

- **Political System**—A system comprised of any grouping of primarily civil roles and institutions, both formal and informal, that exercises authority or rule within a specific geographic boundary or organization, through the application of various forms of political power and influence.
- **Military System**—A system comprised of the armed forces and supporting infrastructure, all of which are acquired, trained, developed and sustained to accomplish and protect national or organizational security objectives.
- **Economic System**—A system composed of the sum total production, distribution, and consumption of all goods and services in a country.
- **Social System**—A system that is a network of social relationships that is organized and integrated and shares a common value system. (Alternate) Social System is an interdependent network of social institutions, statuses, and roles that support, enable, and acculturate individuals and that provides participatory opportunities to achieve personal expectations and life goals within hereditary and nonhereditary groups, in either stable or unstable environments.
- **Infrastructure System**—A system composed of the basic facilities, interconnections, services, and resources to support the functioning of a community or society (e.g., electrical power, water, sanitary, food supply, transportation, etc.).
- **Information System**—A system comprised of the entire infrastructure, organization, personnel, and components that collect, process, store, transmit, display, disseminate, and act on information. (JP 1-02)

Prescriptive Model—A model used to convey the required behavior or properties of a proposed system; for example, a scale model or written specification used to convey to a computer supplier the physical and performance characteristics of a required computer. Contrast with: Descriptive Model. (DoD M&S)

Reasoning—The deliberate thought processes that seek a solution by applying logic, argumentation, imagination, creativity, and evaluation. A *line of reasoning* is the specific framework or path that is used to move from evidence, via argument, to a conclusion or judgment.

Retroductive Reasoning—The feedback process that occurs when a new conceptual hypothesis is conjectured that causes a return to the pool of information to seek evidence to match (or test) this new hypothesis.

Simulation—A method for implementing a model over time. Models are essentially static representations, while simulations add dynamic (temporal) behavior. (DoD M&S)

Sensemaking—The thinking process by which people assign meaning to experience by placing information in context to create understanding and develop beliefs about things, associations, and causality.

Situation Awareness—The perception of the elements in the environment within a volume of time and space, the comprehension of their meaning, and the projection of their status in the near future.

State—The complete set of properties that describe the unique condition of a system at a point in time.

Stochastic Model—A model in which the results are determined by using one or more random variables to represent uncertainty about a process or in which a given input will produce an output, according to some statistical distribution. Opposite: Deterministic Model. (DoD M&S)

Structured Analysis—A mechanism by which internal thought processes are externalized in a systematic and transparent manner so they can be shared, built upon, and easily critiqued by others.

Theoretical Model—A model that represents the internal elements and functions of a situation or system, based on some theory of how the system operates. The model is referred to as a *causal model* because it attempts to explicitly represent causality—the relationship between external driving causes and the effects (or outputs) of the system.

Transactive Memory (also called "Group Mind")—The set of individual memories operating in combination with the communication that takes place between individuals. It is this collective and shared memory that enables collaboration processes.

Use Case—A detailed narrative description of a single, specific activity in a business process from an end-user perspective. Use cases describe how an end-user will conduct his day-to-day activities using the software application being developed. The use case identifies preconditions, data inputs and outputs and performance/timing requirements and interfaces with external applications. Because a workflow may have many different paths (or "threads") through the business process, multiple use cases are used to describe the many different ways that a user may use an application.

Validation—The process of determining the degree to which a model and its associated data are an accurate representation of the real world from the perspective of the intended uses of the model. (DoD M&S)

Validity—The measure of how appropriate the model is for it intended use and *validation* is the process of determining the degree to which a model or simulation is an accurate representation of the real world *from the perspective of the intended uses of the model or simulation.* (DoD M&S)

Variable—An object whose attributes may assume any one of a set of values

Verification—The process of determining that a model implementation and its associated data accurately represents the developer's conceptual description and specifications. (DoD M&S)

Wargaming—A conscious attempt to visualize the flow of the operation, given joint force strengths and dispositions, adversary capabilities and possible courses of action (COAs), the operational area, and other aspects of the operational environment. (Joint Publication 5-0 *Joint Operational Planning*)

Work Flow—A narrative and/or graphical description of the general or typical process steps of a business cycle (e.g., military planning process, intelligence cycle, etc.); the description articulates the actions of people and associated automated processes. The workflow describes the steps, the actions, and the decisions at each step, alternate paths, and the flow of information that moves from problem to solution.

Appendix B

A Course in Modeling, Simulation, and Analytic Gaming for Intelligence

In this appendix we introduce a recommended 12-section course to provide the background necessary to acquaint intelligence analysts with the theory, principles, literature, and application of these capabilities and apply them to a wide range of analytic problems.[1]

MODELING, GAMING, AND SIMULATION COURSE DESCRIPTION

This course introduces the concepts and methods of developing explicit models of analytic thinking and intelligence subjects and teaches the techniques to apply those models to intelligence problems. The course introduces the methods of analytic modeling, the use of analytic games, and computational models and simulations to support the analytic process. The course focuses on the translation of mental models to conceptual representations and then to computational models, emphasizing practical examples of the use of modeling and simulation tools in intelligence problems.

Learning Objectives

- Distinguish the roles of mental, conceptual, and computational models in intelligence analysis.
- Understand and distinguish the basic schemas (narrative, spatial, temporal, and causal) for quantitative representation of information in models.

- Understand how to translate mental models to explicit qualitative and quantitative conceptual representations.
- Be able to represent the analytic thought process in a model of the structure of analysis.
- Be able to represent target subjects (physical, nonphysical, and human systems) in explicit static models and dynamic simulations.
- Understand the potential benefits and the limits of models, games, and simulations to analytic problems; know when such methods are appropriate analytic tools and when they are not.
- Apply the method of dynamic analysis to support planners' requirements to assess potential outcomes of alternative courses of action.
- Report the results of model, analytic game, and simulation methods in analytic products that communicate the knowledge provided by these means.

Course Design

This course is designed to introduce the student to the appropriate role and application of quantitative and computational modeling, analytic gaming, and simulation to challenging intelligence problems. The course provides appropriate reading assignments, eleven 4-hour classroom lectures and discussions, class assignments that introduce explicit analytic methods, and team class projects that involve small teams of students applying the methods on representative intelligence problems.

Final Project:

Students will work in small teams to select an operational problem to be modeled and analyzed using at least one method to represent analytic thinking and one method to represent the subject of analysis—a target system. The project results will be presented at the last class, in the form of an intelligence briefing describing the results of analysis.

Required Texts

- Waltz, Edward, *Quantitative Intelligence Analysis: Applied Analytic Models, Simulations and Games*, Lanham, MD: Rowman and Littlefield, 2014.
- Dörner, Dietrich, *The Logic of Failure: Recognizing and Avoiding Error in Complex Situations*, New York: Basic Books, 1997.
- Sterman, John D., *Business Dynamics: Systems Thinking and Modeling for a Complex World*, New York: Irwin/McGraw-Hill, 2000.
- Law, Averill. *Simulation Modeling and Analysis*, 4th edition, New York: McGraw Hill, 2006.

- Heuer, Richards J., Jr., The Psychology of Intelligence Analysis, Washington, DC: Center for the Study of Intelligence, 1999.
- Heuer, Richards J. and Pherson, Randolph H., *Structured Analytic Techniques for Intelligence Analysis*, Washington, DC: CQ Press, 2010.

Optional Texts and Materials

- Davenport, Thomas H. and Harris, Jeanne G., *Competing on Analytics: The New Science of Winning*, Harvard Business School Press, March 2007.
- Davenport, Thomas H. "Competing on Analytics", *Harvard Business Review*, January 2006.
- Kott, Alex and Citrenbaum, Gary (eds.), *Estimating Impact: A Handbook of Computational Methods and Models for Anticipating Economic, Social, Political and Security Effects in International Interventions*, Springer, 2009.
- Waltz, Edward, *Knowledge Management in the Intelligence Enterprise*, Boston: Artech House, 2003.
- Clark, Robert, *Intelligence Analysis: A Target-Centric Approach*, 3rd edition, Washington, DC: CQ Press, 2009.

Handout Readings

- ESRI Geospatial Intelligence Applications (Digital format copies).
- The 9-11 Commission Report, Washington, DC: GPO, 2004 (chapter 11, Foresight and Hindsight).
- *Report of the Commission on Intelligence Capabilities of the United States Regarding Weapons of Mass Destruction*, March 31, 2005 (chapter 8, Analysis).
- Strategic Plan 2007–2012: Leading the Defense Intelligence Enterprise, Defense Intelligence Agency, PCN 2822, p.13, 14.
- National Research Council. (2011). *Intelligence Analysis for Tomorrow: Advances from the Behavioral and Social Sciences.* Committee on Behavioral and Social Science Research to Improve Intelligence Analysis for National Security, Board on Behavioral, Cognitive, and Sensory Sciences, Division of Behavioral and Social Sciences and Education. Washington, DC: The National Academies Press.
- Report of the Defense Science Board Task Force on Understanding Human Dynamics, Office of the Under Secretary of Defense for Acquisition, Technology, and Logistics, Washington, DC, March 2009.
- Moore, David T. *Critical Thinking and Intelligence Analysis*, Occasional Paper 14, National Defense Intelligence College, May 2006.

- Moore, David T. *Sensemaking: A Structure for an Intelligence Revolution*, National Defense Intelligence College, 2010.
- Noel Hendrickson, *Counterfactual Reasoning: A Basic Guide for Analysts, Strategists, and Decision Makers*, National Intelligence University, Office of the Director of National Intelligence and the Center for Strategic Leadership, U.S. Army War College, The Proteus Monograph Series, Vol. 2, Issue 5, October 2008.
- Davis, Jack, Combating Mind-Set, *Studies in Intelligence*, Vol. 36, No. 5, 1992.
- *Illuminating the Path: The Research and Development Agenda for Visual Analytics*, National Visualization and Analytics Center, Pacific Northwest National Laboratory, 2006.

Curriculum Structure

The following pages describe a representative 12-week curriculum, describing the objectives for each of the classes, the learning objectives that will be achieved by class participation covered in class, and the pre-class class reading and post-class written assignments.

CLASS 1—EXPLICIT ANALYSIS IN INTELLIGENCE

Reading Assignments

- Waltz, Edward, *Quantitative Intelligence Analysis: Applied Analytic Models, Simulations and Games*, Lanham, MD: Rowman and Littlefield, 2014 (chapter 1, The Intelligence Analysts and Synthesis).
- The 9-11 Commission Report, Washington, DC: GPO, 2004 (chapter 11, Foresight and Hindsight).
- Strategic Plan 2007–2012: Leading the Defense Intelligence Enterprise, Defense Intelligence Agency, PCN 2822, p.13, 14.
- *Report of the Commission on Intelligence Capabilities of the United States Regarding Weapons of Mass Destruction*, March 31, 2005 (chapter 8, Analysis).
- National Research Council. (2011). *Intelligence Analysis for Tomorrow: Advances from the Behavioral and Social Sciences.* Committee on Behavioral and Social Science Research to Improve Intelligence Analysis for National Security, Board on Behavioral, Cognitive, and Sensory Sciences, Division of Behavioral and Social Sciences and Education. Washington, DC: The National Academies Press (chapters 1 and 2).
- Report of the Defense Science Board Task Force on Understanding Human Dynamics, Office of the Under Secretary of Defense for Acquisition, Technology, and Logistics, Washington, DC, March 2009 (chapters 6 and 7).

Written Assignment

Prepare a table of explicit methods identified by the National Research Council (NRC) and the Defense Science Board (DSB) and the potential analytic applications of each to intelligence problems.

Class Objectives

At the end of class you will be able to:

- Describe the contrast in the activities of analysis (evidence decomposition) and synthesis (hypothesis and model composition).
- Identify at least five types of descriptive models and their use in intelligence analysis.
- Demonstrate knowledge of the benefits of explicit representation of analysis, evidence, inference, and judgment.
- Describe how explicit analytic methods (structured analysis and quantitative methods) address the shortfalls identified in *Commission on Intelligence Capabilities of the United States Regarding Weapons of Mass Destruction*.
- Describe how explicit methods comply with Intelligence Community Directive 203 "Analytic Standards."
- Describe the categories of explicit modeling methods recommended by the National Research Council to enhance intelligence analysis.
- Identify the explicit methods recommended by the Defense Science Board to support the analysis of human systems.

CLASS 2—MODELING: MENTAL, CONCEPTUAL, AND COMPUTATIONAL

Reading Assignments

- Waltz, Edward, *Quantitative Intelligence Analysis: Applied Analytic Models, Simulations and Games*, Lanham, MD: Rowman and Littlefield, 2014 (chapter 2, Modeling in Intelligence).
- David T. Moore, *Critical Thinking and Intelligence Analysis*, Occasional Paper 14, National Defense Intelligence College, March 2007 (chapter 1, What Is Critical Thinking; chapter 4, How Can Intelligence Analysts Employ Critical Thinking?).
- Noel Hendrickson, *Counterfactual Reasoning: A Basic Guide for Analysts, Strategists, and Decision Makers*, National Intelligence University, Office of the Director of National Intelligence and the Center for Strategic Leadership, U.S. Army War College, The Proteus Monograph Series, Vol. 2, Issue 5, October 2008.

Written Assignment

Prepare a paper summarizing the basic methods of critical and counter-factual reasoning, describing the role of mental and conceptual models in these methods of reasoning.

Class Objectives

At the end of class you will be able to:

- Demonstrate knowledge of the critical thinking and counterfactual reasoning processes.
- Define the explicit, coherent, and correspondence characteristics of rigorous analysis.
- Describe the top-level taxonomy of modeling terms and provide an example of each term.
- Distinguish between *descriptive* models and *action* models.
- Discuss the challenges to understanding the dynamics of systems.
- Identify the benefits of explicit models and simulations for collaborative analysis; describe three levels of depth of collaboration and explain how explicit models enable "shared thinking."
- Discuss the levels of confidence in the value of applying models to analytic problems.
- Identify the seven challenges to modeling that must be addressed by the modeler to respond to reasonable questions from intelligence consumers.

CLASS 3—ANALYTIC MENTAL MODELS

Reading Assignments

- Waltz, Edward, *Quantitative Intelligence Analysis: Applied Analytic Models, Simulations and Games*, Lanham, MD: Rowman and Little-field, 2014 (chapter 3, Mental Models in Intelligence Analysis).
- Heuer, Richards J., Jr., *The Psychology of Intelligence Analysis*, Washington: Center for the Study of Intelligence, 1999 (chapters 1–3).
- Davis, Jack, Combatting Mind-Set, *Studies in Intelligence*, Vol. 36, No. 5, 1992.
- Kahneman, Daniel, *Thinking, Fast and Slow*, New York: Farrar, Straus and Giroux, 2011 (chapters 1–9;11–12, 16, 18).
- [Optional] George, Roger Z., Fixing the Problem of Analytical Mind-sets: Alternative Analysis, in Roger Z. George and Robert D. Kline, eds., *Intelligence and the National Security Strategist*, pp. 311–26.
- [Optional] Polanyi, Michael, *The Tacit Dimension*, Garden City, NY: Doubleday, 1966.

Written Assignment

Choose an example intelligence assignment (e.g., all-source, GEOINT, COMINT, etc., analyst dedicated to a particular country or target domain) and prepare a paper describing how an area analyst uses mental models of the subject domain in conducting analysis and reporting. [Note that the selected problem will be used in written assignments in classes 4, 6, and 8 in a progressive development of the chosen example. The student should choose the intelligence assignment and domain such that it is suitable for progressive development in all four written assignments.]

Class Objectives

At the end of class you will be able to:

- Discuss the distinctions between intuition and analytic reasoning processes, and tacit and explicit knowledge—and provide examples of these cognition and knowledge types in GEOINT, SIGINT, HUMINT domains.
- Describe how mental models are used in intuitive (system 1) decision-making processes.
- Describe how mental models are used in deliberate (system 2) analytic reasoning and decision-making processes.
- Demonstrate knowledge of current understanding of the types of cognitive mental models.
- Describe how mental models are artifacts of human thinking.
- Identify the potential analytic risks posed by mental models that become mindsets.

CLASS 4—TRANSLATING MENTAL MODELS TO CONCEPTUAL MODELS

Reading Assignments

- Waltz, Edward, *Quantitative Intelligence Analysis: Applied Analytic Models, Simulations and Games*, Lanham, MD: Rowman and Littlefield, 2014 (chapter 3, Mental Models in Intelligence Analysis).
- *Illuminating the Path: The Research and Development Agenda for Visual Analytics*, National Visualization and Analytics Center, Pacific Northwest National Laboratory, 2006.
- [Optional] Tufte, Edward R., *Envisioning Information*, Cheshire, CT: Graphics Press, 1990.
- [Optional] Nonaka, Ikujiro, and Takeuchi, Hirotaka, *The Knowledge-Creating Company: How Japanese Companies Create the Dynamics of Innovation*, New York: Oxford University Press, 1995.

Written Assignment

Continuing the paper prepared in the Class 3 written assignment for a chosen analyst and target domain, extend the paper to show how the analyst frames the domain problem, selects schemas and represents a target subject explicitly to conduct a rigorous analysis.

Class Objectives

At the end of class you will be able to:

- Demonstrate knowledge of challenges and issues that analysts have for expressing their mental models of their analytic thinking and targets or objects of study in explicit representations.
- Describe the process of "framing" an analytic problem or situation and choosing schemas to represent the mental models an analyst is developing to understand it; identify the common schemas and their use in intelligence analysis.
- Describe how visualization of models performs as "external cognition," and explain the role of visual analytics in exchanging tacit and explicit knowledge.
- Apply the knowledge of tacit-explicit capture by translating and growing a conceptual model of a situation described in class, based on evidence, contextual information, and prior knowledge. Demonstrate situation framing, selection of schema(s), and conceptual representation. Explain the role of system 1 (intuition) and system 2 (analytic reasoning) in model development.
- Explain the attributes of analytic rigor and how the explicit representation of mental models contributes to rigor.

CLASS 5—MODELING IN STRUCTURED ANALYSIS

Reading Assignments

- Waltz, Edward, *Quantitative Intelligence Analysis: Applied Analytic Models, Simulations and Games*, Lanham, MD: Rowman and Littlefield, 2014 (chapter 5, Explicit Models in Structured Analysis).
- Heuer, Richards J., and Pherson, Randolph H., *Structured Analytic Techniques for Intelligence Analysis*, Washington, DC: CQ Press, 2010 (chapters 1–3).
- Cooper, Jeffrey R., *Curing Analytic Pathologies*, Center for the Study of Intelligence (CSI), December 2005 (chapters 2 and 3).
- *Tradecraft Primer: Structured Analytic Techniques for Improving Intelligence Analysis*, U.S. Government, released March 2009.

- Pirolli, Peter and Card, Stuart, The Sensemaking Process and Leverage Points for Analyst Technology as Identified Through Cognitive Task Analysis, *International Conference on Intelligence Analysis*, 2005.
- Fishbein and Treverton, Rethinking "Alternative Analysis" to Address Transnational Threats, Occasional Papers: Vol. 3, No. 2, Sherman Kent Center, 2004.

Written Assignment

Prepare a table of qualitative and qualitative analytic methods, distinguishing methods of expert judgment, structured analysis, and quantitative analysis. The table must summarize each method, the appropriate uses of the method, and an example problem appropriate for each.

Class Objectives

At the end of class you will be able to:

- Describe the distinctions between (Qualitative) Expert Judgment, (Qualitative) Structured Analytic Methods and Quantitative Methods using empirical and expert-generated data; explain the role of mental, conceptual, and computational models in each of these methods.
- Enumerate the benefits of structured analytic methodologies identified by the Intelligence Community.
- Identify the cautions in using structured and quantitative methods and the appropriate application of models to mitigate subjective human bias and judgment.
- Demonstrate knowledge of a sensemaking model of the analytic process and the role of modeling in developing schemas to represent information, and in developing hypotheses to explain evidence.
- Provide several examples of structured analytic methods and quantitative analytic methods, and explain the appropriate use of each in intelligence analysis.
- Distinguish data-driven and hypothesis-driven sensemaking processes.
- Explain the process of developing an *analytic framework* and distinguish: 1) the analytic methodology, 2) the representation method that explicitly represents a problem in conceptual models, and 3) the method to synthesize a computational model.
- Select the appropriate methods of structured and quantitative analytics for a range of intelligence problems, and explain the reasons for applying the methods to achieve rigor, openness to examination, sharing, and openness to alternatives.

CLASS 6—MODELING ANALYTIC THINKING

Reading Assignments

- Waltz, Edward, *Quantitative Intelligence Analysis: Applied Analytic Models, Simulations and Games*, Lanham, MD: Rowman and Littlefield, 2014 (chapter 6, Explicit Models of Analytic Thinking).
- Heuer, Richards J., and Pherson, Randolph H., *Structured Analytic Techniques for Intelligence Analysis*, Washington, DC: CQ Press, 2010 (chapters 7 and 8).
- [Optional] Schum, David A., *The Evidential Foundations for Probabilistic Reasoning*, Evanston, IL: Northwestern University Press, 2001.

Written Assignment

Continuing with the intelligence domain selected for Class 3 and 4, prepare a paper that develops a representative informal concept mapping of an argument for a typical problem in the domain, then translate the argument to a form as a formal structured argument tree, or in a spreadsheet as quantitative argument suitable to be represented in a computational network.

Class Objectives

At the end of class you will be able to:

- Demonstrate knowledge of empirical (empirical, data-driven) and conceptual (contextual, theory-driven) thinking and their roles in intelligence analysis.
- Enumerate and describe the major elements of analytic thinking that can be explicitly represented.
- Describe the methods to represent an analytic argument and explain the appropriate use of each in intelligence;

  o Informal concept mapping of an argument
  o Formal structured argument tree diagram
  o Quantitative argument represented in a computational network

- Define the methods to develop alternative hypotheses based on available evidence and contextual knowledge.
- Apply the technique of alterative competing hypotheses by representing hypotheses in a spreadsheet or ACH tool.
- Discuss and compare the characteristics of both qualitative and quantitative comparisons of alternative hypotheses.

CLASS 7—COMPUTATIONAL MODELING AND SIMULATION

Reading Assignments

- Waltz, Edward, *Quantitative Intelligence Analysis: Applied Analytic Models, Simulations and Games*, Lanham, MD: Rowman and Littlefield, 2014 (chapter 7, Explicit Models of Targets of Analysis).
- *GIS in the Defense and Intelligence Communities*, Redlands, California: ESRI Publication, Vols. 1–4, n.d.
- Sterman, John D. *Business Dynamics: Systems Thinking and Modeling for a Complex World*, New York: Irwin/McGraw-Hill, 2000 (chapters 1–4).
- Zacharias, Greg L. et al. (eds.), *Behavior Modeling and Simulation: From Individuals to Societies*, Washington, DC: National Academies Press, 2008 (chapters 3 and 4).
- [Optional] Law, Averill, *Simulation Modeling and Analysis*, 4th edition, McGraw Hill, (2006).
- [Optional] Shiflet, Angela B., *Introduction to Computational Science: Modeling and Simulation for the Sciences*, Princeton University Press (2006).

Written Assignment

Prepare a table enumerating at least 10 computational modeling and simulation approaches, a summary description of each, and the potential application of each to a counterproliferation intelligence problem.

Class Objectives

At the end of class you will be able to:

- Describe the process of *abstracting* a real-world intelligence target in terms of a target system suitable for analysis.
- Distinguish the methods of empirical data modeling and theoretical (causal) modeling; explain the modeling roles for each method.
- Demonstrate knowledge of empirical data modeling methods and the types of intelligence problems where data are available for such analysis.
- Demonstrate knowledge of theoretical modeling methods and the types of intelligence problems where such models are suitable for analysis; distinguish *causal explanation*, *causal inference* and *causal modeling*.
- Distinguish the purposes of abstraction, ensemble, and virtualization models that represent human behavior.

- Discuss the use of deterministic and statistical models.
- Apply the knowledge of target system modeling to:

    o Select an approach to model the behavior of a weapon manufacturing process—for the purpose of understanding how the process can be disrupted.
    o Select an approach to model the behavior of a terrorist organization, focusing on its recruitment process—for the purpose of developing methods to minimize recruitment effectiveness.
    o Select an approach to implement a hybrid model that represents a narcotics organization, its financial operations, and its physical shipping process—for the purpose of developing methods to target its financial viability.

CLASS 8—DYNAMIC MODELING OF TARGET SYSTEMS

Reading Assignments

- Waltz, Edward, *Quantitative Intelligence Analysis: Applied Analytic Models, Simulations and Games*, Lanham, MD: Rowman and Littlefield, 2014 (chapter 7, Explicit Models of Targets of Analysis).
- Sterman, John D., *Business Dynamics: Systems Thinking and Modeling for a Complex World*, New York: Irwin/McGraw-Hill, 2000 (chapters 5–8).
- Zacharias, Greg L., et al. (eds.), *Behavior Modeling and Simulation: From Individuals to Societies*, Washington, DC: National Academies Press, 2008 (chapters 5 and 6).

Written Assignment

Continuing with the intelligence domain selected for Class 3 and 4 and continued in Class 6, prepare a decomposition paper that abstracts a representative intelligence situation, develops a conceptual model of the target system, and selects an appropriate modeling or simulation approach. The paper should provide the high-level specification suitable for an analytic methodologist to build an appropriate model.

Class Objectives

At the end of class you will be able to:

- Demonstrate knowledge of the major alternative methods of computational simulation, including: Bayes Nets, System Dynamics, and

Agent-based simulation and their application to dynamic modeling and simulation.

- Describe the appropriate use of computational models for intelligence analysis in each of the following categories:

  o Spatial modeling with geographic information system (GIS) tools;
  o Physical system modeling with system dynamics tools;
  o Human behavior and social system modeling with agent based models.

- Describe how to abstract and decompose an alternatives analysis problem into a Bayesian network and explain how to implement that network in a Bayesian modeling tool, such as Netica™.
- Describe how to abstract a physical system problem in causal diagrams, and then describe how to represent the system in a system dynamics model that distinguishes stock, flows, and relationships; demonstrate the ability to implement the model in a system dynamics tool, such as Stella™ or VenSim™. Explain how the model can be used to simulate dynamic behavior and represent the major characteristics, operating vulnerabilities, and instabilities.
- Describe how to abstract a human system problem and then describe how to represent the system in an agent-based simulation using appropriate agent-model building tools. Explain how the simulation can represent group decision-making behavior.

CLASS 9—ANALYTIC GAMING

Reading Assignments

- Waltz, Edward, *Quantitative Intelligence Analysis: Applied Analytic Models, Simulations and Games*, Lanham, MD: Rowman and Littlefield, 2014 (chapter 8, Analytic Wargaming in Intelligence).
- McCown, Margaret M. Strategic Gaming for the National Security Community, *JointForces Quarterly*, Issue 39, 2009, pp. 34–39.
- Hanig, Rachel K. and Henshaw, Mark E. To Improve Analytical Insight: Needed—A National Security Simulation Center, *Studies in Intelligence*, Washington, DC: Center for the Study of Intelligence, Vol. 52, No. 2, June 2008.

Written Assignment

Prepare an analytic game design paper, describing the design of a game to develop a range of alternative collection approaches to understand the decision-making calculus of a closed regime.

Class Objectives

At the end of class you will be able to:

- Explain the unique role of analytic gaming in exploration and learning, assessment, and training.
- Distinguish between "analytic games" and "analytic methods" applied in operational analyses; explain the relative roles of each method and how they are complementary.
- Discuss why analytic games are never identical nor repeatable and why the elements of human behavior, interaction, and decision making contribute to their analytic value.
- Describe the categories of analyses, games, and operational exercises.
- Explain how an analytic game may be applied to representative intelligence collection, operations planning, or analysis problems.
- Apply the principles of game development to a representative intelligence problem, identifying the appropriate type of game for the problems, the major steps in developing the game, and the key design choices that must be considered.
- Explain the role of computational models and simulations in analytic games and the different ways in which they can be applied.
- Apply knowledge of analytic games by participating in a classroom analytic game exercise.
- Explain how studies have shown that the activities involved in games can contribute to intelligence work group effectiveness.

CLASS 10—MODEL-BASED SUPPORT
TO COLLECTION AND OPERATIONS

Reading Assignments

- Waltz, Edward, *Quantitative Intelligence Analysis: Applied Analytic Models, Simulations and Games*, Lanham, MD: Rowman and Littlefield, 2014 (chapter 9, Model-based Support to Collection and Operations).
- Joint Chiefs of Staff (2009) Joint Publications (JP) 2-01.3, *Joint Intelligence Preparation of the Operational Environment*, June 16, 2009.
- Waltz, Ed, "Anticipatory Intelligence Analysis: Integrating Multiple Models for Joint Intelligence Preparation," *Proceedings of IEEE Conference on Intelligence Security and Informatics; Workshop on Predictive Analytics for Intelligence Security Applications*, May 2010.
- Klein, Robert M., "Adaptive Planning," *Joint Forces Quarterly, JFQ* Issue, 2nd quarter 2007, pp. 84--88.

Written Assignment

Prepare a paper applying the Multidimensional Analysis (MDA) methodology to develop a conceptual model of narcotics organization, and explain how the model could be translated to an appropriate computational model to develop probes to test the hypothesis that the organization is factional and unstable.

Class Objectives

At the end of class you will be able to:

- Describe the process of Joint Preparation of the Operational Environment (JIPOE).
- Describe the concept of model-based approach to data fusion and demonstrate knowledge of roles of models and simulations to support Intelligence Surveillance and Reconnaissance collection for difficult target systems.
- Describe the elements of a model-based analytic approach and explain the closed-loop process that develops and tests hypotheses, then refines models.
- Describe the role of conceptual and computational models in the model-based approach.
- Explain the fundamentals of Activity Based Intelligence (ABI) and provide examples of *patterns of life* for typical human target systems.
- Apply the model-based Multidimensional Analysis (MDA) methodology to structure the analysis of a foreign organization.
- Explain how models are used to aid in *model refinement* and in *hypothesis testing*.
- Describe the appropriate conditions for applying, and the methods of implementing, computational models of organizations and their activities or processes.
- Demonstrate the ability to apply a model-based approach to the JIPOE process for a difficult target system, such as a foreign weapons of mass destruction (WND) threat.
- Explain the potential roles of explicit models in Joint Intelligence and Operations coordination.

CLASS 11—VALIDATION OF MODELS [OPTIONAL]

Reading Assignments

- Waltz, Edward, *Quantitative Intelligence Analysis: Applied Analytic Models, Simulations and Games*, Lanham, MD: Rowman and Littlefield, 2014 (chapter 7, Explicit Models of Targets of Analysis).

- Conceptual Model Development and Validation, Defense Modeling and Simulation Office (DMSO) RPG Special Topic, September 15, 2006.
- A Practitioner's Perspective on Simulation Validation, Defense Modeling and Simulation Office (DMSO) RPG Reference Document, August, 152001.
- Zacharias, Greg L., et al. (eds.), *Behavior Modeling and Simulation: From Individuals to Societies*, Washington, DC: National Academies Press, 2008 (chapter 8).

Written Assignment

Prepare a paper summarizing the basic methods of validation of physical system and human target system simulations, describing the relationship between of the purpose of the models and the methods of validation. Include in the paper a specific intelligence problem, the purpose of a simulation to support analysis, and the method of validation appropriate for that purpose.

Class Objectives

At the end of class you will be able to:

- Demonstrate knowledge of the roles of verification, validation, and accreditation of computer models and simulations.
- Describe model and simulation validation and its importance.
- Describe a simulation conceptual model, the development, assessment, and management approach.
- Discuss the fundamentals and approach to validate a conceptual model.
- Describe a seven-step approach to a successful model or simulation study that validates the programmed simulation.
- Define the basic techniques for developing valid and credible models and simulations, and the guidelines for obtaining good data.
- Distinguish the challenges with validating simulation models of physical target systems (physics-based models) and human target systems (social science– and human behavior– based).
- Distinguish between "validation for understanding and exploration" and "validation for action" for behavioral simulations (see Zacharias, chapter 8).
- Define precisely the "purpose" for an intelligence simulation and from that definition, derive an appropriate procedure for validation.

- Apply the methods to develop a process for conceptual model validation and then simulation development and validation for a hybrid simulation including physics-based and human behavior models.

CLASS 12—FINAL PROJECT PRESENTATIONS

Class Objectives

During Class 12, each project team will present the results of their operational analysis in the form of a 30-minute intelligence briefing. Students should carefully follow the standards of Intelligence Community Directive 203 "Analytic Standards" in preparing the project presentation.

Class Presentation

The final project presentation should, at a minimum, include:

- statement of the intelligence problem;
- description of problem framing and representation;
- explicit representation (model) of the analytic thinking in hypothesis development and assessment;
- rationale for selecting quantitative modeling representations;
- assessment of the key issues using model, game or simulation methods;
- as appropriate, demonstration of the modeling method; and
- intelligence judgment.

Project Assessment

Each project team will be evaluated on the approach to the operational problem, the clarity of presentation, and the appropriateness of the explicit analytic methods applied:

- the framing of the problem and representation in a quantitative schema;
- the selection of explicit methods to represent analytic thinking and the target system;
- the degree to which modeling, analytic gaming or simulations methods are applied to addressing the intelligence problem; and
- the degree to which the selected modeling methods support the analytic conclusions.

NOTE

1. This section follows the curriculum format adopted in Moore, David T., *Critical Thinking and Intelligence Analysis*, Occasional Paper Number 14, Washington, DC: National Defense Intelligence College, March 2007.

Index

About the Author

Ed Waltz is a Distinguished Member of the Technical Staff at Virginia Tech, working within the Intelligence Community. Previously from 2004–2013 he was the Chief Scientist, Intelligence at BAE Systems Technology Solutions, where he led intelligence research. He has led numerous hard target and counter denial & deception programs, applying computational modeling and simulation to understand target dynamics over the past decade for different agencies of the IC and DoD. He led the development of capabilities to understand physical target systems (underground facilities, dual-use facilities), foreign leadership, and foreign social systems. Mr. Waltz holds a BSEE from the Case Institute of Technology and an MS in Computer, Information and Control Engineering from the University of Michigan. He has over forty years of experience in developing and deploying signal processing, data fusion, and analytic capabilities for intelligence. He is a recipient of the DoD Joseph Mignona Data Fusion Award (2004); he became a Veridian Technology Fellow in 2002 and a BAE Systems Engineering Fellow in 2009. He is a senior advisory panel member for the strategic intelligence curriculum at the Patrick Henry College, where he is also a lecturer in advanced analytics.

Prior to 2004, he led research at General Dynamics (and acquired predecessors at Veridan and ERIM 1993–2004). Prior to this, he developed capabilities in data fusion technology while at Allied-Signal (1968–1993) and deployed systems for overhead reconnaissance, airborne non-acoustic anti-submarine warfare, a Space Shuttle payload, and air combat target recognition.

Other texts by the author:

- *Counterdeception Principles and Applications* (coauthor), Artech House, 2007.
- *Knowledge Management in the Intelligence Enterprise*, Artech House, 2003.
- *Multisensor Data Fusion*, Hyder, Shahbazian and Waltz (eds.), Kluwer Academic Publishers, Netherlands, 2002.
- *Information Warfare: Principles and Operations*, Artech House, 1998.
- *Multisensor Data Fusion* (coauthor), Artech House, 1990.